A puppy called Wolfie

A passion for
Free Will Teaching

Kathie Gregory

Hubble & Hattie

The Hubble & Hattie imprint was launched in 2009, and is named in memory of two very special Westie sisters owned by Veloce's proprietors. Since the first book, many more have been added, all with the same objective: to be of real benefit to the species they cover; at the same time promoting compassion, understanding and respect between all animals (including human ones!) All Hubble & Hattie publications offer ethical, high quality content and presentation, plus great value for money.

More great books from Hubble & Hattie –

Among the Wolves: Memoirs of a Wolf Handler (Shelbourne)

Animal Grief: How animals mourn (Alderton)

Babies, kids and dogs – creating a safe & harmonious relationship (Fallon & Davenport)

Because this is our home ... the story of a cat's progress (Bowes)

Bonds – Capturing the special relationship that dogs share with their people (Cukuraite & Pais)

Camper vans, ex-pats & Spanish Hounds: from road trip to rescue – the strays of Spain (Coates & Morris)

Canine Aggression – Rehabilitating an aggressive dog with kindness & compassion (McLennan)

Cat Speak: recognising & understanding behaviour (Rauth-Widmann)

Charlie – The dog who came in from the wild (Tenzin-Dolma)

Clever dog! Life lessons from the world's most successful animal (O'Meara)

Complete Dog Massage Manual, The – Gentle Dog Care (Robertson)

Detector Dog – A Talking Dogs Scentwork Manual (Mackinnon)

Dieting with my dog: one busy life, two full figures ... and unconditional love (Frezon)

Dinner with Rover: delicious, nutritious meals for you & your dog to share (Paton-Ayre)

Dog Cookies: healthy, allergen-free treat recipes for your dog (Schöps)

Dog-friendly Gardening: creating a safe haven for you & your dog (Bush)

Dog Games – stimulating play to entertain your dog & you (Blenski)

Dog Relax – relaxed dogs, relaxed owners (Pilguj)

Dog Speak: recognising & understanding behaviour (Blenski)

Dogs just wanna have Fun! (Murphy)

Dogs on Wheels: travelling with your canine companion (Mort)

Emergency First Aid for dogs: at home & away Revised Edition (Bucksch)

Exercising your puppy: a gentle & natural approach – Gentle Dog Care (Robertson & Pope)

For the love of Scout: promises to a small dog (Ison)

Fun and Games for Cats (Seidl)

Gods, ghosts, and black dogs – the fascinating folklore & mythology of dogs (Coren)

Harry & his Grownups – A guide to training Parents (Dicks)

Heart-felt dogs – The canines behind the art (Cowburn)

Helping minds meet – skills for a better life with your dog (Zulch & Mills)

Home alone – and happy! Essential life skills for preventing separation anxiety in dogs and puppies (Mallatratt)

Hounds who heal: It's a kind of magic (Kent)

Know Your Dog – The guide to a beautiful relationship (Birmelin)

Life skills for puppies – laying the foundation for a loving, lasting relationship (Zuch & Mills)

Lily: one in a million! A miracle of survival (Hamilton)

Living with an Older Dog – Gentle Dog Care (Alderton & Hall)

Miaow! Cats really are nicer than people! (Moore)

Mike&Scrabble – A guide to training your new Human (Dicks & Scrabble)

Mike&Scrabble Too – Further tips on training your Human (Dicks & Scrabble)

Mike&Scrabble 2018 calendar (Dicks & Scrabble)

My cat has arthritis – but lives life to the full! (Carrick)

My dog has arthritis – but lives life to the full! (Carrick)

My dog has cruciate ligament injury – but lives life to the full! (Haüsler & Friedrich)

My dog has epilepsy – but lives life to the full! (Carrick)

My dog has hip dysplasia – but lives life to the full! (Haüsler & Friedrich)

My dog is blind – but lives life to the full! (Horsky)

My dog is deaf – but lives life to the full! (Willms)

My dog, my Friend: heart-warming tales of canine companionship from celebrities & other extraordinary people (Gordon)

Ollie and Nina and ... Daft doggy doings! (Sullivan)

No walks? No worries! Maintaining wellbeing in dogs on restricted exercise (Ryan & Zulch)

Partners – Everyday working dogs being heroes every day (Walton)

Puppy called Wolfie – a passion for free will teaching (Gregory)

Smellorama – nose games for dogs (Theby)

Swim to recovery: canine hydrotherapy healing – Gentle Dog Care (Wong)

tale of two horses – a passion for free will teaching (Gregory)

Tara – the terrier who sailed around the world (Forrester)

The little house without a home (Sullivan & Burke)

The lucky, lucky leaf: A Horace & Nim story (Bourgonje & Hoskins)

The supposedly enlightened person's guide to raising a dog (Young & Tenzin-Dolma)

The Truth about Wolves and Dogs: dispelling the myths of dog training (Shelbourne)

Unleashing the healing power of animals: True stories about therapy animals – and what they do for us (Preece-Kelly)

Waggy Tails & Wheelchairs (Epp)

Walking the dog: motorway walks for drivers & dogs revised edition (Rees)

When man meets dog – what a difference a dog makes (Blazina)

Worzel goes for a walk. Will you come too? (Pickles & Bourgonje)

Worzel says hello! Will you be my friend? (Pickles & Bourgonje)

Winston ... the dog who changed my life (Klute)

Worzel Wooface: For the love of Worzel (Pickles)

Worzel Wooface: The quite very actual adventures of (Pickles)

Worzel Wooface: The quite very actual Terribibble Twos (Pickles)

Worzel Wooface: Three quite very actual cheers for (Pickles)

You and Your Border Terrier – The Essential Guide (Alderton)

You and Your Cockapoo – The Essential Guide (Alderton)

Your dog and you – understanding the canine psyche (Garratt)

www.hubbleandhattie.com

All Wolfie illustrations courtesy of Mighty Dog Graphics

First published May 2018 by Veloce Publishing Limited, Veloce House, Parkway Farm Business Park, Middle Farm Way, Poundbury, Dorchester, Dorset, DT1 3AR, England. Tel 01305 260068/Fax 01305 250479/email info@hubbleandhattie.com/web www.hubbleandhattie.com ISBN: 978-1-787110-70-0 UPC: 6-36847-01070-6 Readers with ideas for books about animals, or animal-related topics, are invited to write to the publisher of Veloce Publishing at the above address. British Library Cataloguing in Publication Data – A catalogue record for this book is available from the British Library. Typesetting, design and page make-up all by Veloce Publishing Ltd on Apple Mac. Printed in India by Replika Press.

Contents

Foreword
by Lisa Tenzin-Dolma

I was enchanted by Kathie Gregory's previous book, *A tale of two horses*, so greeted the news that Kathie was writing a book about raising Wolfie, her beautiful Irish Wolfhound, with eager anticipation. Kathie's method of Free Will Teaching, which is a framework based on animal behavioural science and a blend of human cognitive and behavioural therapies, includes offering choices, fostering independence, and focusing on learning opportunities. It's practical and highly effective, and is applicable to all species.

Kathie and I have been friends for several years, and her compassionate wisdom and gentle way of communicating shine through in both her daily life and her work. *A puppy called Wolfie* distils and shares her vast knowledge in such a way that we naturally absorb understanding while being engrossed in the story.

Puppies are immensely loveable, and can also be much harder work than a new caretaker may expect. Kathie's behaviour tips throughout the chapters, accompanied by lovely illustrations by Denise O'Moore of Mighty Dog Graphics, help to make rearing a pup a joyful and rewarding experience. A key saying among force-free behaviourists is 'Set the dog up for success,' and Kathie expands on this by reminding us that our puppy "… can only be successful if we set ourselves up to be successful at managing and teaching him."

A great deal of research into the emotional lives of animals is being carried out, and studies have revealed that there's a close similarity between the emotions in humans and non-human animals, with the same areas of the brain activated in dogs as in people when emotions are experienced. Kathie's method of teaching the animals in her care to control the emotional mind, instead of becoming overwhelmed by it, form the essence of her philosophy.

Another aspect is communication through conversation. We all talk to our dogs, but Kathie guides Wolfie through teaching him words and phrases that he comes to recognise and associate with objects, requests, information, and behaviours. The two-way relationship is further enriched through mutual understanding.

This wonderful book is more than a story about a couple and their beloved Wolfhound puppy (and the subsequent arrival of Remy, a French Barbet pup). Kathie weaves in useful scientific information that's easily absorbed, and offers a great deal of sound guidance about how to help a puppy mature into a well-rounded, confident dog.

I hope you enjoy reading this illuminating book as much as I did!

Lisa Tenzin-Dolma

Principal of The International School for Canine Psychology & Behaviour, founder of The Dog Welfare Alliance, co-chair of The Association of INTODogs, and chair of ICAN, the International Companion Animal Network.
https://theiscp.com/
www.dogwelfarealliance.com/
http://intodogs.org/

Chapter 1
New beginnings

We have a puppy.

These four words trip off the tongue, in different languages, of every new puppy owner all over the world, bringing excitement, hope, and anticipation of the relationship to come.

This is a very exciting event for us to anticipate, too, although, along with the excitement is sadness for the dog we have just lost. Indie, our Great Dane, was such a wonderful, happy boy. Mum (me) was the best thing in his world, closely followed by Dad (Matt, my husband), and then puddings – his favourite treat. The relationship Indie and I shared was so close and special, and time together reinforced how much I loved him, and he loved me.

Our relationship was so good because of the time I spent nurturing it; the quality of that time, and the trust that was built between us. Indie and I were perfectly in tune, and being with him was an absolute pleasure. I can't tell you how much I miss his little face, the look of love in his eyes just for me, the times we had, and his delightful personality. We had ten-and-a-half wonderful years with our Indie.

After Indie died, we quickly discovered that being without a dog was just too lonely. There seemed no reason to go for a walk – the motivation was lost. What fun was a walk without Indie? We missed him 'helping' around the farm: being with us as we got on with the things that needed doing. Often, Indie's 'job' was to oversee things: lying comfortably in the cool grass, or on a bed we'd brought outside for him, Indie made sure that all was going to plan.

Matt and I made a decision: it was time to welcome a new boy into our lives, to nurture, love, and be a part of our family.

The single most important question at this point is one that every potential dog owner should ask themselves: which is the right dog for me? There are a few to choose from, for example a pedigree breed, a cross breed, a puppy, an adult, or rescue dog? Perhaps one or other of these better fits with your situation, or maybe you have a particular preference?

If you're leaning towards a pure bred animal, consider all of the breed's characteristics and inclinations; if a cross breed, determine which breeds make up the dog to understand how they come together to form the dog's personality.

Often the answer to this question is based on existing criteria (a breed you have always wanted/ another example of the breed you've always had/ characteristics/temperament, etc).

Asking yourself a few more questions can help with the choice of which is the dog for you –

WHAT'S MY LIFESTYLE, AND HOW MUCH TIME DO I HAVE TO DEVOTE TO A DOG?

If yours is a fairly sedentary lifestyle, and you like it that way, you should cross off your list all of those breeds and types who like/need a lot of exercise. Likewise, if being out and about with a dog is what you like to do, getting a dog who doesn't require much exercise due to size or physical capability would be a mistake.

A puppy called Wolfie

HOUSE AND GARDEN SIZE: HOW MUCH SPACE DO I HAVE FOR A DOG?

Big dogs need a lot of indoor space – right? Not necessarily.

Matt and I live in a two-bedroom bungalow, that is small and very limited, space-wise, but Indie lived here happily for seven years. We own a small farm with land, so there is no lack of outdoor space, and our lifestyle involves spending time outside. Because of this, the size of our home was not an important consideration, because we did not need a lot of indoor space for activities. I work mostly from home, and we do not have a busy social life, so a lot of the time Indie was out and about with us for most of the day. Our previous home did not have land, however, apart from a small garden, so if Indie had needed to spend most of his time here, there would not have been enough room for him to have a good run about. Luckily, back then, we had time to take Indie on walks near and far, as well as visit parks and fields where he had the space to run.

Given our small home here, and small garden at our previous place, a small dog would be the obvious choice, although that does not best suit our lifestyle, and how we spend our days.

WHAT IS THE MOST IMPORTANT ATTRIBUTE I'D LIKE MY DOG TO HAVE?

If you receive lots of visitors, you may want your dog to be good with people, and comfortable with whoever is in his home/garden. If you already have dogs, or live somewhere highly populated with dogs, you may want a dog who is good with other dogs. You may live somewhere where a very reliable recall is essential; maybe you'd like your dog to be always by your side, taking direction from you, or possibly one who is more independent.

WHAT CHARACTERISTIC/TRAIT WOULD I FIND THE MOST DIFFICULT OR UNREWARDING TO MANAGE?

One answer to this question is, of course, the opposite to that of the previous question. If you want an independent dog, you are less likely to enjoy a dog who looks to you for direction all the time.

Think also, about your answers to these questions –

- do I have the time to groom my dog every day? Every two days? Every week?
- how much time do I have to provide regular exercise for my dog?
- how much time do I have to play with and teach my dog?
- for what periods of time must my dog stay home alone?
- should I have a male or a female dog?

Every dog, regardless of breed, size, or exercise requirements, should spend quality time with his family, and not be left alone for long periods (in excess of four hours).

Now think about how your dog will fit into your environment.

Will you be out at work for part of the day? A dog who prefers company, and doesn't cope well on his own is obviously not the best fit in this instance, and will suffer accordingly. If you own a farm or have land, will he be off-lead most of the time? If so, he may need to be able to manage himself around livestock and machinery as the land is worked. Are you in an area where there is only common land on which to exercise him? A breed with a high prey drive/chase tendency is more likely to need plenty of ongoing training if he is to be reliable about not chasing sheep, etc. All dogs have a degree of prey drive, so will require careful management when off-lead around livestock.

Are you somewhere that is difficult to fence? A very small dog is likely to become an adept escape artist if he can get through gaps that you cannot secure.

Do you want to take him with you to shows? The pub? Gardens? Will you want to take him with you when you visit family and friends who also own dogs? A dog with a nervous disposition, or who prefers to be quiet, may not appreciate the stress and change in routine of going to different places.

Matt and I have a preference for large dogs,

and also want a dog who enjoys plenty of exercise, as we would rather be out walking with our dog than socialising. We don't mind hair about the house, and we have time for grooming, so both long and short coats are fine. We don't want a dog who hangs on our every word, waiting to be told what to do next. Luckily for us, we have our own fields, so don't have to rely on parks, or common land which often homes livestock, for our off-lead exercise.

The short list that we drew up when considering which dog was right for us consisted of specific breeds, as well as cross breeds –

- Great Dane
- Mastiff (kind undecided)
- Irish Wolfhound
- Beagle
- Elkhound
- Deerhound
- Transylvanian Hound
- A cross breed including one of the above breeds

Our next step was to research each breed, looking at personality, health, and typical breed traits, crossing off our list any breed we were not sure about. This whittled our choices to –

- Great Dane
- Mastiff (kind still undecided)
- Irish Wolfhound
- A cross breed including one of the above breeds

We looked at plenty of websites and read all about the breeds on our short list, then made our choice. An Irish Wolfhound was definitely the dog for us, and a puppy who we could rear, rather than an older dog.

Now we had to find a good, reputable breeder, which involved more research and chatting to breeders. Whilst we were assessing breeders, they were also assessing us, to determine whether we would provide an Irish Wolfhound with the best possible home. Debra Greenwood of Barachois Newfoundlands and Irish Wolfhounds was our

The puppies have been born – and one will be ours!
(Courtesy Debra Greenwood)

breeder of choice, as she is a really nice, genuine breeder with lovely dogs, and was happy to answer all of our questions. That she is a very long way from Devon, where we live, didn't matter, as it was far more important for all of us to be sure we were the best carers for one of her puppies. The most difficult part was waiting, keeping our fingers crossed that, a) a litter of lovely puppies would be born, and b) we would receive one of them.

Finally, we get the news we'd been waiting for: a litter of gorgeous Irish Wolfhound puppies had been born, and there was one for us, if we wanted him. Yes, please! The pups were black and brindle colours: which would we like? Brindle is a lovely colour and patterning, but we were smitten with the black ones. There were three to choose from ... but how to decide which one?

We had just a glimpse of their personalities at this stage, and, based on this, were able to decide that one of the three was not for us. From the two remaining we chose the one who gave us the best feeling, and, from this initial decision, Debra assessed each puppy's personality as it developed, to check whether the chosen puppy was still the right fit for us.

It's essential to visit the puppies with their mother before making a final decision. Good breeders will have been with the puppies from the time they were born, so will know their personalities and breed traits, and the environment and lifestyle they will best suit. A good breeder will already have in mind which puppy is right for each new owner. Visiting the puppies in their home environment will allow you to gauge their behaviour, as well as provide insight to their personality. Meeting your puppy also marks the start of the bonding process as you focus on him, in anticipation of taking him home.

It is not advisable to choose your puppy from a photo, and meet him for the first time when you arrive to take him home. The rest of the litter may be reserved or sold, and you may well find your puppy's personality is not right for you.

WHAT TO LOOK FOR WHEN CHOOSING A PUPPY

Your lifestyle, and how your puppy will fit into this is a vital consideration in this respect. If you have a very busy, lively home, the quietest, most timid puppy may find himself out of his depth, and not cope well in this situation. On the other hand, the most outgoing puppy may prove too much to manage if you have a busy schedule and limited time.

Consider these points with your head ... but also with your heart. Which puppy responds to you; which one do you feel drawn to? Of course, you can't be sure how a particular puppy will fit into your home, or how he will develop – how you teach him will make a huge difference – but the personality he was born with will remain the same, in essence, so whatever traits you see in the puppy when you visit him are likely to stay with him as he grows into adulthood.

The most helpful thing you can do at this stage is listen to yourself. Your first impressions matter, and you should listen to what your gut is telling you. Ignoring an initial doubt or niggle is probably the biggest mistake we make when choosing a puppy. The concerning trait you've glimpsed will most likely always be present, influencing personality and ability to learn, so don't dismiss it, Ask the breeder what their interpretation of what you've observed is: by discussing it, you can determine whether this affects your choice.

For example, the puppy who initially shies

away before becoming friendly may always have that trait. The puppy who is the most difficult to distract and engage may always find refocusing that much harder to do. The puppy who is easily distracted may initially find it difficult to concentrate. How you teach him and work with his personality makes a big difference to his development, of course, and whether existing personality traits are developed or played down. If there is an aspect of his personality that you feel you might not be able to cope with, change your mind and choose another puppy.

Behaviour Tip

Personality comprises a number of factors –
- the puppy's innate personality
- personality traits inherited from his parents
- learned behaviour from watching the responses/ behaviours of parents and siblings
- learned behaviour from his own experiences

He will already have learnt from his short life experience, and will have developed responses to this, in addition to those responses that are a part of his personality. How he is taught and encouraged to develop can have a lot of influence on his adult personality. By taking things slowly, being reassuring, and not asking for things that are outside his comfort zone, he will become more confident, and develop lots of coping strategies.

OUR PUPPY

At three weeks old, our pup is much too young to take home, so we have a few weeks before picking him up. How exciting!

Less exciting was what we needed to do in preparation of this. Of course, our home was already dog-friendly, as Indie had lived here for years, but, as Indie was an adult dog when we moved here, and not a puppy, our home was most certainly not puppy-proof. All of the gaps that were far too small for Indie to squeeze through were perfectly puppy-sized – and there were a great many of them, but there was no way we could secure them all. The only solution was to fence that part of the land the house sits on – the 'garden' – to make a secure area for our new puppy to wander and play in. The rest of the farm could be explored on-lead until he was either too big to get through the gaps, or, we have taught him not to go through them.

Once the fencing was sorted, we turned our attention to the rest of our home, and removed everything that a puppy should not have access to, but which will prove too tempting to leave alone. This is a great way to stay tidy – at least until our puppy has learnt what he should and should not play with! Once everything was ready, we took a trip out to buy a new bed and some toys for him.

Three weeks old and adorable.
(Courtesy Debra Greenwood)

Teaching Tip
Have a good look around your home and garden, and remove the things that a puppy is definitely going to want to play with, but shouldn't! It's obviously not possible to remove everything, of course, but do temporarily remove temptations such as cushions, or clothes on the sofa, the remote control on a table he can reach, and put away shoes. Your time will be better – and more enjoyably – spent teaching him how exciting toys are rather than trying to retrieve one of your shoes from his mouth!

The final ingredient you need when preparing to welcome your new puppy is to have time for him. An obvious statement, I know, but you'd be surprised how much time a puppy uses up. If you go out to work, arrange time off so that you are there to help your puppy settle in, and in which to begin teaching him. This gives him a head start so that when you go back to work he already has some learning in place.

Think through your lifestyle and routines, and come up with some ideas in advance of your puppy arriving. What will you do at meal times if he is making a fuss? Have you time to supervise him in the mornings, or will you be too busy getting yourself ready for work, and the kids for school? What will you do with your puppy if that is the case? Time your routine to accommodate your puppy's needs so that life does not become too chaotic. Puppies can be unpredictable, though, so don't expect to have a completely reliable routine for a while. Be ready to adjust as you go along.

Puppies learn quickly, and allowing time to teach him is essential. This is the best time to begin teaching him; don't leave this until he starts getting into trouble, or you realise that his behaviour is becoming more difficult. New owners sometimes don't take the time to teach their pup when he is young because they have been advised that he will be calmer as he ages, making teaching him easier, but this is only true if he has had an opportunity to manage his own behaviour from a young age.

Chapter 2

It's never too early to begin teaching

We make the 15-hour round trip to collect our new puppy, staying overnight, and returning home the following morning. Our puppy is nine weeks old now, and a fair bit bigger than he was at three weeks of age. We have a short list of potential names – I wonder which one will suit him?

Finally, we are here, and couldn't be more excited! We are greeted by the sight of several Irish Wolfhounds running and playing together in a field: they look so happy. Next, we meet our puppy, who is totally gorgeous with very large paws. I wonder if his paws will keep growing with him, or if he will grow into them. Looking at him I suspect the former: they'll just keep on growing. It looks like he's going to be a big boy then! We've already fallen in love with him, of course.

The journey home to Devon is a long one, so we have plenty of time to sit and do nothing except look after puppy, and decide his name. Our short list consists of Paddington Bear, Storm, Wolfie, Hercules, and Shadow. I prefer Paddington Bear, but it's not quite right. Matt likes Storm best ... but he's not a Storm, either. Looking at his little face, there really is only one choice: Wolfie.

We have to make several stops on the way back, which provide our first teaching opportunity. Clients often ask me when they should begin teaching, and whether they should wait until their puppy is a little older. The answer is to start straight away: you want to make the most of every moment to help your puppy develop into a confident and well-balanced dog.

It's a long journey home ...

(❀) *Behaviour Tip*

Life is all about learning, and your puppy will learn, whether or not you actively teach him, but teaching him from the start will give him the best education.

We have to put a harness on Wolfie every time we get out of the car. As we show him how to move himself so we can do this, it becomes our first teaching exercise. We say 'put on your harness' as we place it over his head, and 'give me your paw' as we lift a leg to fit the harness. When the harness comes off, we say 'head down' as we take it over his head, and 'give me your paw' to finally remove it. (Note that if your pup is lying down, 'give me your paw' will involve having him in a sitting position.)

After doing this five times on the way home, Wolfie has definitely got the idea, and is doing the movements with just a little assistance, going from a lying position to sitting up on his own, ready for his paw to be lifted to put on the harness, and lowering his head ready for it to come off. Of course, we could have left the harness on him for the entire journey, but since he didn't mind it going on and off, we decided not to do this. And it also meant, of course, that we could begin teaching this exercise.

(😺) *Teaching Tip*
How you continue with an activity or action depends on your puppy's response to it. If he's unsure about a harness going on and coming off, it's better to leave it on if you need to make a stop before getting home, so that you minimise any stress he may be feeling. Instead, perhaps practise putting it on and taking it off once he has settled into his new home.

Finally, after nearly eight hours, we arrive back, and our first job is to settle Wolfie into his new home. The second is to put on the kettle – we really need a cuppa!

Wolfie is a little overwhelmed by his new surroundings, so is quite hesitant. We let him wander around outside, saying encouraging things such as 'Well done; are you okay?' 'You're a lovely boy.' The words mean nothing to him now, as he hasn't yet learnt them, but the reassuring tone of voice helps.

After a while he looks into the house. He's not at all sure he wants to come in, so we don't try to entice him: he'll be a little braver in a few minutes, when he's had chance to process things and realise there is nothing to be scared of. He comes a little closer and has another look in. Nothing has changed! 'Hello,' we say, 'are you okay?'

Home at last!

As Wolfie is exploring the garden he comes across a bucket. We have many buckets of water here, so he has plenty of options for drinking outside. He looks at the bucket and warily takes a step back. He has another look and does the same thing. I talk to him, tell him it's fine, and scoop up some water in my hand, which I offer to him. He sniffs it and then licks at what little water is left. I do this a couple more times, and then he is brave enough to try the water from the bucket. Once he realises what it is, he keeps going back for a drink.

This exercise worked well as I took it at Wolfie's pace, and did not try to encourage him to

A puppy called Wolfie

approach the bucket, which was clearly worrying him. Instead, I showed him what was in it so he could connect the bucket with the water. As soon as he realised this, he felt brave enough to investigate.

This wariness about objects is common and will occur often – on a walk, say. It's important not to over-encourage your puppy to investigate whatever it is that's concerning him, as his behaviour is telling you he is anxious and wary, and pushing him is likely to result in his becoming fearful.

The next time that he approaches the house, Wolfie musters the courage to come in, and we praise him: 'Well done, aren't you clever!'

Our first evening goes well: Wolfie is such a little pudding! He has some dinner, settles down for a sleep, and then gets up for a play. Periodically throughout the evening we take Wolfie out into the garden in case he needs to toilet, praising him when he does. He is whining a lot, but this is to be expected, as he must be missing his mum and litter-mates, and he doesn't know us yet, so is very much out of his depth. The temptation is to give him a big cuddle and fuss, and of course we do, but we must be careful not to make this the only response. We do not want to teach him that we are his emotional crutch, and an alternative to developing his own self-confidence. Our aim is to reassure him that he is fine, giving him all the love and support he needs to cope with the move to a new home, whilst allowing him the freedom to express himself and learn about his new life, which will help him to develop self-confidence and self-reliance.

(☺) Behaviour Tip
Aim to include three different strategies in your response –

- cuddle and reassure
- distract him with play or an activity
- use your voice to reassure him as you go about your business

Cuddling Wolfie every time he needs reassurance means he will always expect this response from us, which will not help him learn how to cope himself. If we begin to build his self-reliance by using a range of reassuring and comforting responses, there is less chance of Wolfie developing an over-dependence on us, and more chance of him learning to rely on himself, with our support. If our only response is to cuddle him throughout the day and evening every time he is unsure, by the time we go to bed, this will be the response he will expect if he feels insecure in the night. When that response is not forthcoming, he will experience increased emotional distress, and has no other strategy to help himself.

It can be very damaging to a developing mind to ignore an insecure puppy in distress. It is much better to go to him and reassure him briefly. How often you need to do this depends on the puppy and his personality. Listen to him, and rather than going to him the moment he barks, wait. Some puppies will settle down after initially whining or barking, but, if not, will escalate their vocalisations, which means you need to go to their aid. The key is your reassurance, which lets your pup know that everything is fine, enabling him to cope alone for longer and longer periods.

Remember, though, that this brief relief from the distress reinforces his sense of insecurity at being alone, and vocalisation (crying/barking) of his distressed state is what brings comfort in the shape of Mum or Dad. This is where problems at bedtime start if the only reassurance given is hands-on cuddling, as each time you leave that support leaves with you. Even a more confident puppy, who is not in distress but is experimenting to see what brings a desirable response, will quickly learn the association between his vocalisation and your arrival. Dogs are social animals who like and want company, and whether or not he is able to cope on his own is immaterial: if he's discovered a way to summon company, he will use it. All dogs need to be on their own sometimes in their life, and it is up to us to help him develop a healthy sense of self-reliance for his emotional well-being. The three strategies mentioned provide three different responses to his attempts to get attention. Using them means you are beginning to teach him to manage his emotions, and cope with changes and different outcomes.

Wolfie has done well this first evening. He is a cute (and not very small!) bundle of fun, and we've really enjoyed being with him. We are exhausted, though, after a very long day, and it's time for bed. But before we can get some rest, we must decide –

- do we sleep in our bedroom or the same room as Wolfie?
- if he is quiet, do we get up in the night to check him?
- do we wake him to go out to toilet, or leave him?

We choose to sleep in the same room as Wolfie – well, Matt volunteers! – because we have been travelling all day, and have only been home for three hours, so Wolfie has not had much time to get used to his new environment. If we'd been here all day, he would have been a little more comfortable, more settled, and we might have both gone to bed if Wolfie was asleep. As it is, we don't want him to panic and be unable to cope if left alone this first night.

Reinforcing our decision is evidence to suggest that allowing puppies to sleep in the same room has benefits for both of you, plus a new puppy will have been through quite a traumatic time leaving his mum and siblings, and coming into a completely new environment. It can add considerably to the stress he is already feeling if he then has to sleep on his own for the first time, rather than with his litter-mates. Options to minimise these effects are –

- sleep downstairs with him
- let him sleep in your bedroom
- keep doors open, and be just a room away so you can reassure him if he wakes

Taking things slowly – but always with the aim of building his self-reliance – will make the transition to sleeping on his own much easier, if sleeping in the bedroom with you is not possible.

The next morning, I'm excited to see Wolfie. Matt got up twice in the night to take him out, and each time Wolfie settled down to sleep easily.

Our life with Wolfie has begun. Now it is up to us to teach, nurture, love, and keep him safe; ultimately, to guide him and help him be the best he can. This is a big deal: how we teach him will influence how he grows, and how his personality is shaped. We can't change the personality he was born with – and wouldn't want to, as it is part of who he is – but the experiences we give him, how we manage his behaviour, what we reinforce, will make a difference to how his personality develops.

THE FIRST WEEK

This period is all about getting to know Wolfie. Matt and I have been dog owners for a number of years, so do understand what puppies are like, and, as

Discovering the garden ...

A puppy called Wolfie

a professional animal behaviourist, I also have a vast amount of knowledge about dogs of all ages. However, we don't know Wolfie, yet, and he doesn't know us.

At this stage, teaching Wolfie is not about him learning specific exercises such as a sit, but about helping him understand his new life: when his mealtimes are, where his bed is, what he can play with, what to do when he's outside, how to cope, and what to do when we are not here. He also needs to get to know us; trust us, and love us. These emotional responses take longer to achieve as they are products of a good relationship, which we won't have until we know one another.

It is easy to mistake dependency for trust. At this very early stage in our relationship, Wolfie may consider us the best bet if he is anxious or scared. This is not trust, but simply that we are the only other living beings in his new home. Since we have been nice to him and not made him afraid of us, he may choose to come to us if he finds himself in a situation he does not know how to cope with.

As it is, in the first few days, Wolfie finds safety in the house more than he does with us, which is not surprising, as in the house is routine, dinner, and his bed. Why not in us, you might ask? One reason is that all dogs are different in this respect: some are 'people' dogs, some are 'dog' dogs, and some are simply more self-contained.

Another reason is that establishing trust cannot be rushed; it takes time. It is very easy to create dependency, however, which we do not want to do, so I have not rushed to Wolfie every time he has whined, or not known what to do. I have helped and supported him, loved him, and understood him, but not treated him as if he is incapable. As a result, he has begun to be self-reliant, and not overly-dependent on me.

However, he is retreating to the house when he is scared. Fear often involves an element of panic, which requires a different response to anxiety. In these instances, rather than try and reassure at a distance, I follow Wolfie into the house for the first couple of days as the closer contact helps resolve his negative emotions. I return to whatever it was I was doing, then, and talk to Wolfie at a distance for additional reassurance.

We gradually progressed to providing more reassurance at a distance, and reducing the time I was with him in the house. It took just a few days for Wolfie to be able manage his fear response and cope with the situation, rather than run away from it.

It's day two, and, whilst we have taken time off work to help Wolfie settle in, we do have things to do around the home. Wolfie is lying happily in the lounge, and, as I am about to leave the room, Matt says he would like to water his greenhouse, but will wait until I get back, so that Wolfie is not left alone, but this is a mistake. As Wolfie is not currently in play mode, and is not trying to play with the furniture instead of his toys, there is no need to supervise him. Having one of us stay with him at all times over the next few days is going to create the expectation that this will always be the case, and is normal in his new home. It also means Wolfie will not develop self-reliance if he always has us to rely on, and separation anxiety may be the result when he is eventually left to cope on his own.

After this period of being with him all day, every day, we will go back to work, and although most of my work is done from home, Wolfie will have to be on his own when I am busy with clients or need to go out. If, by this time, we haven't taught him that being on his own is fine, that we always come back, and he can just relax and wait for us, he may panic at suddenly being left, and be unable to cope.

All young animals naturally have an alert cry, part of the panic system in their brain, which they use to tell mum they are feeling vulnerable, so that she can reduce the distance between them and keep them safe. This response switches off in the mother once she has finished weaning. As they get older, stronger, and learn more about the world, youngsters are increasingly capable of looking after themselves, and will start to wander further away from mum, and for longer periods of time. When a puppy is collected and taken to his new home, this natural progression towards self-reliance is interrupted, and instead of a progressive ability to cope on his own, the pup takes a step backwards as the support from his mum is suddenly gone. Once he has settled into his new home, the progression towards self-reliance continues with the support of his new carer, of course. However, if a pup's continually been around his new carers day and night for several weeks or months, there's a good chance he will not have developed any self-reliance, and as he does not have a coping strategy for being left alone, will develop separation anxiety.

Having told Matt to carry on and water his greenhouse, Wolfie has the option to follow him outside, although he doesn't. I also then leave the room, telling him 'I won't be a minute.' Wolfie doesn't know what this phrase means, yet, but if I say it every time I leave, he will begin to associate it with this action, and what he does whilst on his own.

As I do not want to come home to chewed furniture, or find he's tearing about causing havoc, I time leaving him on his own to coincide with when he is tired, calm, and relaxed. The process of leaving him involves –

- the phrase, 'I'll be back in a minute,' which lets him know I am going to leave
- the knowledge that this happens when he is settled and relaxed, so less likely to panic, and his first experience of being alone is when he is in a positive and contented state of mind
- him learning that I always come back

This process should enable him to remain calm and not panic, along with eventually using self-restraint to settle and remain that way.

Teaching Wolfie this strategy begins with leaving him the first few days for a minute or two when he is quiet, gradually increasing the length of time he is alone by a few minutes. When he is having a good sleep, I can leave him for longer, checking every so often that he is still asleep. As the first week goes by, I vary the period of time I leave him: sometimes it is very short; sometimes a little longer. Puppies do not learn in a linear manner,

so increasing the period that Wolfie is alone by the same amount each time does not usually work. His ability to cope depends on the emotional state he is in, and what influences there are. Sometimes, he may cope with being left consecutively for twenty minutes several times, but then manage two minutes only. The key to success is to assess how he is feeling before I leave, and decide how that will affect his ability to cope, then adjust the length of time I am away, or when I check on him, accordingly. As I increase the length of time he is on his own, I always check in to make sure he is okay, and to reassure him that he is fine, by telling him that he is a clever boy, which also reinforces the idea that relaxing is a good thing to do when I am not there. Leaving again, I tell him that I won't be long. Sometimes, I leave the back door open so that he can go into the garden.

If Wolfie is playing quietly when I check him, or has gone into the garden, this tells me that he was bored, and has found something appropriate to do, so I say to him 'Well done, you're playing with your toy,' or 'Are you relaxing? That's lovely.' If he then becomes excited, I'll stay and play with him, before going back to what I was doing. Puppies can't regulate their emotions, and simple associations are easily made, so if I ignore his excitement and leave him, he may associate my leaving with his current excited state. He will also need to expend that energy, so, rather than becoming quiet when I leave, he is likely to turn that excitement into playing, and without my presence to guide him, may choose something he shouldn't play with, rather than a toy. This can then form the basis of what he does when I leave, which is why I address his excitement and play a little, leaving when he is calm.

An inquisitive and excited puppy is likely to play with anything that catches his attention, such as the furniture, or will dig in the garden, both activities that will be reinforced without any input from me, as they're enjoyable. This will then mean I will not be able to trust him not to do this when left alone, and supervision will be necessary.

After applying my strategy each day this week, we're at the stage where I can leave Wolfie for

A puppy called Wolfie

between a couple of minutes and a couple of hours, and trust that he will settle and not cause havoc in the house. More importantly, he is not concerned at being left on his own, and does not panic when I leave, which I know to be the case because, when I began teaching him to be fine on his own, I remained close enough to hear and look in on Wolfie, which allowed me to deal with any issues quickly.

Reassured that there were none, as I increased the time he was left alone, I observed his body language and the area he was in to determine how he had been. Dogs who are not coping may damage furniture, or chew inappropriate items, If they panic, they may harm themselves, cause destruction in the home, or toilet inside the house.

Conversely, some dogs shut down and become very fearful, and don't acknowledge you when you return, or their mood is very dull and flat.

All of the foregoing will have begun as slight changes in your pup's general demeanour, or the behaviour he exhibited in the early stages of being left alone. Spotting these changes early will allow you to adjust when you leave him so that they do not become the problems described.

(☺) *Management Tip*
Timing is important when you leave your puppy on his own. Do this only when his mood is happy and contented, as this enables him to cope without you, and reduces the likelihood that he will panic. Returning whilst his mood is still happy and contented is essential for him to associate your return with positive emotions, and not relief from anxiety he is experiencing.

Ideal situations for practising leaving him on his own (remain close by in order to monitor these) –

- leave him when he is asleep, and return when he is still asleep
- leave him when he is asleep and return when he is still dozing
- leave him when he is engaged with a toy that is safe for him to be alone with, and return whilst he is still playing with this
- leave and return when he is content and relaxing

Begin by leaving him for between a few seconds and a minute if he is awake; longer if asleep, then gradually increase and vary the time. Be guided by how well your puppy copes, not a specific time-scale.

I always tell Wolfie I'll be back soon, even if he is asleep. I also always say 'I'm back, well done, aren't you a clever boy?' when I return. My tone of voice has a big impact on how Wolfie feels, and how he views my absences, so it's always reassuring and calm. I do not speak in an excited tone when I return as I do not want to change his relaxed state to one of excitement.

Limited time on day one means that we also begin teaching Wolfie to toilet outside on day two. A pup's need to toilet is not necessarily regular, but when Wolfie toilets outside, as he is actually going, we say 'Go for a wee,' so that he begins to associate the action with these words. Once he has finished, we follow it up with praise.

If engaged in something inside, such as playing, and Wolfie begins to wander about, I take him outside and ask him if he needs a wee. If he is relaxed after we've been playing, I wait until he decides he wants to do something again before suggesting we go outside first. If we have been inside for a long time, I take him out, just in case.

It hasn't taken long for Wolfie to understand the question 'Do you need a wee?' so now that he does, we begin using it to ask if he needs to go when we are outside. To ensure he knows not to toilet inside, we also ask the question, immediately following it up with 'Come on then, let's go out,' and once outside, say 'Go for a wee.' This teaches him to be aware himself of whether or not he needs to toilet, and every instance is followed up with praise, voiced in a reassuring and happy tone.

Doing activities outside helps with toileting in the first days, as the association with toileting outside and noting when Wolfie goes for a wee outside, as he has understood where this should happen, so there is no need to continue to reinforce this. Once that association has been made, it's not necessary to praise your puppy for doing something that comes naturally. If I should happen to see Wolfie toilet, I will occasionally reinforce the action, but now the focus is on increasing self-awareness so that he remembers to go outside if we are indoors; reinforcing his leaving the house to toilet. We progress again a few days later to reinforcing his going outside on his own when I ask him to. He is aware of needing to toilet, and is now going outside of his own accord.

⊛ Teaching Tip

Once you have established the initial association between your puppy being outside when he goes to the toilet, progress to reinforcing him when you encourage him to leave the house, and when he leaves of his own accord. Reminding your puppy that he might need to go out for a wee is more about timing going outside to when he has finished one activity, and is possibly wandering about, rather than taking him outside at set times.

Various methods exist that teach your puppy not to toilet indoors during the night. A popular one is to use training pads, which are placed on the floor for your puppy to toilet on. Once your puppy knows to toilet on the training pad, it is gradually moved closer to the external door, and then outside.

There are both benefits and drawbacks to this approach. The pads are very handy, and save cleaning up if you haven't let your puppy go outside to toilet during the night, but you will be teaching your puppy to toilet in the house, creating the impression that it's okay to do so. A second drawback is that using this method will mean that house-training will take longer, as, once you stop using the pads, it will be necessary to watch your puppy all the time during the day, so that you can

Outside activities help with toilet training.

is made. I take the computer, paperwork, or a book so I can work whilst Wolfie is outside. I also leave the door open so Wolfie can go in and out. Checking whether your puppy needs a wee is more important on cold or wet days, when he may be less inclined to go out, and the door is closed when he has not yet learnt how to ask to go out.

Particularly excitable puppies are sometimes unable to control their bladder. If he has been left alone, take him outside as soon as you return, walking him to a toileting area so that he knows to toilet here, even though he is excited. Establish a routine of getting home, going straight out to wee, then cuddles whilst you teach him to be calmer when you come home, and in control of his bladder. It's also wise to greet visitors outside until your puppy has more control to prevent any accidents inside the home, making it easier for him to learn that he should toilet outside.

After the first four to seven days of Wolfie being with us, I no longer make a point of knowing take him outside before he toilets in the house (which is what you have taught him to do).

I much prefer the quick and effective method of teaching a puppy to toilet outside in the first place, and my daytime strategy is easily adapted to night-time use.

I get up two or three times in the night to take Wolfie outside, mostly timing these to before he has woken up and gone for a wee inside. Puppies don't usually need to toilet as often in the night as they do in the day, but if they wake up, they probably will need to toilet. A good guide is to check on your puppy every two to three hours for the first few days. You will then have a better idea of his night-time pattern, and you can adjust when you get up so that it coincides with him.

I do the same as I do during the day: ask him if he needs a wee, and encourage him outside. During the night I watch and reinforce Wolfie when he does toilet, using a morsel of food to call him back to me to return inside. By the end of the first week, I am getting up just once each night, occasionally a second time if I am already awake to check whether he needs to go out (half the time he does not).

(☺) *Teaching Tip*

Week 1
Get up every two to three hours and take your puppy outside to toilet. At this very early stage, pick him up and take him outside if he doesn't do this himself.

Use the same phrase you do when he toilets during the day: we say, 'Go for a wee.'

Week 2
Reduce getting up to two times during the night, and encourage your puppy to get up to go out, rather than pick him up. This is a particularly important point for those of you with giant breeds – your puppy will soon be too heavy to pick up – but is also important for every dog.

You want to teach your puppy to be aware of when he needs to toilet, so that he will decide he needs to get up and go outside to do so.

Week 3
Reduce getting up to once a night. By this stage, your puppy will begin to decide for himself whether or not he needs to toilet. This is what you are aiming for.

Wolfie has been with us for three weeks, and is now twelve weeks old, and becoming quite big. I can still pick him up, but not so easily. I need Wolfie to be aware of when he needs a wee, and make the decision to do so himself. If this doesn't happen, the chances are we will regress, and he will begin to toilet in the home rather than outside.

GOING FORWARDS
All puppies develop at different rates, and Wolfie's toilet training has been based on a relaxed natural timescale, without rushing things. Wolfie went through the stages a little quicker because we were at home, with plenty of opportunity to teach him. Adjust how many times you need to get up for your puppy, and also how long you continue to do so.

Your puppy will only be able to hold his bladder for so many hours, so, in order to ensure your puppy continues to toilet outside, make sure you do not leave him longer than he is capable of waiting: this would be unkind and damaging to his well-being.

Chapter 3

First steps

A new puppy becomes part of your life from day one, so setting yourself up to succeed from the start is essential if you are to teach him all the skills he needs to fully integrate with your life, behaving as you would like him to, in whatever situation he is in.

Your puppy has limited – if any – impulse control or self-restraint when he first arrives with you at eight or nine weeks old. He doesn't know you, or his new home; he has no idea what he can bite and chew, where he can sit, where he should toilet, and what he should and shouldn't do in general.

In order to set up Wolfie to succeed, we've also done the same for ourselves when it comes to managing and teaching him. Removing all of the things that are not appropriate for him to chew – such as the TV remote control, or clothing on the floor – is one of the first things we do, because he will find these items much more interesting than his toys! He doesn't know that he shouldn't play with them – nor does he have the necessary self-restraint to resist them – and trying to prevent him simply taking them at the moment is likely to require a lot of extra supervision. It will be so much easier to teach him not to take things that aren't his when he has learnt a few basics, and understands some language.

There's also another good reason for doing it this way: Wolfie will find it easy to learn what to play with, as play items will be the only things around.

This ensures that everything I do will give him good, positive experiences. I will also have a tidy house, if I make sure everything is away and out of reach, which has got to be a good thing, as housework is not my strong point!

Not adopting this approach could result in significant problems that can have a negative impact on other aspects of Wolfie's behaviour. Firstly, it would mean that I am *behind* his actions, not in front of them, which is a very poor way of teaching, as, instead of guiding and shaping his actions, I am correcting them. Secondly, he learns that he can take what he wants, but I then take it from him. Two other things he learns from this are 1) the object is more interesting and important because I take it away from him; 2) if he takes things that he shouldn't he will then try and avoid me when I approach him, to prevent my taking them from him. This then becomes a fun game, as he runs away and I have no option but to chase him to retrieve the object. He may even take this a step further and swallow the object! Essentially, he will not trust me not to take away something he has, and whilst this may only relate to things he knows he shouldn't take, it may also extend to things he can have, with possessive behaviour and resource guarding the result.

So, everything Wolfie can reach but shouldn't have, goes away. Those things that he can't yet reach lose their novelty value, but may become temporarily interesting again when he can reach them. By that time, he will have learnt plenty of language, as well as some self-restraint. As he will not have had experience of me taking things from him, he won't feel the need to pick up what he can now reach and run away with it, so I can let him sniff

A puppy called Wolfie

and investigate these items, telling him what they are and that we don't eat them. Once Wolfie has familiarised himself with the items, they will most probably no longer interest him, and I won't have to manage him or constantly clear up – which is great for developing his self-restraint.

Another aspect of setting up Wolfie to succeed with regard to things he shouldn't have involves play. We play games that are part of teaching Wolfie to exchange objects, so if he does pick up something he shouldn't we can easily exchange it for something it's okay for him to have.

Toy exchange is good for this, and involves having two equally exciting toys, of a type that you and your dog can easily hold on to: tug toys or soft toys are good.

I have both toys with me, and play tug with Wolfie with one of them. After a while, I show Wolfie the other toy and encourage him to play with this one instead. I continue swapping the toys, making sure that Wolfie is excited about the exchange, adding a voice cue that means Wolfie should let go of the toy: something like 'Give,' or 'Let me see,' so that he becomes used to relinquishing a toy when he hears the word or phrase.

It's possible to progress this game to teaching your pup to retrieve toys from a bucket, for example, enabling him to learn how to disengage from one object and find another.

Another strategy is to give Wolfie something nice to eat when he is lying down with a toy. I ask him 'Would you like one of these?' and drop one of his favourite foods on the floor near him. I then walk away, and ask 'Was that nice?' when he's eaten it. This is to help him realise that if he has something he wants (the toy), he can let go of it for something

Dropping a tasty treat nearby helps Wolfie learn that he can let go of toys.

else he wants (the food), and no one will take away his toy.

The final strategy is one we employ as we go along, to teach him what is and what isn't for him. We guide Wolfie as he investigates things, so that he has an awareness and develops some self-restraint, and he doesn't take those things that are not for him.

Of course, there are occasions when Wolfie does take something he shouldn't – he's a puppy, after all, and still learning – but employing all of the above these strategies makes it easy to retrieve this from him. The things that Wolfie is most likely to take are Matt's socks and my gloves, and, if he gets hold of either of these, I firstly find something nice for him to eat, rather than immediately follow him, so that he's not prompted to run from me, and I have something to exchange for what he has. As I wander outside to find him, I also pick up a toy.

I usually find that Wolfie is either sitting down with what he has taken, or standing waiting for me, his tail wagging. If standing, he usually trots a little further away before stopping again, and, if that happens, I don't follow him, but walk in a different direction and circle back to him. I talk to him as I'm doing this, telling him what we are going to do next, so that I can begin to change his focus from the object to something else.

When I'm close enough I can drop some food, and if I have his favourite chew, say to him 'Would you like one of these?' This usually results in him dropping the object as he can't resist the chew. I follow this up with 'Here you are then, go and eat that, lovely boy.' I might also play toy exchange with him to retrieve the object, telling him that it's Dad's sock; not Wolfie's.

If he is sure that he doesn't want to let go of whatever he has, I tell him to bring it with him as I walk away, him following, and may go into the house and ask him what he wants from the fridge, or I might go to the gate to go out to the field. It doesn't matter what I do, I'm simply reducing his focus on the object. He may let go of the item as we do this, but, if not, when we get to the fridge or gate I say, 'Okay, give me Dad's sock, then, and we'll open the fridge/

go through the gate.' I may have to repeat this two or three times, but eventually Wolfie gets the idea, and lets me have the object. I tell him 'Thank you, what a clever boy you are, now let's do such-and-such,' so he gets reinforcement from vocal praise, and to do something he wants to in exchange for Matt's sock.

I've begun to keep a daily diary to chart Wolfie's progress, as it's a really good way of getting into the habit of observing him, in order to appreciate and understand what his emotional state is, why he does what he does, and what is likely to happen in different situations. This information makes is easy to adjust, time, and choose activities and interactions to the best advantage for your puppy.

WOLFIE'S DIARY

June 8
Day 4 with us: nine weeks and 3 days old

AM

6.15:	Breakfast, play, mad half-hour – 10/10 (excitement factor)
7.40:	Morning snooze
8.40:	Awake, small snack, lying in the garden
9.30:	Bitey – 8/10
9.40:	Calmed down
9.45:	Settling down for a snooze, but not quite getting there – translate to doesn't know what to do, so doing random things: biting sofa, pawing door, etc!
10:	Asleep
11.30:	Awake, nice play
11.50:	Lunch, play, not too excitable – 6/10

PM

12.45:	Asleep
2.55:	Awake
3.15:	Dinner, play, manic puppy – 7/10 – but not for long
4.10:	Asleep
5.10:	Awake and comfy
5.20:	Bitey – 4/10, play, walk

A puppy called Wolfie

6.00:   Dinner, lying in garden, chewing
6.15:   Manic puppy – very bitey – 10/10 – had
             to leave him outside to play on his own.
             Play, run around, biting furniture, etc.
             A couple of chews. Final food of the day
8.30:   Finally asleep for the night

NOTES

Another good night, with no inside toileting, and settling well after going out to do so. Very playful and mouthing everything. Nearly had Matt's breakfast sandwich – he was just about to take it, so I removed the plate saying, 'Oh no, you can't eat Dad's breakfast, let's get you something.' Played by himself, but kept coming back to us to pull clothes, the sofa, and anything else he got his teeth around. In fact, anything other than toys!

Went for a walk to use up some of his energy. He walked well down the lane, and Chilli the cat came with us. He sat when Chilli went past, then ran after her, but he was easy to distract from this with the word 'Carefully.' A happy, waggy-tailed boy. It wasn't until a half-hour after we got back before he calmed down.

Wolfie had a small meal as he's always hungry after play and walks, before sleeping, snoozing for a couple of hours. Tried toast and butter – yum! Tried sausage – yum! Walk to pond. Met Charlie and Star [my horses], and was really good. Barked a couple of times once he'd been there for a few minutes, then sat and lifted his nose to Star to sniff her. She sniffed back. Wolfie then whined, he was a little anxious, and wanted to go back to the house. He was also very tired and needed to sleep. This is a really good response: he returns to the house if he is scared or tired. When he's settling, he whines a few times, then changes pitch to more of a groan, which means he's settling and about to sleep.

Note that I didn't let Wolfie investigate Matt's breakfast. Having just explained how to guide Wolfie when around items he shouldn't have, at this point in time, it cannot apply to food. Food provides a different motivation to inanimate objects, and Wolfie will require better self-restraint before he is able to resist eating something tasty that has been left about.

Puppies very often have a mad half-hour where they go completely bonkers, and aren't able to listen or respond to anything. This is quite normal behaviour as play, food, motion increase excitement levels, and cause the mind to become over-aroused, resulting in the puppy running around at top speed, jumping about, chasing balls, grabbing, shaking, and running about with toys, or directing this energy at a person. Once in this state, trying to subdue, control or ask a puppy to do something incompatible with this manic behaviour – such as sit, say – is impossible. He is simply unable to think coherently, and needs to release this excess energy.

The safest option in this case is to direct his energy as best you can so that he is somewhere appropriate, and interacting with something suitable. If he is running across the furniture, take him outside so he can run around in the garden. If he is trying to grab items that are not toys, take these away and redirect him to his toys. If a person is his focus, removing that person from the area is the best way of redirecting him to interact with something else.

Sometimes, a mad half-hour occurs because a puppy becomes very over-tired, and even if he is physically tired, if he's still mentally aroused he may keep going. In fact, his physical over-tiredness can be what's preventing his mind from calming, keeping it in a heightened state of awareness long past what is healthy for mind and body.

I leave Wolfie to his mad half-hour unless I know he is too tired and overdoing it, in which case I will intervene and try to help him calm down, rather than leave him to settle in his own time. Using my body language, tone of voice when repeating calming words, and bringing him back to self-awareness all help to quieten his mind.

Two things woven through every aspect of life, from birth to death, are impulse control and self-

Resting after his mad half-hour!

restraint. Without these, life can be chaotic, as the emotional mind is unable to regulate itself, resulting in mania, over-indulgence, and a discontented or dysfunctional life. In addition, learning and decision-making are impaired, as the intellectual mind is at the mercy of the emotional mind.

With a mind that is balanced and content, the intellectual mind is in control of decision-making, and regulates the emotional mind, keeping behaviour and responses on an even keel. The emotional mind only takes over in times of significant emotional stimulation, such as when we become over-excited or anxious, or when the survival instinct (flight or fight) is triggered.

It is clear from this just how important it is to teach impulse control and self-restraint to our dog, as these give him the ability to control his emotional state; not be swept along by it. Behaviour becomes reliable and balanced, as the dog uses his intellectual mind to regulate his actions and responses. I teach impulse control and self-restraint as part of life; they are core behaviours for all of us to learn, both animals and people. If your dog is to be able to manage himself and make good decisions about what he does in any given situation, you must also teach awareness and understanding right from the start.

A reward-based method is the best way to train, as it is ethical, effective, and motivational. It is important to understand the difference between training and behaviour, and the outcomes you may see because of this difference.

Training involves teaching an action – a conditioned response associated with a specific stimulus (often a voice or body signal) to give it a cue – then practising this until it becomes reliable, and the dog performs the action on cue.

An animal's natural behaviour is shaped by his personality, and, as already noted, this comprises the puppy's own innate characteristics, personality traits inherited from his parents, learned behaviour from watching his parents' responses, and learned behaviour from his own experiences.

Let's take self restraint as an example.

Clients often book in for a session with me as they are unable to manage their dog's behaviour, now that he has grown, although they were able to do so when he was a younger and smaller puppy. Almost all of them have done some training with their dog, and cannot understand why his behaviour can become so over the top and out of control on occasion.

They have taught their dog some self-restraint by training and practising specific exercises, one of which is often a 'sit and wait.' In many cases, the client has worked really hard to take this exercise to an advanced level, whereby their dog can sit and wait for food, amidst distractions, for a good length of time, until given the go-ahead to take it. This demonstrates how good the dog is at the exercise, and is one example of self-restraint, but if we look at this in detail we can begin to see its limitations, and understand why dogs who have this level of self-restraint in this exercise may not have any at other times.

We typically train our dogs to give a specific response to a specific cue. In the 'sit,' we may use a hand signal or a voice cue of 'sit' every time our dog does so, so that he associates the cue with the action of sitting. Once he has learnt what the cue requires him to do, we can give this in advance of the action, and our dog will respond accordingly.

Throughout the learning process we reward and reinforce the action with food, play, and affection, which gives our dog the incentive to do what is asked of him. But, what has our dog learnt, what is he thinking, and what context is applied to this exercise?

Wolfie sits on cue.

Our dog has learnt that, when a particular cue is given, he should carry out the action associated with that cue (in this instance a sit) in order to receive a reward. Most dogs can learn to remain in the required position for an increasing length of time until the reward is given at the end of the exercise.

When teaching a new exercise, food is often used to actually guide our dog toward the desired action. This is called luring: the food is held in the hand, and the dog follows the hand with the food. Often the action is taught in steps, called shaping, and our dog receives a food reward in stages as he progresses towards performing the complete action. Once the action is learnt, luring might continue to be used to encourage our dog to perform the action, or only given once the action has been performed. In each case, the food performs dual roles of incentive and reward.

The most likely probability during this exercise is that our dog is anticipating and thinking about the food, whether it is being used to lure him, or only given once he has performed the required action. If this is what he is focusing on, he is taking less notice of everything else, and how much this impacts on how and what he learns depends on the individual animal.

In the example of teaching a sit, as this is a natural movement for a dog he doesn't really need to think about *how* to do it, so focusing on the food does not impair his ability to carry out the action. In fact, it's often the case that compliance is very quick and precise as our dog practices it and anticipates the food.

For some dogs, food being taken out of the equation results in poor execution of an action, which is where reliance on luring falls down. The food provides the motivation to perform an action on cue, and without it the dog has no incentive to do this.

Additionally, if our dog has focused on the food too much and this is subsequently removed, it may be the case that he has not properly learnt the action required, and may not know what to do.

Instinctively he knows what to do for the specific (food) reward previously offered for the action, although he has not really taken in the action, and, without the food association, does not know what it is that's required of him.

Sometimes, context can be so powerful that a dog can only perform a cued action when all the things that make up that context are present, from where it is practised to the mood our dog is in, and a specific reward can become an integral part of learning the action. Change or take away any one of these elements and our dog cannot perform the action: a change in the situation means he no longer understands what is being asked of him.

Sometimes, context is so strongly attached to an action that our dog is never able to perform that action at any other time, or in any other circumstance, despite attempts to teach him that the action is separate from the context.

Our dog's emotional state and motivation also make a difference. When he is motivated to achieve something, he is far less interested in performing a particular action, especially if that action does not help him achieve his goal. So whilst he may be at an advanced level in training sessions, all the things that catch his interest when he is in a different environment are likely to be more compelling than responding to a cue. This may result in a less reliable response in a real-life situation compared to his usual response in a training session. His arousal level will rise, and his emotional state, which might range from excitement to fear, further boosts this, resulting in the emotional mind taking over. Thinking becomes impaired, and it is very hard or even impossible for him to respond in the way we want him to.

Every dog and every perspective is unique, although observation and experience reveals common scenarios.

- Food is relied upon to prompt him to perform the action, and he will only do this if he knows the food is there, and, in some cases, has to see this in advance. In this instance, without the guarantee of a food reward, he is either unwilling to participate, is unable to as the food has become an intrinsic part of the action and he can't comply without it, or he does not understand the cue on its own without the food, and therefore does not know what to do

- He can and does carry out the action, but then resumes what he was doing immediately afterwards. This often happens when a dog is asked to perform one action in order to stop him doing something else. Although he has been temporarily interrupted, his focus has not changed, and he is still motivated to do what he was doing before the interruption

- He is so well conditioned that he does not do anything outside of the parameters of his training. Owners find it difficult to achieve any variation or different response when the situation requires it

A puppy called Wolfie

- A cue is relied upon to prompt him to perform the action. His training will determine how reliably this occurs

- No cue is required as he has learnt the routine, and always does the same thing so there is no need for further training. This reliability breaks down when something alters the usual parameters, demonstrating that the dog hasn't actually learnt the action out of context. This is often seen with recall. If a dog naturally stays close to his walker, the need to teach a recall may not be realised until circumstances change

- In the foregoing scenarios, the dog has learnt responses in specific contexts that are not necessarily applied to general behaviour

Some dogs spend their entire lives waiting for and responding to specific cues, and are considered very intelligent, when what they actually demonstrate is an enhanced ability to follow instructions. Dogs who are predisposed to this way of learning find it rewarding and fulfilling, but there are many who do not. Teaching a dog to respond to specific cues is essential, but there is so much more that they can learn, develop, and benefit from.

The way we are taught, and the reinforcement and rewards for learning become part of what we expect and anticipate, and when these elements change, we can become unsure about what to do. Different approaches to teaching result in a mind that is more versatile, more open, and with the capacity to learn more.

Often, self-restraint is only taught as a specific exercise, and just like the foregoing example, it is specific to particular criteria, rather than a way of life. And therein lies the problem.

There is so much focus on how to train dogs to perform specific exercises, achieve set goals, and progress through different levels, we've forgotten that these achievements are a very small part of life.

And, anyway, most of the time a puppy is not capable of being calm enough to sit and wait, or

the action is not an appropriate response to many of the things that happen each day. In reality, direction from you needs to be in a more adaptable form than specific training exercises, if he is to learn how to behave calmly and manage himself.

😊 *Behaviour Tip*
Just because your pup does something without being actively taught it, this does not mean that the behaviour will remain, or be reliable.

I don't want to train Wolfie to have set responses to how he lives his life. Learning set responses is only one ability that the canine mind is capable of, and his life is much more than learning specific cued actions chosen by someone other than him. Imagine if you were told what to do and when to do it, all day, every day ...

Whilst some of us find decision-making difficult, having no choice at all is a very stressful way to live, and our dogs, however positively they have been trained, are very often in this situation. We decide when they get up, when they eat, what they eat, when they exercise, what type of exercise they have, and when they sleep. We may even also control how they act and respond in every situation they find themselves in.

What is often overlooked in this situation is that, by controlling our dog's actions, and freedom of choice, we may also be controlling his emotions.

For example, a dog who is anxious around other canines may feel uneasy about an approaching dog, and would rather move away. If he is asked to sit and stay as the dog passes him, we control and prolong his distressed emotional state, and he therefore has two options –

- suppress his natural emotional response (of which his carer is presumably unaware)
- show his natural response to a situation he finds difficult to cope with

Both situations compromise his emotional welfare, as well as increase the possibility of an altercation between the two animals. In general, the dog may feel a range of negative emotions at this happening, such as disappointment or reluctance, if not allowed to express themselves and have some control over their daily life.

Wolfie is a living being, with self-awareness, and likes and dislikes, so training him to do only what I ask, when I ask is limiting his mind, his choices, and his right to free will. Relying on food as his primary motivation to do what I ask is also limiting. By changing the focus from training specific actions to teaching awareness and an ability to understand life, Wolfie will be free to do what he wishes within the boundaries of what is and isn't appropriate in any given situation.

My approach to training embraces Wolfie's rights as an autonomous being, his right to choose how he lives his life, within the boundaries of safety and a harmonious relationship with the humans he lives with. Free Will Teaching focuses on working with his free will to increase intellectual and emotional cognition, understanding, awareness, and the ability to apply this knowledge in different contexts so that he can live life for himself.

In our day-to-day life, Free Will Teaching is the biggest component of Wolfie's learning experiences. I provide a framework within which he can learn, experience, investigate, and explore himself and the world around him. Problem-solving, developing his personality, finding out what makes him interested, happy, content; what he doesn't like to do, and what he wants to do more of are all considerations.

This is an advanced and productive method of teaching and learning, to allow competent and peaceful navigation through life, along with other essential types of learning that complement Free Will Teaching, and is where training classes and activities come in. Learning actions on cue is one type of learning your puppy will enjoy and benefit from. Variety in learning boosts brainpower and knowledge. Puppy training classes can equip him

Wolfie: a living, feeling, thinking being.

with skills that, together with Free Will Teaching, will enable him to participate in a number of activities, such as trick training, agility, and Canicross, whilst maintaining a healthy and balanced emotional mind.

Many dogs find activities such as these too exciting, and become over-aroused, often experiencing frustration and irritation as a result, and needing time to return to a balanced state of mind. Being able to feel excited about and engage in these activities, without the detrimental state over-arousal brings, is an advantage, keeping the mind focused and engaged on the activity, ensuring a positive state of mind throughout. Apart from anything else, with other dogs invariably around at such activities, a frustrated mindset is not at all helpful or conducive to keeping the peace. Other activities are possible, which can progress to exceptionally high levels of advanced training, such as search and rescue, assistance dogs, and scent detection.

The biggest obstacle to allowing our dogs to have the freedom to make choices is the ill-considered and obsolete dominance theory, formed from inaccurate studies with captive wolves, which asserts that we must always be the alpha in our relationship with our dog. In a wolf pack, every member plays a part in maintaining the group, working together for its benefit. An order does exist, it's true, but the pack exists and flourishes due to mutual co-operation. And the same is true for dogs, who want only to be a part of our 'pack,' with no desire whatsoever to dominate us!

Partnership is about giving all members of a group the ability and freedom to express themselves and make choices, within the confines of what is mutually beneficial. But, in order to do this, guidelines must be ascertained, learned and observed – if we were to allow a young puppy free will, for example, he would undoubtedly chew the sofa, dig holes the garden, destroy our plants, and eat our shoes! He will need to learn impulse control and self-restraint, and understand what is and isn't appropriate to interact with, before he can be relied upon to manage himself.

And how do we achieve this? By spending most of our free time with him, teaching and guiding.

Puppy first

In the first few months with your new puppy, you will have almost no time for yourself, as it will all be spent with him! But by putting in the time with Wolfie now, I am ensuring that, in a few months' time, I will not have to manage or supervise him, or check that he is not getting into trouble.

By this time, I will be able to leave him to potter about and do his own thing, knowing that I can trust him. I have no desire to have to watch my boy like a hawk for the whole of his life, or never be able to leave him on his own in case he does something I

don't want him to. It's much better – for us both – to dedicate all of my time to him now for a few months, than have to continually manage him for the next 12-15 years.

The following section outlines the ethos behind Free Will Teaching, and is a guide to achieving a reliable and trustworthy dog who is happy, balanced of mind, and loving life.

Free Will Teaching

- I am his teacher, helping him to understand how to interpret this world he lives in
- As he learns, I become his guide, suggesting a good course of action for a given situation
- As he becomes aware, he become *my* guide; I honour his choice as long as it isn't dangerous, or completely wrong for the situation we are in
- As our relationship of trust, understanding, and awareness develops, we each contribute to what we do that day, and how we solve any difficulties experienced along the way

At this point, Wolfie and I are at the very beginning of our relationship, and I am still his teacher. It is fairly easy to teach a young puppy how he should manage himself when he hasn't yet learnt very much, but more difficult to teach an older puppy how to manage himself in a way that is acceptable to our world, when he has spent several months discovering for himself how to behave from his point of view. It also makes it easier if he already has some learning behind him, before becoming a teenager and his hormones kick in, meaning he just can't think!

The sooner you begin teaching him, the sooner he will learn, and when you are teaching him, it is important for your puppy to experience a good balance of different activities, so that he learns and understands his part in the routines of daily life, and all the different situations with which he may be faced. This includes going away from the home, playtime, being content to be in the garden or the home, time away from owners, and time to simply sit and watch the world go by.

It can be difficult finding the time to manage a puppy as well as everything else in daily life, but this is for a relatively short period of time, because, as his learning progresses, your need to supervise him reduces.

Some people don't teach certain things as they don't seem relevant, or are not an issue at the time. But is waiting until something becomes an issue the best way to teach? That depends on *how* you teach.

If your methods are based on set exercises or responses, there will be things that you will not teach unless you need them. For example, how likely are you to teach your puppy to lift his paw and hold it there just in case he has an injury that requires attention? It's not an obvious exercise to teach, despite being a good way to check paw pads.

By basing your teaching on increasing your puppy's self-awareness and understanding, confidence and calmness, then you encompass all the qualities he will need to easily work through unexpected events such as injuries, along with usual, day-to-day life.

Living with a giant breed means that your puppy will grow much bigger, and much faster than other breeds, which makes many more things necessary to consider as a matter of course, rather than addressing them if you find your dog doesn't have the skills for a particular situation. One of these is, of course, his being able to reach the table or kitchen counter. I *have* to teach Wolfie self-restraint around food, but even for those with puppies whose nose will never reach the kitchen counter, there's huge benefit to teaching self-restraint in this context, in addition to teaching it at your puppy's meal times.

Approaching teaching as a way of life, rather than as a way of training specific exercises to control specific responses, your puppy will learn to apply this learning to different contexts and situations, making life very easy for both of you. The true value of impulse control and self-restraint is when an individual applies it of his own volition, throughout his life, to regulate his emotions and actions to the benefit of himself and the world he lives in.

Wolfie is too small to reach the worktop ... yet!

At the moment Wolfie is far too small to reach certain things, but, in barely three months' time, his nose – then his mouth – will be in reaching distance of any food around, so it is definitely not a good idea to wait until this becomes an issue before teaching him self-restraint around food.

How will he be able to resist? It is very likely that the temptation to take food will prove almost irresistible, and if he hasn't already learnt some self-restraint, I will have quite a problem on my hands. I cannot control his access to food once he can reach it himself, unless I shut him out of the kitchen when there is food about, or I am standing right next to it, watching for his nose to appear at the counter edge. But if I shut him out of the kitchen, how will he ever learn? And if I have to watch him every second, how will I get anything done?

If this lesson is incorrectly taught, it will only be my presence that will prevent Wolfie from helping himself, which would mean that, when I'm not there, he will snaffle any food that's about. Better to begin teaching self-restraint now, so that, by the time he can help himself, he will choose not to.

And one thing is certain: he will soon be far too big to pick up and remove from the area (which is not a sensible strategy, anyway).

Of course, it's not possible to teach a puppy self-restraint, and choose not to help himself to food that is on the kitchen counter if he can't yet reach this, which is the case with Wolfie. But there's one thing in the kitchen he will definitely want to get his nose into, and where I can begin teaching: the fridge.

I'm sure most of you have experience of your puppy trying everything he can think of in order to get his paws on food he can smell but can't get to. This behaviour can be addressed in a number of ways –

- shut him out of the room/area
- ask him to go to his bed
- ignore him
- distract him with a toy or food

All of the above may have the desired effect, but none will actually teach him to manage himself around food, making it difficult to know whether you can trust him when to not help himself if food is in reach or when you are not around? I need to be able to trust Wolfie to have enough self-restraint to choose not to take food that is not for him, since he will be able to reach anything that is out, may pick up dropped food, or take advantage of the opportunity if I leave the fridge door open by mistake.

Rather than decide upon a set routine or response for teaching this, I prefer to keep Wolfie with me, and teach him how to manage himself when I have food, so that he understands the situation in each case. In this respect, I work with whatever Wolfie gives me of his own free will, which entails

teaching in a certain way. It's not about Wolfie giving a correct or incorrect response, as there is no 'right' or 'wrong' at the start of teaching, since he doesn't know which is which.

Every response he gives is the right response, and I use it to guide his actions, giving him the freedom to choose what he does, rather than teaching him a specific action. I use this approach to develop his abilities rather than try to change his response head-on, or limit his options and allow him to make only the response I want. (This does involve him helping himself to Matt's Yorkshire pudding, but, as you will read, this was a learning stage from which we have since progressed. And Matt did get another Yorkshire pudding, so everyone was happy!)

Ordinarily, teaching impulse control begins the moment a puppy acts on an impulse. For Wolfie, some of these are when I open the gate to go for a walk, and he rushes through; he sees Chilli the cat, and tries to chase her; I open the fridge and he sticks his nose in; he sees his food bowl and jumps to get it. As far as I am concerned, however, addressing impulse control as described above does *not* begin when Wolfie acts on an impulse, as this means that we are once again behind the behaviour, not in front of it. A dog who is displaying a lack of impulse control is showing the results of this in his actions: the lack of control has already occurred in his mind, which is where I want to concentrate my teaching.

Wolfie has been with us for two days, and is still finding his feet, so is not confident or sure of things yet. He is not overly-excited about going for a walk, as this is new to him, and he does not yet associate seeing his lead with going out. He has not yet tried to chase Chilli when he's seen her; he's simply looked. And he has not yet associated the fridge with yummy food, so is not jumping in anticipation of his meals. This is the perfect time to begin teaching Wolfie impulse control.

If your puppy is more enthusiastic about these things, and has engaged with everything as soon as you bring him home, you can still use this strategy, but will need to time your teaching to occur in advance of what your pup becomes excited about, so that your input is just in front of everything he does, and you are working *through* his excitement, rather than, in Wolfie's case, *before* he becomes excited. I worked like this when teaching Wolfie to manage himself when I came home with the shopping, as you will read further on in the book.

The first step is to put language in place so Wolfie can learn what to do around each situation. I can begin to teach this now, before Wolfie makes associations and becomes excitable in anticipation of an event. If he has learnt how to behave in these situations before impulsive behaviour occurs, he has the tools in place to enable him to control his impulse with more ease than if he did not already know what to do. Of course, this will take time, and, as you will discover, Wolfie can be as impulsive as the next puppy, but by beginning the teaching process ahead of this, his mind is in a receptive state, and he finds it easy to learn.

At this stage he learns the language around each situation, which makes it easier for him to learn the routine of daily life, and know what to do.

(😊) *Behaviour Tip*
What is the difference between impulse control and self-restraint?

The answer is determined by which part of the mind is responsible for each action. The impulse to do something is an instant response that comes from the emotional mind; it is not a product of thinking things through, and happens reflexively as a response to stimuli. Self-restraint is a conscious decision to cease acting on that impulse. The initial impulse to respond to stimuli may have passed, but the desire to carry out the actions may not have. There is often still a drive to respond, and, whilst this is not impulsive, it still requires self-restraint to not act upon that drive. This stems from the intellectual mind, and is a chosen course of action.

Continued exposure to said stimuli may cause another impulsive response, and this pattern may be seen: impulse to act controlled by the dog, who then seems to settle as he demonstrates self-restraint, only to be followed by another impulse to

act, which may not be so successfully controlled, or, if it is, the self-restraint is not as strong.

As Wolfie is very quickly going to associate the fridge with yummy food, this is the perfect place to begin teaching him impulse control and self-restraint around food. We open and close the fridge several times a day, which provides a great opportunity for Wolfie to learn not to take food that he has not been invited to take.

Imagine the scenario: I'm in the kitchen preparing dinner, and Wolfie is mooching about around me. The first step is to teach him the language. It goes something like this. I open the fridge and Wolfie wanders over. 'Ah, yes,' I say. This is the fridge. Lots of yummy things in here. Can you smell them?' Wolfie is sniffing at the fridge, but has not got his nose right in it, as this is only day two, and he is still sussing things out rather than going in with enthusiasm. 'Right, let's get this out for dinner, your nose is better off somewhere else! Excuse me,' I say as I close the door slowly so that he can remove his nose.

Over the next couple of weeks we have many conversations at the fridge. One of my guiding principles when teaching is that every response is correct, and I work with whatever Wolfie gives me, guiding him towards understanding. So when he puts his nose right into the fridge, I ask: 'Well, do you fancy that?' 'Okay, let me get there and have a look. Mind your nose, and we'll see what there is for you. Oh, look what I've got here, would you like that?'

We progress to 'Well, hang on a minute then; let me have a look and see what there is.' If there is nothing for Wolfie, I show him what I have as I take it out of the fridge, so, he gets to sniff vegetables, an egg, a jar of jam, etc. This satisfies his curiosity, prevents him over-anticipating, and teaches him which things are boring and which things might be for him. I talk him through each thing, saying 'Would you like some of this?' as I take out a joint of roast

'Ah, yes, this is the fridge.'
(Courtesy Mighty Dog Graphics)

'Well, do you fancy that?'
(Courtesy Mighty Dog Graphics)

beef. Or 'Oh no, this carrot is for dinner, not you, but would you like a carrot, too?'

I do not use the word 'no' in the context of telling him off, and I use the same kind and soft voice as usual, because constructive feedback is vital to effective learning. Once he understands, Wolfie can then decide whether he wants something when I offer it, and also dismiss those things that are not intended for him. If he decides to try and take something anyway, I can say 'That's not for you, silly boy, you can't help yourself. Now then, what do you think you should do if you want something?' all in a positive tone because I am not telling him off.

It doesn't take long for Wolfie to decide to wait and see what I'm doing at the fridge, rather than try and help himself. I give loads of positive feedback: 'Clever boy,' 'Well done,' and 'That was very restrained, you wait there.' The whole experience is engaging and rewarding; he is learning and understanding, so his self-restraint is not dependent on specific rewards such as food.

With regard to food, Wolfie needs the assurance that his food is *his*, whether this be his meal or a treat. The practice of taking food away from a dog is not one I advocate. It is often done to demonstrate that the owner is the alpha, but as already discussed, it has no value or purpose at all, and only serves to confuse and frustrate the dog.

It's also sometimes done in an effort to teach a dog to give up objects, but it's far preferable to do this using the toy-for-toy exercise described previously, substituting food for toys. Your puppy's food is never *not* for him, and taking away his meal can only lead to confusion. Every living thing has an instinct to guard what is theirs, especially if someone tries to take it away, so the likely response will be that he will tell you he doesn't want you to take his food. As he lacks the option of saying 'Excuse me; that's mine,' he will use his own language, which is a growl. This is usually interpreted as the puppy 'showing dominance,' when all he is saying is 'Please don't take my dinner!'

Don't forget, our dogs are dependent on us to provide their food, and as food is necessary for

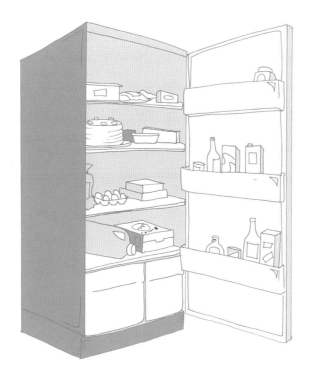

'Clever boy ... well done!'
(Courtesy Mighty Dog Graphics)

survival, it's no wonder if they respond in this way. And, as your puppy cannot know whether or not you will try this again another time, he may decide to protest in advance by growling at meal times, even if no attempt is made to take his food. This is resource guarding caused by human action. (Some puppies and dogs may already resource guard when they arrive at your home – there will be a reason for this.)

I want Wolfie to feel safe around food, so the only thing I am going to do is give him more. I can do this by giving him a smaller portion initially, and then, when he has finished this, say, 'Would you like some more?' and give him the rest of the portion.

If you want to follow my example, wait until your puppy has settled in, and has been left to eat in peace so that he already has a sense of security around food. Some puppies need a little time before you give them more, and going straight to the bowl the moment he has finished eating may cause him to think you are about to take his bowl. Some puppies are happy to sniff the food as you are putting it in the bowl, whilst others may prefer to wait until you have moved away. Get to know what your puppy's preference is before you begin adding food to the bowl, and do this calmly and without fuss.

How does your puppy respond to you at meal times? What does he do when he is finished? I am in the same area as Wolfie when he eats, but I leave him alone, and do not watch over him. Unless he lets me know that he is uncomfortable with me around, I do other things in the kitchen whilst he is eating, and when he is finished, I wait until he has

A puppy called Wolfie

moved away from the bowl before asking 'Have you finished? I'll pick this up, then.'

I watch for any sign that Wolfie is uncomfortable with any part of this, but he isn't, and is quite happy for me to be around him whilst he eats, and for me to pick up his bowl afterwards. I progress to asking him if he wants some more, and show him the food in my hand. Giving him some from my hand, I say, 'Let's put the rest in your bowl.' The next stage is to place the food in his bowl without giving him something from my hand first.

In the early stages, when he's finished I don't pick up the bowl until Wolfie's attention is elsewhere, and again I talk him through it, asking, 'Are you finished? Let's pick this up, then.' As long as he remains comfortable, this progresses to picking up the bowl before he has moved away from it.

Chapter 4
Conversation is education

Looking at the principles of teaching, my Wolfie's personality is pure sunshine. What has this got to do with teaching, you may ask. Well, part of what makes up Wolfie's personality is his nature – who he is – and part of it is nurture: how he has been brought up. Imagine how happy and content your puppy will be, and what a wonderful outlook on life he will have if you are always lovely to him. Should Wolfie act in an unacceptable way, I can address this by telling him he's a silly boy, and should we do this instead, in a positive way so that he's happy, or I can shout at him, tell him he's a naughty boy and make him unhappy. But why would I want to make him unhappy, when I can guide him toward doing the right thing, all the while praising him for being the lovely, clever boy he is?

Free Will Teaching uses a mix of well established and cutting edge human therapies, that include both research- and theory-based evidence, transposed to apply to animals. Established elements of good therapy are upheld, along with the therapist's ability to understand, apply, and tailor their advice to each individual animal's needs. Giving a dog a choice between A and B, or even A-D, is *not* free will, however, which is why I say that training conditioned responses is great for certain things, but not a way of life. Can you imagine living your life within the confines of limited options for everything you do? Giving a dog the freedom to express himself as he wishes develops and nurtures his soul. Of course, there are boundaries and rules, but these are restricted to the framework that we teach dogs

to work within, just as we are restricted within our own framework of abiding by society's laws, common decency, and appropriate behaviour.

As well as providing a framework for teaching and resolving behavioural issues, Free Will Teaching becomes a state of mind. Yes, I get frustrated at times: Wolfie is a puppy, and life does not always go according to plan, but I remain in control of my emotional state and my actions so that I behave as usual, and do not retaliate. When it seems as if all's going to pot, I remember that Wolfie can't help himself, it's not his fault, and, although it's difficult at the time, we will get through whatever it is that's causing the problem. And this state of mind applies to both Wolfie and me, as we each learn and benefit from interacting with one another; a process that enriches our lives, and gives us so much.

WOLFIE ...

Because Wolfie's life is so happy and rewarding, he can easily switch from one activity to another without any damage to his emotional well-being. Wolfie is just as happy to turn his focus and attention to me as he is to focus and engage with other dogs, people, or anything else. It is why he doesn't overly focus on things and become single-minded or obsessive, meaning that undesirable traits that are often ongoing in some dogs are transient for Wolfie. He does not become unduly frustrated, irritated or defensive, practise avoidance, have behavioural problems or ignore me. Well, sometimes he ignores me, but that's normal. No one listens *all* the time!

A puppy called Wolfie

Wolfie is happy to go along with what I ask, or may suggest something else, as he's confident enough to tell me what he does and doesn't want. He's proactive in seeking out those things in our day-to-day life that keep him content and happy. We have no problems, and it is all because of his state of mind. We have moments where things may go in a different direction to what is wanted, but Wolfie is a living being, not a machine, so it's easy to take this into account because of the way I teach. On a more profound level, the way I am with Wolfie has significant positive effects on his psyche, and contributes to everything he does.

... AND ME

Our way of life promotes my happy state of mind, and I can view setbacks without negative connotations. On a more profound level, it facilitates a state of mind whereby I can actually ignore certain pain levels (an old injury) and just concentrate on being with Wolfie. The feeling of love I have for him when we are actively engaged and doing something together eclipses is paramount.

I hope you are beginning to understand why Free Will Teaching is not a case of black and white: simple input and output, set cues and precise, robotic responses cannot encompass the intricacies of a feeling, thinking mind. What I do depends on what Wolfie does; there's no script to follow.

When I'm doing the washing, I talk Wolfie through what I'm doing, and do the same when putting on his harness to go for a walk.

Wolfie gets excited about my coming home with the shopping, jumping up to try and get his paws and head into the bags as I carry them from the car to the kitchen. Obviously, a routine is needed, so, the next time I bring in the shopping, I talk Wolfie through this.

It starts with asking him to come to the car with me. Once there I tell him 'Okay, we're at the car, let's get a bag.' As he becomes excited, trying to get his nose into the bag, I walk off, saying, 'Come on, let's put it in the kitchen, then we'll see what's in there for you.' If I have more than one bag, I say,

'Come on, back to the car for the next one,' until all are inside. I walk quickly from the car to the kitchen so that he has to speed up to follow me, which takes some of the momentum out of trying to get his head in the shopping bag. In the kitchen, I make my tone of voice more exciting so that Wolfie is more interested in following me back out to the car than staying in the kitchen and jumping up to the counter to reach the bags.

Once all the shopping is in I say 'Well, we'd better have a look and see what's in here for you.' and, as I retrieve whatever it is I've bought him, I tell Wolfie 'Hold on, then, I've got to unwrap it; give me a minute,' as his excitement and anticipation grows.

It doesn't take long for Wolfie to learn the routine, and less encouragement from me is needed for him to accompany me to and from the car, as he waits for me to get his treat out of the bag when we are finished.

I progress to only sometimes bringing something home for him, and say, 'Oh dear, there's nothing in here for you! Let's get you something from the cupboard.' when this is the case, thus ensuring that he does not always expect something then. The next stage is to tell him that he can have something from the cupboard in a little while, rather than straight after arriving home.

The end result is that Wolfie may choose to be part of the shopping routine if he is interested; is very happy if I bring something back for him, and is content to wait for something if I don't. He is developing his own self-restraint, and managing his excitement level and what he does, without any direct instruction from me. I do not teach him to sit, wait, or walk with me on cue, I only teach him what the routine is and leave the rest to him.

Teaching language means I talk Wolfie through his days, so that he understands what is going on and his place in this new life with us. Along with this, I also begin teaching specific word association, to which there are two elements –

• word association for objects, so that Wolfie learns the names of things

• word association to movement, so that he associates what he is doing with specific words

I tell Wolfie what an object is called as we come across it, and apply this to all of the things at home and in the garden, as well as when we're out and about. Taking the gate as an example, once I've told him 'We're at the gate' a few times, I say 'Let's go to the gate' in advance of getting to it, and 'Here we are at the gate' once we arrive there. In this way, Wolfie is learning what 'gate' means, and the phrase that tells him we are going to it.

I also point out landmarks. Most of the lanes hereabouts look pretty much the same with trees, gateways, and sheep and cows in fields, so not much scope for teaching actual landmarks, when there are so many of each thing! But this is easily resolved by progressing the basic word association to applying context and directional information, such as 'Shall we go to the next field?' or 'Come on, let's find the next tree,' or 'There are more sheep up here,' etc, etc.

To apply word association to movement, I simply say what it is that Wolfie is doing in the home, garden, and out on a walk. As he begins to walk from a standstill, I say 'Let's go.' When he moves from one side of the lane to the other it's 'Other side.' If he's scenting, I ask him 'What can you smell?' The emotional mind becomes more involved and dominant when the senses are used, which is why you may think that your dog has become deaf when he's scenting. The intellectual mind is in the background, and although he can hear and understand what it is you're saying, until input from the emotional mind reduces, he's unlikely to respond. It's like talking to someone whose mind is elsewhere: they've heard you but not taken in what you are saying. "What did you say?' they ask once they realise what's happened, which is exactly what happens with your dog, be he scenting, focused on watching something, or trying to achieve something. His mind has to disengage from the emotional focus, return to the intellectual focus, and be attentive to you before he is able to think and respond.

(*Courtesy Mighty Dog Graphics*)

It's easy to see this change when Wolfie is scenting as he lifts his head when done, at which point his mind is most likely to be transitioning from emotional to intellectual state; it is now that I ask 'Are you ready?' which engages his attention. Once he responds to me, I know he is listening, and can continue the conversation. As Wolfie learns that this phrase is associated with his shift from emotional to intellectual mind, I can use it to get his attention and help him disengage when his emotional mind is still at the forefront. In essence, he is learning to allow intellectual input to cut through the emotional state and not become swept away by it.

A puppy called Wolfie

When he turns back to sniff something, it's 'Turn around,' and, once again, it's not long until he associates the words with what he's doing.

Use only those words that come naturally to you when teaching word association, using normal conversational language. For example, I use the word 'together' to describe Wolfie for walking by my side, but some clients use 'close,' 'stay with me/by me,' etc. It doesn't matter what phrases you use, your puppy will pick them up. It doesn't matter, either, if other family members use different phrases, as your puppy is quite capable of learning your choice of phrase compared to someone else's. The consistency you need between family members is the Free Will Teaching ethos and framework.

From a human perspective, going for a walk is sometimes about getting from A to B and back again, and if this happens at a sensible pace without too much messing about, we consider it successful. But, from your puppy's point of view, this would be a very unrewarding and unsuccessful walk, as dogs interact with the environment, not just walk through it. (Well, some do, but there are reasons for that, and there are reasons why some dogs don't want to go out at all that I'm not exploring here.)

A rewarding walk for a dog is one during which he can have a good sniff to tell him what other dogs have been there, scent other animals, explore and investigate, and scent mark. They enjoy these activities at all ages, but for puppies or those dogs with limited experience of the outdoors, they are also a huge part of the learning experience. Some dogs, such as Remy (Wolfie's brother, who appears later), are highly motivated to *get* somewhere, whilst others (like Wolfie) enjoy sitting and watching the world go by. Otherwise, they like to sniff about, investigate and explore, so the more I can accommodate them the better, which might mean we end up going backwards, round in circles, a bit further, and then back again, which all make up an enjoyable walk for a puppy. Having your puppy lead you where he wants to go (as long as it's safe and you are able to follow him), provides a great opportunity to teach him more words and phrases, and apply what he has

From a dog's point of view, a walk is all about investigating the environment.

already learnt around the home and garden to your walks.

I use the phrase 'no further' when we cannot walk somewhere, and begin doing so when Wolfie is on-lead. Our first experience of this is our open woodland down the lane, which is not safe or even possible for me to walk through. Wolfie would manage to traverse it quite well, but it's not safe for him either; nor do I want him somewhere that I cannot be with him.

We get to an opening where we can walk a little way into the woodland, and have a look. Obviously, Wolfie wants to go further, and pulls on his lead. I stand still and tell him 'no further.' It's important that I do not pull him away when he does this, because he will learn that 'no further' means I will move him, which is no use whatsoever when he is off-lead, or when he is an adult and strong enough to pull me with him! Aside from that, pulling him back denies him the choice of changing direction and not going further that way. This is part of him having the self-control to disengage from one thing and move onto another. It also needs to be his decision in order for his choice of response to be reliable when he is off-lead.

So, I stand there and tell him 'no further,' and the moment his lead slackens as he turns his head, or makes any movement other than trying to go forward, I say something like 'Well done! Come on, then, let's go this way instead.' If he returns to looking forward, as if still contemplating moving in this direction, I leave him for a minute and then ask 'Are you coming? No further: we can't go that way.' I again praise him, and offer an alternative course of action for any positive response he gives. If he pulls again I repeat 'No further,' followed by another alternative.

It takes a couple of minutes, but Wolfie eventually looks around at me, and the tension on his lead slackens. His response gets loads of praise and enthusiasm from me, followed by engaging his attention in what we will do next. It takes just a little encouragement for him to turn, ready to continue down the lane. We continue to practice this whenever the opportunity arises.

'Steady' is the word I use for teaching Wolfie to maintain a constant pressure on-lead, and not pull to go faster. Quite important, this one, as I have no desire to be pulled along behind a fast-moving adult Wolfhound!

Teaching this concept begins with acknowledging that puppies can be excitable, and will pull to get somewhere, so expecting them to walk calmly beside you is unrealistic, when there are things they want to get to and investigate. Some puppies don't pull on the lead, but most do, either some of the time, or all of the time, depending on the puppy.

Wolfie has some self-restraint, but he is still a puppy, and will pull when he wants to get somewhere quickly. His size and strength mean it's quite a strain on my arm if he suddenly decides he wants to chase a butterfly as we are walking down

the lane. We also run when we are out on-lead, and Wolfie is very fast already – I can't keep up!

When Wolfie pulls, I speed up to a pace that is comfortable for me, and which I can sustain for a while, then I say 'Steady' so that he learns to associate the word with how much he is pulling, and the speed we are going. If he continues at this speed, I will repeat the word, and also say 'Clever boy, that's great.' If he pulls more to go faster, I say 'Whoa, hang on a minute,' or 'Wolfie, look here,' to interrupt the walk and slow us.

Sometimes, I have to slow right down and bring Wolfie to a halt in order to calm him and return his mind to intellectual mode, but this is never done by tugging on the lead, or pulling him back, as he is the one on the end of the lead, and I do not want him to accept this as routine behaviour. Apart from the sudden force of tugging not being good for him physically, he may also come to associate lead walking with sudden movements like this, and not the continuous pressure between us that I want him to. I need Wolfie to learn to adjust his pace himself, which is much easier to achieve by us gradually slowing, and only stopping if necessary, rather than coming to an abrupt halt and beginning the exercise again.

All of these things I teach Wolfie have so many benefits, and can be used in so many different contexts. By talking to him, I maintain a bond with Wolfie when we are out walking, and he learns to cock an ear to listen for me, making it easier for him to hear me through his emotional state. This also means that Wolfie's emotional mind is less likely to tip him over into manic behaviour, because he is using the intellectual side of his mind, and he is not as likely to lose the plot when he becomes excited, unless things are arousing enough for the emotional mind to take over completely.

Be aware, though, that simply nattering away is neither teaching nor educational. If what you are saying to your puppy doesn't mean anything, he is more likely to perceive your voice as background noise rather than something to listen to with interest.

A puppy who knows what to do and where he

A puppy called Wolfie

is going has a purpose, which gives him enthusiasm, and also means that you will be going the same way, with less pulling and lunging. Off-lead work will also become a lot easier, as you will have voice cues in place. It is much easier to engage a dog and have him come with you if you give him a reason to do so. You can even direct him to meet you at a landmark, tell him which way you are going, or ask him to turn around as part of teaching a reliable recall.

Having knowledge gives your puppy confidence, which usually means that he may be more easygoing. He will also have the means to deal with unfamiliar or worrying situations, as his mind will focus on you talking to him, rather than the situation.

WOLFIE'S DIARY
June 9
Day 5 with us: nine weeks and four days old

AM

6.20:	Breakfast
6.30:	Manic – better with clear yes/no voice cues
6.50:	Settled
7.20:	Asleep
7.35:	Awake
7.40:	Second breakfast
8.05:	Manic – 6/10
8.35:	More breakfast! Play, explore, bitey. Tried to get on sofa, legs far too little to do it!
9.15:	Zonked
10.05:	Awake. Tesco delivery arrived; Wolfie had a nice cuddle from the delivery man
10.20:	Lunch. Play
10.50:	Whining, then play
11.10:	Relaxing

PM

12.45:	Awake; walk up the hill
1.30:	Lunch. Wolfie likes apples and carrots, and keeps sitting in front of the fridge. Mad playtime, but some self-restraint apparent, as he didn't lose the plot so much. My hands nipped once only instead of several times as he took his toy!
2.06:	Relaxing on the beanbag
2.30:	Asleep
3.30:	Awake. Visitor, Neville: Wolfie was anxious; didn't want to greet him. Left him bumbling around the garden whilst we got on with some work
4.00:	Dinner. No mad half-hour, just relaxed
4.30:	Asleep.
5.00:	Awake and playing
5.35:	More dinner for Wolfie: as a fast--growing puppy, he sometimes needs extra meals
6.00:	Settled on the beanbag with the door open so he could go into the garden whilst I taught puppy class on exercise yard. Checked him twice – comfy, happy, relaxed – then went to sleep
7.00:	Class finished. Dad home. A walk and then a play
7.30:	Supper for Wolfie: he is a hungry boy today. Mad half-hour – 5/10
8.00:	Asleep for the night. (I got up twice only)

Everyone assumes that puppies will be excited to meet new people, but this is not always the case, as strangers can make puppies anxious. At this point in their lives, they will have met only a small number of people, and are not necessarily confident enough to greet new people straight away. Once Wolfie had settled in for a few days, friends began coming over to meet him, and we arranged this so that Wolfie would not be overwhelmed, asking that visitors be quiet in movement and voice; greeting Wolfie if he approached them, but not engaging with him otherwise. I wanted Wolfie to go at his pace and be comfortable around new people; I also wanted to ensure he didn't go over the top with excitement.

How visitors act can make a big difference to how a puppy perceives the situation. It's natural to want to cuddle a pup, and give him loads of fuss, but this might not be best for your puppy. A shy puppy is likely to be overwhelmed, anxious, or scared, making his early experiences of strangers less than positive. Trying to engage a shy puppy to make him interact can cause him to fear those he doesn't know – sometimes for the rest of his life.

If pushed too far, and he is forced to endure interaction he does not want, or being picked up, he may panic when he is not able to get away, and feel he must defend himself, usually expressed as teeth-baring or growling, since passive strategies are not possible, or have not been understood. Dogs do not like conflict, but, when given no choice, let you know they are not coping in whatever way is possible. Body language, such as lip-licking, looking away, yawning, trying to actually wriggle away, or staying still, are all signs that a dog is anxious, but if none of these produce the desired effect, more direct body language may result, and may include stiffness, laid-back ears, bared teeth, growling or snapping. None of these actions mean that your puppy is being aggressive: he is simply trying to communicate the extent of his distress.

Consider this scenario. At work, someone we have just met puts their hand round our wrist and holds on, making us feel anxious and want to pull away. At this point, we're unlikely to make a big fuss about the situation, although will probably ask that they let go of our arm. If this does not happen, our anxiety may go up a notch or two, and our actions and voice become more panicked. We might try other things: moving away, keeping still, looking down at the ground. If we are still not released, our survival mode may take over and we will try and remove the unwanted hand from our arm using physical force. This is exactly what happens with a puppy (or any dog) who is put in a situation he is unable to cope with or resolve.

The extremely unfortunate possibility here is that the dog's carer is completely unaware of their puppy's distress, subjecting him to similar situations when the next person comes to visit. As a result of his traumatic experience, the puppy has learnt to be afraid of people. The next time he meets someone new he may be okay until his tolerance level is reached, and he can no longer cope, or he might even growl or snap as soon as the new person gets close to him, so damaging was the previous encounter. The real tragedy about this is that, at some point, most people might incorrectly deduce that the puppy is aggressive, and decide that something needs to be done about it, which is usually bad news for the dog ...

The flip side to the foregoing is an over-excitable puppy. Puppies have little control over their arousal level, regulating it takes time, and until they learn how to do this, it rises as the result of additional stimulation. Enthusiastic and keen visitors will move their arms quickly, talk in a higher-than-normal voice, and be very interactive with the puppy, all of which increase his level of arousal, and he ends up going over the top, often becoming manic.

In this state, he may run around madly, wee, become jumpy, bitey, or grab and pull clothes. It is usually impossible to get through to him until he has calmed down, which can take some time. Being in a manic state can cause huge frustration, because, as far as his mind is concerned, it is trying to achieve something, but never manages it. This is very relevant because, when the mind reaches natural resolution (the satisfaction of achievement) it naturally calms down. A mind that does not reach natural resolution must still find some way to do so, but the two options it has are neither natural or healthy because the emotions and drives that are fuelling the arousal must either dissipate or escalate. If they escalate, this results in an intense expression of action, often expressed as manic jumping and biting, after which arousal levels drop and the puppy calms.

If the puppy's emotions and drives do not *not* escalate, the mind will dissipate these in order to reduce his arousal level, and this can often only happen when a factor is removed from the situation that changes the situation and allows dissipation

A puppy called Wolfie

Wolfie is very excited about a new box.

to occur. The continued presence of those present prevent dissipation, and fuel escalation, so leaving the room can help, but this results in disappointment for the pup, and an inability to achieve. When the mind calms in this way, it can leave the puppy feeling unfulfilled, and the mind unresolved. Both escalation and dissipation can lead to feelings of dissatisfaction, irritation, or resignation, and are expressed as anger or by opting out.

Ensuring that a puppy is not subjected to this situation in the first place may seem an obvious answer, but until the puppy has learnt to regulate his emotional mind, it's pretty much unavoidable. And although it's not a healthy state, that can have lasting negative effects if not handled correctly, it *is* necessary, because a mind that is never allowed free expression will become severely damaged and dysfunctional.

To ensure that your puppy's mind stays as healthy as possible, addressing his arousal levels

in the right way is vital. Minimise amplification of the arousal level by tailoring what you do, how you do it, when, and where, to your puppy's emotional state. Refer to the arousal infograph in Chapter 5, and assess where your puppy is at any given moment to guide you about where his arousal level will be when you add different stimuli. For example, if Wolfie is already 'up,' taking him somewhere that's really busy is likely to increase his arousal level. Think about what interests your puppy, and what his drives are. Wolfie is a sight hound, so movement will increase arousal, as will a windy day in summer. Grass, bushes and leaves that are moving catch his interest; so, too, birds, bees and butterflies flying about. Each of these on their own raise his arousal level, so all of them together really rack it up. If I was to then add a visitor to the mix, or take him for a run along the lane, Wolfie's arousal level would go sky high!

Instead, I tailor our activities so that he doesn't experience so much stimulation that he tips into mania. Once his arousal level reduces, I still need to be careful, however, as more stimulation before the mind has calmed completely will send Wolfie straight back up.

If your puppy's state of mind has already become manic, don't force a resolution through escalation. Although further excited play with a puppy in high arousal might seem like a sensible decision (the thought being that it will expend his energy and he will calm down), this is not necessarily the case. Certain activities will simply feed mania, and an intense explosion of activity is often the result once a factor in the situation changes: finishing the game, turning and walking away, or another dog engaging with the puppy.

What feeds mania does depend on the individual dog. I have known a few dogs whose manic state was fed by their favourite ball or food, despite these being the things they found most pleasurable in other circumstances. Once the mind was in a manic state, they made things very much worse. For others, a change in movement – such as being let off the lead, or moving from the home to the garden – ensured that the mania continued Sometimes it's a specific object, area, or association, and sometimes it's that something in the situation has changed – moving from inside to outside, or a person, dog or cat appearing – that causes the escalation, or triggers an explosion.

As the weeks go by, we progress our word association to having a conversation. I can ask Wolfie which way he wants to go; what he wants to do. He can reply, as I've given him the means to do so, and crucially, he understands what I am asking him so can contribute to the conversation. Teaching your puppy to understand his choices and make decisions has so many advantages, but more about that as Wolfie progresses.

The next element to begin working on is understanding body language. Having a conversation with your puppy is not just about using your voice: it's about what he does, too. The sooner you can learn to read him, the easier it will be to get through all the stages of puppyhood.

Notice what he does at different times of the day. It won't be long before you recognise his behaviour when he is hungry, sleepy, or about to have a mad half-hour. Once you are familiar with how he acts, look a little closer to begin to see other factors, such as frustration, times when he doesn't know what he wants, or when he shows anxiety, fear, or excitement. Combining your word association and body language then will enable you to understand what he's doing, and why.

Wolfie has been with us for just a few days, but, by day two, I have begun teaching the following –

- how to manage toileting
- leaving Wolfie on his own so that he doesn't develop separation anxiety
- teaching impulse control, self-restraint, word association, and body language

That's quite a bit, but it's easy to put all of these things in place because I do them as I go about my day, and they are often inter-related.

Teaching becomes easy; it's a way of life, and it's not necessary to find extra time every day for specific training sessions. Of course, going to puppy classes is a very good thing to do, as I've already discussed, but the Free Will Teaching type of learning is incorporated into your daily routine.

Reliable recall

Matt and I had been working on calling Wolfie's name, and asking him to follow us, with cues such as 'This way,' or 'Let's go up the hill.' This is the start of recall teaching, and all went well until both Chilli the cat and Winston the chicken decided they wanted to watch. Wolfie looked from one to the other ... then promptly sat down. This was good, as we've been working on impulse control since he arrived last Thursday, but this was not the reason he sat down, of course. I could see his little face first light up, and then – glancing from Chilli to Winston – take on a rather confused look: what a decision for a puppy – who should he try and play with first?

There's a lot more to successfully teaching a reliable recall than calling your dog and giving him a food reward when he comes to you. This simple strategy works for some dogs, but, in my experience, it always falls apart at some point. This can be when the puppy gains more confidence, when his hormones kick in, when he associates the recall with the end of his off-lead play, when other dogs, people, or practically anything else is more interesting, when the food reward is not good enough to compete with being off-lead, when the pup does not consider the recall sufficient motivation to return, or simply because he just doesn't want to!

I like to have a range of recall options available to cover all outcomes. Firstly, in order to have a great recall, you have to be part of the walk with your dog. If you let him off the lead when you arrive at your destination, and leave him to do his own thing, only calling him when you want to leave, it's quite likely that he will not want to return. Although he loves you, and wants to be with you, this does not apply when he is outside having fun, and you represent the end of that fun.

A puppy called Wolfie

The language that I teach around the home and garden can apply to when Wolfie is off-lead. Let's go this way, up the hill, to the gate, etc, are all good directional phrases that tell your dog what you are doing, and gives him a purpose; something to do. Doing this also keeps his mind at least partly in intellectual mode, because if he has half an ear listening to you as you are saying something relevant to him that he can engage in, his mind will not go so far into emotional focus, where he can't think or respond. Another benefit is that you become an interesting and important part of the off-lead experience, which increases the value of your input.

Things that dogs love to do have a very high value for them, and if the alternative is of a much lesser value, the dog is not going to choose this. Reducing the value gap makes it a lot easier for your dog to disengage from one activity and focus on another. I also play games such as hide-and-seek, ball, Frisbee, running with Wolfie, all backed up by positive feedback.

OH, OH, IT'S THE VET ...

The next thing to tackle is Wolfie's first visit to the vet. It's up to the individual to decide when to begin the usual vaccinations, and often, people prefer to wait until their new puppy has settled in for a few days. I would rather get them started as soon as possible so that we can begin going out without risk to Wolfie.

Day two sees us off to the vet for Wolfie's first vaccination. We carry him from the car park into reception and tell them we are here. Wolfie is already quite big and getting heavy – he's going to weigh more when we come back in two weeks' time for the next one! The reception staff make a fuss of him. I watch him to make sure he is not overwhelmed by the attention, and is enjoying it.

There's a certain reluctance to ask people to stop interacting with your puppy, but it's important to have this ability when taking out your new puppy, or when others are around any of your animals. I do not let embarrassment or lack of confidence prevent me from asking people to stop stroking Wolfie if he

is not enjoying this attention, because I want him to feel comfortable with every aspect of his life if he is going to grow into a balanced confident adult. If he does not enjoy this attention, he is likely to associate people with his negative feelings, from where it's but a short step for him to try and avoid contact. If he can't avoid this, his only option is to tell others not to get close – usually in the form of a growl, particularly if he is on-lead, and therefore has limited choices.

As previously mentioned, do not make the mistake of thinking you have an aggressive puppy: he is simply communicating his anxiety in the only way available to him. The same may happen when he finds himself in other scary or worrying situations, so your job is to read his body language to prevent situations like this.

If you find that your puppy is beginning to become anxious, the simplest thing is to ask the person involved to stop stroking him. Another strategy, which may seem less unfriendly, is to speak to your puppy, and ask him something along the lines of "Are you okay, or have you had enough attention now? It's a lot for a little puppy, isn't it?' This lets the person know that your puppy needs space, without you having to say it directly. It's then easy to switch to talking to the person concerned, saying, maybe 'Thank you for the cuddle, I think he's had enough now, I'm just going to sit quietly with him.'

As well as making it easier to ask someone to stop without offending them, and prevent you feeling embarrassed or as if you are making a fuss, talking to your puppy also takes his mind off the unwanted attention, and thus interrupting anxiety escalation. Obviously, timing is important, so intervene the moment you recognise that your puppy is struggling to cope.

Wolfie likes being stroked, so he has quite a few cuddles from the nurses. Going in to see the vet, we are armed with some tasty treats, and lots of praise for Wolfie. The vet is very nice, and takes the time to say hello to all of us. When he's ready to administer the vaccination, we give Wolfie yummy treats and tell him he is a very clever boy. The whole thing goes smoothly, and Wolfie is not worried. We also weigh him and, at eight weeks of age, he is 13kg (28.6lb).

As this is the first vaccination of the course, Wolfie is not fully protected yet. Huge debate exists regarding when it is safe to take a puppy away from the home and garden: for a walk or to attend puppy class, say. The question must be weighed up between wanting to begin your pup's socialisation as soon as possible by taking him out, or avoiding the risk of disease if the entire vaccination process has not been completed. Unfortunately, vaccinations take several weeks to administer, and, in my opinion, this is valuable time that should be spent teaching your puppy about the world. That said, it does not mean you have to start in a busy, noisy, populated area: my feeling is that it is possible to go out *and* keep your puppy away from risk. Discuss the subject with your vet, and remember that whilst vaccinations are not a guarantee of immunity, they are the best way of keeping your dog safe.

If you decide not to let him walk anywhere until his vaccination course is complete, there are still plenty of opportunities for socialisation. Many people carry their puppy when out and about, so he can begin to experience things whilst remaining safe. This is not quite as easy with a giant breed, for obvious reasons, although it's still possible to visit friends who don't have dogs, and he can run around in a garden that has not had dogs in it, or visit friends whose dogs are fully vaccinated, though careful introductions should first be made between the dog and puppy, and all interactions at the dog's home supervised. If you meet other puppies at the veterinary practice who are also going through initial vaccinations, there is an opportunity to make plans to visit each other.

My strategy is to take Wolfie out once he has had his first vaccination, although we are very careful about where we go with him. We avoid areas where dogs are likely to have been toileting, such as lamp posts, trees, and grassy bits we know dogs frequent, and walk in the middle of the path or lane, rather than along the verges, in areas where not many dogs frequent. We also avoid stagnant water,

or anywhere where rats might have been. That our walks are limited is not a problem, as Wolfie needs to learn about the world a bit at a time, rather than at the park when it is busy. This would be totally overwhelming, and most likely result in the start of Wolfie feeling fear and anxiety towards places, people, dogs, or noise. We take things slowly so Wolfie remains in his comfort zone. We use the same gradual process with every experience, whether it be going for a walk, visitors coming to the house, or seeing new things.

WOLFIE'S DIARY
June 11
Day 7 with us: nine weeks and six days old

AM
6.15:   Breakfast. Play – 5/10
7.40:   Settling down
8.00:   Asleep
10.15:   Awake. Wolfie meets his second visitor. Was a little worried, but relaxed after a couple of minutes. Had a play and then a tummy tickle; then another play
11.00:   Lunch. Manic – 6/10, but only about half as long as yesterday. More play, settles down

PM
12.20:   Asleep
1.20:   Awake. Began teaching 'look' and recall. Went up the hill. Wolfie chased Chilli. Distracted him with tasty food: brilliant! Chilli hid in the reeds like she used to when she ambushed Indie, but she stayed there, and didn't ambush Wolfie – not sure about being that close to him yet; still wary
1.50:   More lunch. Settled down. No play. Looks a bit hot and tired. Some whining as he tried to settle down
2.05:   Asleep
3.30:   Awake; mooches about

4.00: Dinner

4.40: Relaxing after another walk up the hill. Sleepy. No more manic time since this morning

5.15: Awake and on the go. Walk. Dinner. I left him with Matt whilst I went to teach for an hour

7.00: Comfy, excited when I came back in. Play. More dinner. Still on the go at 9.30pm! Couldn't settle, so we went to bed to remove stimulation, so that he could go to sleep

NOTE

Puppies grow quickly, and sometimes need extra food in addition to their set mealtimes. I am guided by Wolfie, and if he is hungry between meals, I give him extra food. As a puppy's tummy is not yet very big, smaller meals fed more frequently are good for him.

HAZARD AVOIDANCE

I notice that, after being with us for a week, Wolfie shows hazard avoidance behaviour. We've been happily exploring the home, garden and some fields, but when I open the gate to the next one, Wolfie is very sure he is scared. His response is to stand and bark a couple of times, his body leaning backwards away from the field. There is nothing different, and as we've been on the other fields, he is used to the open space. Enticing him is no help as he will be moving forward under coercion, with his mind not backing up his actions. This is the last thing I want to happen, so I close the gate and say, 'Come on, we'll go this way instead.' As I am aware that Wolfie is in the hazard avoidance phase, I make sure that what we do is familiar, and I do not expose him to things that are so unknown that they will trigger a fear response. This means thinking about what places we visit and what activities we do during this time.

This behaviour occurs a few more times before it is obvious that the phase is coming to an end, and we can resume our usual investigation of novel experiences, in line with taking things at Wolfie's pace.

The average age for the onset of hazard avoidance is seven weeks. As most puppies go to their new homes at around 8 weeks old, depending on breed, your puppy may be at the tail end of this period, as in the case of German Shepherds, who are usually around five weeks of age when it starts, or your puppy may have just started or be in the middle of it, or, as with the Labrador, may not experience this until he is around ten weeks old.

During your puppy's first week with you it's going to be difficult to determine whether any fear response is due to the unfamiliarity of his new home, or hazard avoidance, so, once he has settled in, your guide will be his breed, and whether you see a fear response to things that he has only briefly encountered, or has not previously encountered. Remember that, just because he has seen something, this does not mean his mind has processed it, and become accustomed to it.

A common fear response is for a puppy to avoid or back away from something/somebody, or maybe stare at or bark at it. If you see this, the best course of action is to reassure your puppy that all is fine with your voice and actions, but don't encourage him to investigate it. When the mind is in a hazard avoidance state, it's conditioned to remember what made it feel threatened. Although encouraging your puppy to interact with what is scaring him may seem like helping him to overcome his anxiety, it will have the opposite effect, and cause him to form an association that it is a threat. The best thing to do is to pay no attention to what is causing the fear response, distract your puppy, and focus on something else.

When his mind has gone through this phase and is no longer in a state of hazard avoidance, he will be more open to investigating something that seems scary. If the puppy is in the right state of mind, and you help him feel comfortable without expecting him to join in, it can aid his learning, so things he is not receptive to in hazard avoidance can always be addressed afterwards.

WOLFIE'S DIARY
June 16
Day 12 with us: ten weeks and four days old

AM

6.15:	Breakfast. Manic – 4/10
7.40:	Comfy, dozing
8.30:	Awake. Walk, play
9.00:	More breakfast. Walk, play, manic, but on his own, not directed at me. Yippee!
9.45:	Asleep
10.15:	Awake, mooching
10.35:	Dozing
11.40:	Went to the pond. As we were coming back he tried to nip me. Managed to get back down to the house with him very excited, and he focused on running downhill for his toy rather than on me

PM

1.30:	Went out and left him at home, the first time away from the house. Up until now we've been on the farm, although not always within eyesight or hearing range. Was out for an hour-and-a-half – don't think he moved, and was still asleep when I got back

NOTE

In the afternoon, Wolfie wanted to interact with me but was not sure how, but had a go. It started well, but then there was too much excitement and he was biting. He's been too hot – he's like a little radiator – and has struggled to get comfy. He definitely wants my company. I have been taking a step back so that he can do things for himself. More and more he's sitting on my knee: how lovely! He only chewed me a little, and was easily redirected to his toys. Didn't go over the top, and got off my knee before becoming too excited.

Everything we do is guided by Wolfie's response. The aim is to keep him relaxed and interested by watching and analysing his body language, which we have already begun to understand as we are taking notice all the time we are with him. Any time he feels unsure, we move away from the object or area, distracting him with words and sometimes food, too, telling him he is a clever boy. The word association we have begun is invaluable for this, as it focuses his mind away from his anxiety, and gives him something specific to do, which is great for confidence-building. This makes it easy for us to move him away from a worrying situation without reinforcing an anxious state of mind, and lets Wolfie know that he can get himself out of situations that worry him.

Chapter 5

Thought creates action, and action creates thought

Understanding how the mind of a dog works is key to understanding him. Free Will Teaching (FWT) focuses on working with the mind to improve cognition – both intellectual and emotional.

Nurturing and supporting every living being, giving them the opportunity to achieve their true potential, is what we should all strive for. I firmly believe that every being should have the right to free will, within the boundaries of what is morally and ethically sound, as this creates a safe environment where every being has the freedom to express themselves. Everything I do in all aspects of my life originates from this perspective.

Whether it's people or animals, it is my job to teach them how to help themselves, how to solve problems, be self-confident and emotionally resilient, and comfortable with who they are. These skills are for life: I feature only temporarily in the lives of the many people and animals I work with, but the skills I teach last forever, enabling each individual to further develop and enhance their lives.

FWT EXPLAINED

Free Will Teaching has four stages, and, in many situations, all are employed during teaching. For applications such as rehabilitation, where time is needed to change existing perceptions, emotions, and responses, each stage is used in turn to achieve the level needed to progress to the next stage.

FWT STAGES
● Subliminal
● Shaping
● Active
● Partnership

Subliminal

Working behind the scenes. Subtle behavioural work that does not fully register on a conscious level. Watching this is like watching paint dry! It appears that nothing really happens, but there is a huge amount going on to allow the animal's mind to relax and feel safe. This is the start of creating trust.

Shaping

Remaining subtle, but increasing awareness. The animal knows something is happening, and gives his side of the conversation. My role is to be a silent partner; not actively contribute. I adjust to what the animal is communicating; nothing more. I am reinforcing the beginning of trust.

Active

This is where my active involvement in the conversation begins; where I respond and have input. We learn more about each other. We develop our understanding of each other's language, likes, dislikes, personality, abilities, and trust.

Partnership

We trust each other. We understand each other's language and can contribute, listen and respond to each other. We know each other well enough to know how we will each behave in situations, what our responses are most likely to be, and how we manage ourselves.

THE SCIENCE BIT

Free Will Teaching is a framework that recognises, supports, and nurtures every aspect of life by integrating elements from different psychotherapy approaches, and applying them to working and living with animals.

Free Will Teaching uses a mix of well established and cutting edge human therapies, that include both research- and theory-based evidence, translating them to working with animals. The established elements of good therapy are upheld, along with the therapist's ability to understand, apply, and tailor their advice to each individual animal's needs.

Cognitive Behavioural Therapy (CBT) (1960s)
With its roots in Rogerian Therapy and Cognitive Therapy, CBT also utilises aspects of other therapies, including those listed below. CBT is the most developed, well established, and scientifically researched modern therapy, which, due to it being the most successful at achieving long term results, remains at the forefront of resolving dysfunctional states of mind.

Our perception of a situation determines how we feel and act, and directly influences our emotions and behaviour. By adjusting negative thoughts we can change our perception, thus changing our emotional state and behaviour.

Key components of CBT are –

• Conceptualization
The therapist understands the perspective of the individual. Everything the individual does makes complete sense if you know where they are coming from

• Developmental experiences
Whereby every experience shapes the mind and personality of the individual, contributing to their current perspective

• Core beliefs and assumptions
Arising from life experience, these are not necessarily a true representation, though they shape emotions and actions

• Collaboration
By working with the client, and guiding them through how to make changes, they then become their own therapist

• Skills for life
The end result is a client who is self-aware, has sustainable and healthy coping strategies, and progresses and develops their self-confidence and abilities

Gestalt Therapy (1940s)
The environment influences and is linked to every person, with context affecting each experience. The focus is on the here and now, developing the ability to trust emotions and acknowledge needs, improving self-awareness. Past experience influences the present state, but is not focused on. Forcing change leads to fragmentation and distress: change from within is the objective.

Dialetical Behaviour Therapy (1970s)
This therapy draws on three theoretical models – Biosocial theory, Zen Buddhism, and Dialetic philosophy – and focuses on acceptance-based strategies for emotional well-being, and teaches emotional regulation, frustration tolerance, mindfulness, and interpersonal skills. Therapeutic stages are stabilization, exploration of emotional state, enhancing quality of life, and progression to the next level.

Self Therapy (1970s)
This was the foundation of modern psychoanalysis. Empathy is an essential part of developing self-esteem, self-worth, and self-value. Therapists have the ability to see things from the client's perspective to aid development. The self is the core of a being's psychological world, and within a healthy

environment that develops this, self-regulation and self-soothing are possible.

Humanistic Therapy (late 1950s)
This is based on the belief that people are inherently good. Ethics, morals and good intentions are said to be the motivations behind behaviour.

Fundamentals of this therapy are –

- we all have free will
- our behaviour is not always preordained
- we each have a desire to reach our full potential (self-actualization)
- each of us and our experiences are unique.

Humanism has contributed to psychology in general, and a number of important therapies have been developed from this movement, such as –

- hierarchy of needs
- person-centred therapy (Rogerian)
- unconditional positive regard – towards the individual
- free will
- self-concept – how we think of ourselves
- self-actualization – the ability to meet our true potential

HOW THE BRAIN PROCESSES INFORMATION

The brain is split into three main areas for evaluating input. *The cerebral cortex* is where the intellectual brain sits, and is where abilities such as consciousness and intelligence are. Thinking and reasoning happens in this part of the brain, enabling problem solving and learning.

The limbic system houses the emotional mind, which interprets the emotional content of input, to provide context and significance based on prior experiences and learning. It works with the intellectual mind to decide appropriate actions and responses to input stimuli.

The basal ganglia is the site of the instinct (reptilian) brain, which is concerned with innate, hard-wired instincts that do not require learning. The genetic make-up of each species contains inherited patterns and responses to facilitate survival.

The brain works by analysing input data, and deciding on a course of action via complex interaction between the intellectual and the emotional mind. If a dog experiences a very strong emotional response, this triggers the instinct brain, with the intellectual part of the mind being inhibited in order to allow the animal to concentrate on survival. If a dog is in a highly aroused state, he will not be able to listen and respond in a rational manner, and his responses will be based on instinct. This is not a matter of choice but a neurochemical response, common to all mammals, and one which we cannot change. This has very serious implications for how we handle a dog, or, indeed, any animal in this state.

LEARNING

When referring to animals, learning is often described as having two main components: learnt responses by association and learnt responses by consequences to actions. Working in a calm environment, when the dog is in the right mood, and using small steps that enables the dog to understand and progress, will help learning be more effective, and pave the way for success.

However, productive learning is so much more involved, comprising many more elements that contribute to its success and achievement level.

TEACHER/STUDENT RELATIONSHIP

Developing a positive-based, empathic relationship with students – be they people or dogs – is essential to learning outcomes, and is particularly important to help young students develop long term emotional resilience. With a difficult-to-teach student, the teacher may experience feelings of dissatisfaction, irritation and frustration, and, however hard they try to be positive, their emotional state colours their body language, voice, and actions. Continuing in this way results in a punitive route, which is widely recognised as unproductive and superficial in terms of compliance (studies have shown that students attribute punitive methods to the teacher, and do not feel that they are in any way responsible for them). This leads to a breakdown in the relationship that can be difficult to overcome, and strong emotions and motivations in the student may manifest as anger, opting out, apathy, helplessness, and resentment.

Teacher personality
Whether you have an outgoing, quiet, or nervous personality, this is not indicative of how capable you are as a teacher. How you act and what you do within the learning environment is what makes you a good or a bad teacher, and also informs your students about whether they can trust you.

It takes just a tenth of a second for students to form an initial impression of a teacher, and whether their emotional state is positive or negative. This is closely followed by an updated impression at two seconds, which involves deciding whether or not the student is comfortable with the teacher. At ten seconds the student's view is shaped by using movement and stance to assess personality, and whether the student likes what they are seeing. Further time determines more of a dialogue with emotions and body language to make a more considered assessment, and explore the possibility of a relationship.

Feedback
In order to learn effectively, feedback needs to be productive and help achieve results. Praise alone does not improve learning; constructive, positive feedback about how to proceed does. Within the learning environment, praise has its place in developing the relationship, and positive feelings towards those involved. Positive feedback refers to affirming whether something is correct, or telling the student that it is incorrect, and then giving guidance about how to progress.

Social modelling and explicit teaching
You can't expect someone to get from A to B without first showing them how to get there. Watching an accomplished example of how to perform something does not provide instruction on how to do it; it needs to be demonstrated in progressive steps, with feedback given.

Observational learning by demonstration occurs when the teacher assumes the role of a model, so that the student may observe the skills required. Verbal instruction, scaffolding, encouragement, and plenty of practice are needed, along with timely corrective feedback to facilitate learning. (Corrective, in this instance, does not mean the common interpretation we use in the animal world – tell him off or punish him – but to point out where he is incorrect in his actions or interpretation, and show him what *is* correct.) This practice ensures you do not fall into the trap of giving continuous positive feedback to the student, which, counter to intuition, actually undermines an individual's self-worth. Every single thing a student does is not worthy of praise alone, without constructive or instructional input.

This approach to teaching gives the student the foundation skills to understand, assess, and interpret data in order to tackle complex tasks and situations. Explicit procedure should be taught as a framework, which can be applied in different contexts for it to be effective. If teaching is narrow, and based on specific rules, this interferes with lateral thinking, and an adaptive, flexible approach.

Acquiring knowledge
Learning does not occur in a linear way, but involves listening, watching, trying, getting it wrong, correcting, and collaboration, and how each individual goes about it is determined by individual perspective.

Six ways in which we acquire knowledge.

● The motivation to learn, and having sufficient time and effort to succeed
We do not learn immediately, nor do we learn without productive feedback and review of what we know. Actively learning means progressing and understanding further knowledge. If we just practise what we already know, this is not learning.

A puppy called Wolfie

- We can only learn when we are able to concentrate

This concentration span typically continues for 15-20 minutes before the mind needs a break, and trying to continue past this point impairs learning. Some individuals are motivated to quickly focus again on the task, whilst others need more time before returning to it.

- It is more effective to practise in small sessions than to try and process information in one long session

Going back to the task means that recognition plays a part, and it becomes easier to learn. This approach is also the most effective for developing procedural skills, as repetition in small sessions over a short period of time allows the mind to process and retain more information than it would in a single long session.

- Prior knowledge influences learning more than any other factor

New information goes through the filter of what we already know, and builds on that. If existing knowledge is based on misconception, this creates an obstacle to further learning. Unlearning and starting again is the solution. Unstructured information is difficult for the mind to understand; hence the mind uses prior knowledge as a building block for new information. Completely new information that can't be related in any way to existing knowledge is quickly forgotten. The key is to know what the student's existing knowledge base is, and teach from there.

- Our brains are wired to acquire information from different sources: a multi media approach

Linking and combining words to visuals results in more effective results than on their own, further enhanced by the mind being able to link to previous experience.

- The mind needs to be active in order to learn

Passivity results in information not being received.

An active mind actually does something with the stimulus and provides an actual response, which makes the information memorable. Observational learning is particularly strong when it does not involve physical or motor skills.

Understanding how the mind learns and acquires knowledge is essential to be able to teach effectively, and can mean the difference between a high and low level of learning, depending on the individual's potential and ability.

WOLFIE'S DIARY
June 18
Day 14 with us: ten weeks and six days old

NOTE
Wolfie has been here for 13 days now. He's getting bigger every day, but not, as yet, growing into his feet! I'm expecting him to reach my shoulders when standing on all four paws the way he's going!

WOLFIE'S ACHIEVEMENTS
Bearing in mind that it takes a lot longer than just 13 days to properly and reliably learn, Wolfie is already pretty good at look, sit, wait, careful, this way, come through, go through, breakfast, dinner, are you hungry?, find a toy, follow your dad, where's mum?, settle down, go for a wee, head down (to remove harness), give me your paw (feet out of harness), and back in a minute.

Some of these are first stages of association; some he is doing on cue.

No toileting inside day or night now, apart from two days ago when I was obviously very sleepy and didn't get up soon enough in the night – alarm wasn't on!

He's still very much in the teething stage, which makes him more bitey and frustrated as he tries to manage any pain and discomfort. When his play gets a little exuberant he's left on his own at that point!

Recall is coming along well; he will come when we call him with 'Come on Wolfie, this way,' and the other recall phrases we have begun teaching. We're also playing games in the garden and in the field. We've visited our local town, walked along the lane by our home, to the vet, local farmers' store, and parts of our farm. Wolfie's met my horses, Charlie and Star, our Hebridean sheep, the ducks (whom he's only chased twice – oops!), the chickens, Cecilia our rather noisy Guinea Fowl (he's not sure about her), and seen a few dogs. And he's had several visitors.

If he gets worried his default is to come to us, or go back to the house – the odd loud and unexpected noise has resulted in that. But once he's experienced something, he is braver the next time, and not so worried. Often, noise sensitivity in a young puppy is just part of the overall experience of leaving his mum and litter-mates, and the insecurity this transition causes, and is not necessarily an indication that he has a noise-sensitivity issue. Being calm and reassuring helps him get through this stage so noise doesn't become a problem, so I tell him what is going on when there is a noise.

Aircraft fly over our area a couple of days every few months, and some are extremely loud. Wolfie's first reaction to these is to run back to the house, and safety. I follow him in and talk him through it, as the aircraft usually make several passes overhead before moving on. I tell Wolfie 'Don't worry, it's just a plane in the sky.' Saying 'Shall we do such-and-such' can sometimes refocus his attention away from the noise; sometimes it doesn't. I might give him a cuddle, saying 'It's fine; it'll be gone in a minute.' Then, once the noise has abated, I tell Wolfie 'There you are: it's gone now.'

Some behaviourists say it's incorrect to comfort a dog who is scared, as this reinforces the idea that this is something to be afraid of, and he is right to be scared. Well, I don't believe that it's as straightforward as that. Reassurance from me is not

going to make Wolfie more scared, but will help him get though a scary situation. Fear exists on a scale – you can be a little scared, or absolutely terrified – and reassuring a dog in a scary situation will help him manage that fear, and prevent it escalating.

The support that Wolfie gets from me will gradually help him manage his fear, and he is already less scared of loud noises. When aircraft fly overhead, I say 'There goes another plane in the sky.' Wolfie looks up to the sky in acknowledgement ... then simply carries on with whatever he is doing.

Having taught Wolfie to happily stay on his own from the start – only a minute to begin with – I can go out and leave him for a couple of hours now without any problems or upset.

We are still working through his over-the-top excitement when he plays, which very quickly turns into playing with us and not his toys. Play bowing, pouncing and biting with us is not how we want to interact with him – particularly as he is the size of an adult Spaniel already, and no longer a small puppy. This is how he would play with another puppy or dog, but would still need help to manage his arousal level and listen to the other dog's side of the conversation in order to facilitate healthy play so that things do not go awry. We'll get there: it takes a little time, but, so far, things are going really well.

Well done, Wolfie!!

Autonomous Nervous System (ANS)

The autonomous nervous system (the part of the nervous system responsible for control of the bodily functions not consciously directed, such as breathing, the heartbeat, and digestive processes), comprises the parasympathetic and sympathetic nervous systems, and is part of the peripheral system (the portion of the nervous system that is outside the brain and spinal cord), and works with the somatic system (the part of the peripheral nervous system responsible for carrying motor and sensory information both to and from the central nervous system).

It regulates internal organs, and comprises three parts: the sympathetic nervous system; the

A puppy called Wolfie

parasympathetic nervous system, and the enteric nervous system. Regulated by the hypothalamus, it controls fight or flight reactions, and functions without conscious thought, although we can learn to control some aspects. The somatic system controls voluntary muscular movements, and when in conjunction with the autonomous nervous system, control is brought about via that route. The autonomous nervous system is always active.

SYMPATHETIC NERVOUS SYSTEM (SNS)
This is split into two parts, both of which are considered stimulating, when the mind is in an aroused state.

Part 1 Threat and protect
Focuses on survival and controls fight or flight responses, creating a state of arousal in the body that generates energy, and inhibits digestion.

Part 2 Appetitive
Controls appetitive behaviours (a behaviour pattern that occurs in response to a stimulus, and which achieves the satisfaction of a specific drive).

PARASYMPATHETIC NERVOUS SYSTEM (PSNS)
Restorative
Often called the rest and digest system, this is part of the involuntary nervous system that serves to slow the heart rate, increase intestinal and glandular activity, and relax the sphincter muscles.

In practical terms, in dogs we want to promote the appetitive part of the SNS, and minimise the threat and protect part of it. Stress is usually regarded as a negative emotion to be avoided, but there are two types of stress: eustress and distress. *Eu*stress is a positive form of stress, with a beneficial effect on health, motivation, performance, and emotional well-being; it can feel exciting and therefore improve performance. However, if it loses its positivity it can cause tension, and become intolerable, leading to *di*stress.

At this point, the state of mind will have

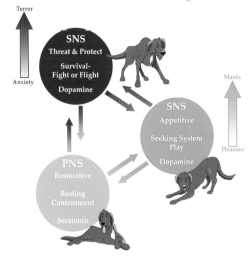

Autonomic Nervous System

(Courtesy Mighty Dog Graphics)

moved from appetitive to threat and protect, as distress is unpleasant, and causes feelings of anxiety and concern. You can see the change from eustress to distress when canine play or other activities go over the top, or become obsessive, when frustration can lead to irritation and anger. If the mind becomes anxious, more protective behaviours emerge. Reading your dog's body language and responses, and helping him stay within eustress is part of teaching him to be aware of his state of mind in order to regulate himself.

It is also very important to promote the PSNS, and restorative state, as this has a big influence on emotional stability and well-being, and is essential to healthy brain function. Teaching your dog to be calm, relaxed, and content helps with anxieties, particularly with those dogs of a more nervous disposition.

Emotions influence every thought and every action, and determine what state of mind our puppy has. How he is feeling affects what the autonomous nervous system does, so his emotional state should be the starting point from which to base every decision we make on his behalf, particularly if experiences and interactions during the sensitive period (see below) are to be regarded positively by our puppy, and help him develop a strong, emotionally healthy mind.

As previously mentioned, the mind comprises intellectual and emotional parts, with the former at the forefront in the normal course of events; the emotional mind providing emotion, colour and context to information that the intellectual mind processes. However, sometimes the emotional mind is at the forefront, and overtly influences perception and, consequently, actions (any strong emotion – positive or negative – can cause this effect). If positive, the sympathetic nervous system is triggered to set the mind in appetitive mode; if negative, the same system is triggered to put the mind in threat and protect mode. When the mind functions effectively, arousal levels are manageable, with emotion subsiding in a timely manner and the intellectual mind returning to the forefront.

For various reasons, this does not always happen, however, and the emotional mind can remain at the forefront too long; in some cases, permanently. Both situations impair the ability of the intellectual mind to function effectively, as high arousal continues.

Every animal (including human ones) is subject to the influence of their emotional mind, the level of which depends on the individual. Those dogs who are always on the go, have a strong work drive, are excitable or easily motivated, have a stronger input from their emotional mind than those who are often described as stubborn or lazy, but who actually just require the right motivation.

STARTLE RESPONSE

The startle response to sound is said to begin at around 19.5 days/nearly 3 weeks old, and is not related to the hazard avoidance behaviour seen in adults.*

HAZARD AVOIDANCE

Puppies have a well-defined neonatal period, a transition period, and a critical (or sensitive) period

(see below), and what happens to them during these periods shapes what kinds of dogs they grow up to be.

The onset of hazard avoidance (fear motor pattern, whereby a puppy avoids or chooses not to interact with something he finds scary), occurs in the critical period of development, with different breeds exhibiting this at different times, although average age is around 49 days/7 weeks old. In some more reactive breeds, such as the German Shepherd, this can happen earlier, at around 35 days/5 weeks old, and for the least reactive breeds, such as the Labrador, it can be as late as 72 days/10 weeks old.

This condition continues for roughly four weeks, with it being very evident the first two weeks, and then gradually reducing in intensity.

SENSITIVE PERIOD

Also called the socialisation or critical period, this is a crucial time in a puppy's life, and spans a period of behavioural development at between 3 and 12 weeks of age, which peaks at between 6 and 8 weeks. Opinion about at what age this period ends varies, with 12 weeks and 16 weeks the contenders, though it has been suggested that the end is more likely to be a gradual decline than a specific stop point.

It is this part of a puppy's life that is considered most important in determining his personality into adulthood, as most of the adult behaviour patterns are formed. These include investigatory behaviour and social behaviour and relationships, which are mostly expressed in a playful manner, but we also see distress vocalisation, location attachment, agonistic behaviour, and escape and avoidance behaviour. It is during this period that puppies are most receptive to learning about the world and how to navigate it, along with forming social relationships with their own and other species.

At around three weeks of age a puppy begins to become aware of and respond to his surroundings, and will see and hear a variety of stimuli which his brain processes. At first, loud noises (startle response) and scary situations make

---

* Scott, J, Fuller, J, 1965. Genetics and the social behaviour of the dog. University of Chicago Press. Chicago, IL.

him run to the safety of his mum. A lack of any physical consequence following these situations, mum's response, and the continuation or repeat of a situation can change that initial perception to one of familiarity, and the situation becomes non-threatening to him. He continues to learn about the world in this way, as he explores and investigates new things, gradually gaining self-confidence.

As his experiences increase, he is able those new to him with better accuracy, and progress his development on all levels. A puppy needs exposure to all sorts of experiences in order to function as a well-balanced dog. When he encounters a new situation, he will respond to it and his brain will store the event, response, and outcome of his response. It is these stored experiences that the puppy refers to when he is older and comes across a new situation. The more experiences he has when he is young, the more information he has to draw upon when older, giving him the ability to relate a previous encounter to a similar, current one.

Brain processes such as hazard avoidance switch on and off at the optimum time for species survival. Scientists have proved that much of the significant brain development necessary for a healthy mind and ability to navigate life competently happens during the sensitive period, at between 3 and 12 weeks of age. It's paramount, therefore, that our puppy's life experiences are appropriate to, and correlate with, these processes, in order for the brain to receive the correct stimulation, and develop properly.

Puppies denied adequate experiences during this period are significantly disadvantaged in terms of emotional health, coping strategies, and overall quality of life. Although we see the biggest developmental changes in the sensitive period, progress is ongoing throughout life, however, and what a puppy experiences as a puppy will not automatically be viewed in the same way throughout his life. Perceptions change due to learning, experience, and age, and unexpected events.

The sensitive period should provide a framework for a puppy to refer to when faced with novel stimuli, and all of the things that may occur during his lifetime, as, of course, it's not possible to experience absolutely everything at just twelve weeks old, and he shouldn't in any case, even if it were. Experiences during this period give the puppy reference to draw on for future situations, influencing responses and providing coping strategies. A strong framework of experiences contributes to emotional resilience.

Quality is just as important as quantity, and if a puppy has a limited number of experiences – even if they are all positive – he will possess a limited amount of learning to draw on. However, if a puppy is overwhelmed by a huge number of experiences that he can't cope with, these will most likely be perceived negatively, and result in his inability to interact successfully in the world, as he has not formed any coping strategies.

Coping strategies are healthy emotions and behaviour patterns that all animals use to respond

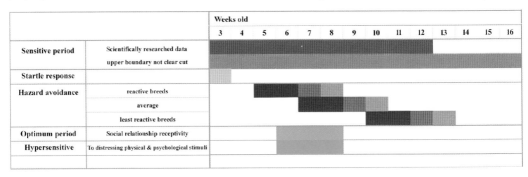

		Weeks old												
---	---	3	4	5	6	7	8	9	10	11	12	13	14	15	16
Sensitive period	Scientifically researched data														
	upper boundary not clear cut														
Startle response															
Hazard avoidance	reactive breeds														
	average														
	least reactive breeds														
Optimum period	Social relationship receptivity														
Hypersensitive	To distressing physical & psychological stimuli														

(Courtesy Mighty Dog Graphics)

to and cope with the stresses and difficulties of life, enabling us to remain emotionally resilient. If we do not have these, dysfunctional emotions and behaviour patterns – reactivity and fearfulness – result, which are not healthy for the mind or body, and can lead to serious distress, an altered perception of reality, and responses that are out of context or extreme.

To achieve a robust framework to provide a reference during the sensitive period, a puppy should experience the world at his own pace, so that his brain can process new information and experiences in a calm and supportive environment. If he is forced to investigate or interact with novel stimuli before he is ready, the threat and protect state of mind will prevail, and his perception will be *negatively* influenced from the point of view of self-protection. Being supported in taking things at his own pace results in an open and exploratory state of mind, which *positively* influences his perception of the situation. Because he has understood that new things can be viewed with an open mind, they are not a threat, so are not automatically regarded with suspicion. This gives him the ability to successfully assess and interpret novel situations that he will undoubtedly come across during his lifetime.

It is important to note that an experience can only be considered good or bad from the perspective of the puppy, and not the teacher, and how he assesses and processes this, and what response it elicits from him.

Socialisation does not create a personality, but shapes the traits already there, and it is perfectly possible to minimise or maximise aspects of a puppy's personality, his perception and responses by how he is exposed to experiences. For example, every puppy responds differently to stimuli, and major differences can be seen in the confidence levels of puppies from the same litter, as well as from different litters from different breeds and backgrounds. The puppy who is naturally quiet and reserved will perceive stimuli in a different way to one who is more outgoing.

Consider the response from all of the

puppies in the litter to the same new toy. Those who are outgoing will investigate the toy, quickly deduce it presents no danger, and will happily play with it. The quieter puppies may advance cautiously to investigate the object, displaying wariness, anxiety, and insecurity, possibly as a result of the boisterousness with which the more confident pups have engaged with it. Some puppies will learn that the toy provides a good experience, whilst others may not: each will have a unique perspective, and will take something slightly different from the experience. Although the same learning opportunities may be available to a litter of puppies, it takes more than just availability of whatever the stimuli is to ensure that all of them react positively.

Similarly, although we know that puppies should meet a variety of individuals of different species, and experience a range of different situations, there's more to achieving a positive learning experience from this than simply exposing the puppies to these.

All experiences are guided and influenced by a puppy's emotional mind. Emotional associations are continuously formed, are very powerful, and not easily overcome. It is essential that a puppy experiences positive emotional responses as he learns about the world, and signs of a negative emotional response should be addressed to ensure this doesn't escalate. Strategies to distract and diffuse the situation by refocusing a puppy's attention, or moving away from it, will prevent this happening. As he matures, he will be better able to cope with being out of his comfort zone when experiencing things that might be a little worrying because his coping strategies develop and progress as he grows.

HORMONES

Hormones come into play for males at around 4½ to 5 months/18 to 20 weeks old, and females when they have their first season, which is from about six months. Hormones are responsible for both physiological and psychological processes in both puppies and adults.

A puppy called Wolfie

MALES

The sex hormone testosterone can influence male behaviour in many ways, one of which is by boosting the confidence to experience new things. Hormones ebb and flow, and a dog will experience surges at developmental stages in his life.

A reduction in testosterone (withdrawal phase) can influence behaviour by producing a lack of confidence, which makes dogs fearful for a couple of days, until the mind acclimatises to the reduced level and perceptions return to normal.

Male hormone phases

The first hormone phase begins at around 4½ to 5 months, when owners talk about their pups becoming 'teenagers.' This continues for around two months. The second phase denotes sexual maturity, and occurs at around 9 to 11 months for most breeds, but often not until 12/13 months for giant breeds. Testosterone levels are now the highest they will be during a dog's lifetime.

The phase continues for around 2 to 3 months, and then testosterone levels slowly drop until around 18 months of age (or getting on for 24 months in giant breeds), where it remains for the rest of a dog's life, although small developmental stages, along with testosterone fluctuations, can still be observed in mature dogs.

Between these major hormone phases, a dog will experience smaller hormone surges.

The male hormone cycle

As noted in the foregoing, whilst a dog is developing, testosterone levels rise and fall, creating a cycle of hormone spike-growth period-withdrawal phase, which influence behaviour. This is most apparent during the major hormone phases (as described above). In between each of these stages will often be a day or two of balance and calmness.

Behaviourally, these stages translate to –

Male hormone cycle.
(Courtesy Mighty Dog Graphics)

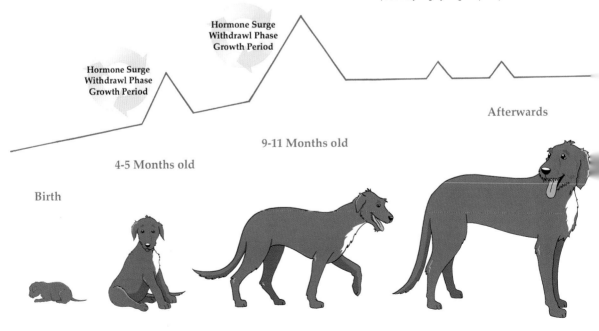

Hormone Surge
Withdrawl Phase
Growth Period

Hormone Surge
Withdrawl Phase
Growth Period

Afterwards

9-11 Months old

4-5 Months old

Birth

• Phase 1: Hormones increase
Hormone spike – manic puppy, biting, jumping, can't think or listen, obsessive behaviours

• Phase 2 Hormones are stable
Balanced – calm, nice play, can think and listen
Growth period – sleepy, less excitable, less energy

• Phase 3 Hormones decrease
Withdrawal phase – a little scared, needing support due to reduction in testosterone

Testosterone levels continuously increase and decrease during these hormone phases, affecting a puppy's mood and behaviour. You may see the clear distinction that I do with Wolfie, though stages may be less distinct, with aspects of the other two running through them: for example, a lack of confidence usually associated with the withdrawal phase as your puppy goes into the growth period, where it then settles, and returns as he moves into the withdrawal phase. It all depends on an individual's testosterone level, and how each puppy's mind copes with changes in this.

You will be able to spot and monitor the change from one phase to another, and how long each lasts. All dogs have different hormone levels, so there will be a variation in how much these hormone periods influence a pup's behaviour. Being aware of what's happening with your pup's hormones will allow you to manage the situation, and help him through this period.

Hormone cycle spikes are more pronounced in the second phase, making behaviour more intense. If you have taught your puppy to manage his emotional mind during the first phase, he should be able to partially regulate himself during the second, thinking through this time of change to some extent, making the second phase easier to get through.

FEMALES
Two main sex hormones are at work here: oestrogen and progesterone. During the female cycle, oestrogen is produced first, followed by

progesterone. Oestrogen affects pain, aggression and sexual behaviours, amongst others. There is evidence to suggest that oestrogen can encourage uninhibited behaviour, and observational evidence supports this, with females becoming irritable and bolder when they are coming into season. This change enables the female to be more active in attracting a male for copulation, and behaviour can become flirtatious when she is receptive to a male.

Following this phase, progesterone increases, which has a calming effect, with easy-going or needy behaviour resulting for a couple of days, until the mind acclimatises to the change in hormones, and she becomes calm due to progesterone influence. This lasts for around two months after a season, and one of its functions is in the social development of the female dog to reduce wariness and enable her to experience and accept new things. Essentially, this is the equivalent of testosterone providing confidence for male dogs to experience and accept new things as they mature.

Female hormone phases
Hormone phases occur each time a female dog comes into season, with the first two seasons particularly intense, possibly. Female dogs often experience fewer hormonal seasons as they mature, with reduced impact on behaviour and responses.

The female hormone cycle
As with a male dog, a female dog will experience a cycle of spike-growth period-withdrawal during a hormone phase, in-between each of which she will appear balanced and calm. The timing is different to males due to the nature of her seasons, but it's possible to notice a similar cycle, caused by changing hormones levels, and the effect these have on behaviour.

Behaviourally, these stages translate to –

• Phase 1: Proestrus
Oestrogen increases. May become growly and irritable, less tolerant, actively repel other dogs, less receptive and more reactive to new things.

A puppy called Wolfie

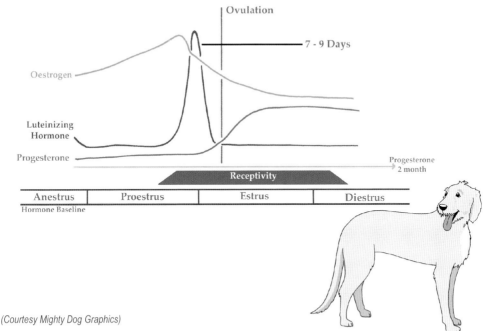

(Courtesy Mighty Dog Graphics)

This is followed by a decline in aggression towards other dogs, then flirtatious and playful behaviour as she becomes more receptive to male dogs. Manic puppy, biting, jumping, can't think or listen, obsessive behaviours

● Phase 2 Oestrus
Oestrogen falls, progesterone rises, luteinizing hormone (responsible for stimulating the ovaries to release eggs) spikes
Receptive to male dogs for mating, may appear soppy, laidback, or needy

● Phase 3 Metestrus or Diestrus
Progesterone dominates. Won't accept a male dog for mating, but calm and receptive to new experiences

● Phase 4 Anestrus
Hormones at their lowest. Rest and recuperation, not attractive to male dogs, personality not significantly influenced by hormones, balanced normal behaviour resumes

Note: As progesterone reduces to base level, aggression and reactivity – much like the behaviour seen in phase 1 – may again be apparent in a small number of females. A dog who displays this will become more aggressive/reactive if spayed, because hormones are no longer present in her body. It is important for a female with this personality trait to maintain a baseline of hormones, so spaying is not in her best interests, unless a medical emergency requires it.

When a female puppy reaches puberty – which may be anywhere between six months and two years, depending on breed – she will come into her first season. Most female dogs have two seasons a year, roughly six months apart, although smaller breeds tend to cycle more quickly and giant breeds more slowly, resulting in some coming into season three times a year, and some just once.

As she matures and is able to manage her emotional mind, her seasons usually tend to be less behaviourally-intense. You will be able to spot and monitor the change from one phase to another, and

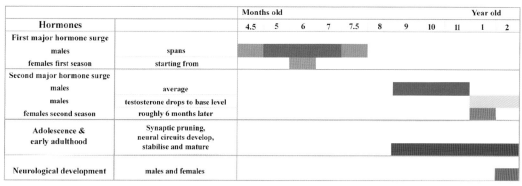

Hormones		Months old									Year old	
		4.5	5	6	7	7.5	8	9	10	11	1	2
First major hormone surge												
males	spans											
females first season	starting from											
Second major hormone surge												
males	average											
males	testosterone drops to base level											
females second season	roughly 6 months later											
Adolescence & early adulthood	Synaptic pruning, neural circuits develop, stabilise and mature											
Neurological development	males and females											

(Courtesy Mighty Dog Graphics)

how long each lasts. All dogs have different hormone levels, so there will be a variation in how much these hormone periods influence a pup's behaviour. Being aware of what's happening with your pup's hormones will allow you to manage the situation, and help her through this period.

If you have taught your puppy to manage her emotional mind during her first season, she should be able to partially regulate herself during the second, thinking through this time of change to some extent. Continue teaching at every season until she can manage herself when they occur.

For both males and females, when hormones run high, behaviours can become manic if not managed and interrupted, although, sometimes, there is a drive to them which compels a dog to perform them, or be redirected to another activity in order to find resolution and calm down.

For example, it's possible to redirect humping to something else, such as play and running about, or, when play is not enough, a little digging helps relieve the desire to hump, although this will also need to be interrupted before the dog becomes manic. At this point, calm talking and slow stroking or massage can help regain calmness.

At sexual maturity, both sexes become very interested in each other, and possibly less tolerant of the same sex during part of the hormone cycle. Frustration is often seen, and activities to alleviate this help to avoid it becoming a part of the adult personality. Dogs are most vulnerable to developing obsessive behaviours at the adolescent stage due to the mind's chemical balance at that point.

Adolescence is also when it's likely you'll be advised that neutering will resolve any behavioural and training issues you may have with your dog, from over-excitement to loss of recall. Please note, however, that neutering only resolves those behavioural issues that are sexual in nature. Most adolescent behaviour is not sexually motivated, but the result of the emotional mind being adolescent. A raised hormone level will amplify matters, true, but this is a transitory period. When hormonal influence reduces, general behaviour is no longer intensified and will also calm down. Continued training will resolve most issues, as your puppy just needs time to learn to manage his emotions.

At this stage in your dog's life hormones are very necessary, and have a significant impact on healthy physiological and psychological development and maturity. For example, if your puppy is experiencing a hormone surge, he is going to become over-excited quickly, so taking him somewhere very busy is not a good idea, particularly if he very easily goes into over-arousal. The balanced phase is ideal for him to try new experiences, but when he is in the fear or reactivity phase you should not do anything that makes him feel out of his comfort zone; neither expose him to new things as he is likely to be anxious about them.

Hormonal phases are also the time when your puppy is less inclined to listen to you, so to

A puppy called Wolfie

help with this, go back to an easier level so that he can learn to think through his hormones (See query below). Essentially, this is pretending he is again a young puppy, and you will be teaching again what he already knows, as his mind is all over the place. This will help your puppy remember that he actually does know things and can do what you ask. This will have effect quickly, as your puppy has already learnt these things, though has temporarily forgotten them. If your puppy doesn't listen, and can't seem to do what you know he is capable of, don't be tempted to try a different tack, as he is even less likely to respond to this because you will be trying to teach him something new at a time when his mind is not receptive to learning. It is far easier to try and remind your puppy of what he actually knows than begin something new.

Practical advice

- When your puppy can't seem to listen to you, return to an easier stage of teaching

- Help your puppy be successful by expecting less when his hormones are at their most potent. Show and guide your puppy to the response you want

- When your puppy is getting into mischief, distract and then refocus him on something else

- Help your puppy calm down and relax. Sometimes an object or person can be the reason for your puppy not being able to do this, so changing the situation can prevent manic behaviour from continuing, and help your puppy transition to a calm state

- Use word association, such as 'settle down' or 'calm time,' when your puppy is being calm and relaxed, and use this when he finds it difficult to be calm

- Add small portions of slow release carbohydrates to his diet between meal times, such as mashed potato. Slow release carbohydrates are a good

way of avoiding or minimising spikes in brain chemistry, as it takes time for the body to break them down, so the subsequent effect on the mind is even and gradual

- It's worth noting that grains such as corn and maize, along with E numbers (colourful food), can have a detrimental effect on the behaviour of some dogs, as can protein, with different effects for different types and quality of protein, and at different stages in life. In the adolescent stage, the mind may be more sensitive to some ingredients, contributing to a state of high arousal

The above are examples of ingredients that may have consequences like this, but others may also do so, depending on the individual dog. Some dogs are very sensitive, and some can eat anything without any discernible effect. Certain breeds are also known to be generally sensitive to specific ingredients.

Control arousal stimuli when your dog is experiencing a hormone surge. Do new things, but when he is in the fear or reactivity phases, do not do anything that will make him feel out of his depth; neither expose him to new things as he is likely to be anxious about them.

Control exposure to new things and progressions of existing situations when in fear (males) or intolerance (females) phases – keep to what they know.

Growth period: a good time for him to experience arousal stimuli, as the mind is less likely to become manic.

Refer to following arousal levels as a guide

Arousal levels

The mind has an arousal baseline, and every mood your puppy experiences affects this. It is further influenced by emotions, hormones, time of day, hunger, food, exercise, movement, sound, novel objects, etc (see diagram, above).

Imagine the mind's baseline as a calm pool of water. All of the things that influence it create excess energy, but a puppy who is unable to calm down due to the influence of his mind will benefit from a more balanced combination of physical and psychological stimulation, that can progress to gradual calming of his mind.

A puppy in over-arousal will be active for far longer than normal due to the sympathetic nervous system remaining in control. In order for him to calm down enough to sleep, the parasympathetic nervous system has to take control, which it cannot do when he is over-aroused. This means that it often takes much longer for his mind to be calm enough for him to relax. If your dog usually settles down 10-20 minutes after a lot of exercise, he may take two to three times longer to achieve this when hormonal, and his arousal level is high.

A good baseline of calm is when a dog is relaxed and content, and able to settle and sleep.

Baseline when calm

Baseline when given exercise and play

= Normal length of time to settle

Baseline when excitable

Baseline when given exercise and play

= Increased length of time to settle

Baseline when hormonal

(Courtesy Mighty Dog Graphics)

ripples in the water: the more stimuli, the more ripples there are, and the greater the arousal. An animal's mind (the pool) may or may not already contain ripples before further stimuli is added, so it's necessary to try and determine where the baseline is, and consider what adding stimulus does to this, and what responses may result.

A common mistake when puppies are hormonal is to give them more than usual physical stimulation and exercise, on the assumption that this will tire them more and they will sleep. They will be more physically tired, it's true, but when their arousal level is high it's their mind that needs to calm down, and physical tiredness does not necessarily achieve this.

Obviously, a lack of adequate physical and psychological stimulation will result in a puppy with

A puppy called Wolfie

Baseline when given exercise and play

= Double the increased length of time to settle

If he is very hormonal

Baseline

Baseline when given exercise and play

This is now mania, and very hard to come down from; often the only option is to leave the puppy on his own to calm down

Limiting exercise and play to try and keep your puppy within lower arousal levels doesn't work, as there is too much pent-up energy, and his arousal level will rise. The key is to give enough exercise and play without it tipping him into mania, and allow the extra time to come down to a baseline of calm so that he can relax and sleep.

If the baseline is already ...

... mania is likely to follow with any excitement, so keep things calm, minimise your body language and voice so you do not contribute to tipping excitement into mania. Play that involves chasing or catching toys and balls, and minimises your involvement is good for puppies who redirect to the person when play gets too excitable. Play that avoids chasing or catching toys or balls is better for those puppies who have a tendency to become obsessed with the game. Any activity or toy that immediately increases his arousal level is best avoided. Unfamiliar activities can be more exciting and stimulating, increasing arousal level, so keep to familiar activities that do not usually over-arouse.

Knowing what to expect during all of the changes as your puppy develops enables you to interpret and understand why he is behaving as he is, and tailor his environment, interactions, and experiences to give him the best opportunity of growing up into a well-balanced dog.

A HEALTHY PSYCHE

All brain processes, conscious and unconscious, make up the psyche. A healthy psyche results in a content animal with a good sense of self, and influences emotional resilience. A healthy psyche and strong emotional resilience comes in part from genetics – the personality we are born with – and in part from nurture and enrichment in our life. To achieve this, all of a dog's needs must be met, biological and physiological, such as safety, love, belonging and social, self-esteem, cognition, and self-fulfilment.

It's also about us as individuals: who we are, and what our body language, tone of voice, actions and responses say about us. As already noted, Free Will Teaching is a state of mind. It's who I am, and it informs every aspect of life, both with my dogs and away from them. It's not a hat I wear when I am actively teaching my dogs.

All of these things impact and shape the psyche and emotional resilience. Although there is a genetic element, changes and enhancements can be made to improve and nurture these aspects.

Many aspects contribute to a healthy sense of self.

WOLFIE'S DIARY
June 19
Day 15 with us: 11 weeks old

NOTES

Just been to the vet for Wolfie's second vaccination. He had loads of cuddles from the staff, and was great with the vet – a different one this time. He now weighs 16.05kg (35.38lb), putting on 3kg (6.6lb) since his last visit.

Wolfie met a Border Collie, who got right up close to his face, almost nose-to-nose. Wolfie was unable to move away or back up, but was fine, in that he did not respond, although I am quite sure that he was not happy about the situation. This was his first close encounter with an unknown dog, who was far too near. She did not move or attempt to use body language to communicate, but just stared at Wolfie, showing no sign of moving away. I politely asked her owner to move her, and was subjected to a load of verbal rubbish about how I should want this type of interaction as this was how to socialise a dog,

and I would obviously ruin my puppy!

As you have already read, this behaviour is most definitely *not* socialisation. If you find yourself on the receiving end of such incorrect nonsense, remember that your main concern is your dog, which will make it easier to stand your ground. Fortunately, Wolfie remained quiet, and, after repeated requests from me that the owner move her dog, she did eventually do so. A lovely Springer Spaniel came in shortly afterward. Wolfie had enough space to move around; wagged his tail; said Hi, and instigated a little play.

It's important to appreciate that, after a negative interaction, the mind does not always immediately return to a receptive state, and so, when meeting the *next* dog, a pup may respond from this perspective (sometimes observed when a puppy or dog responds out of character in a situation that he is usually fine with). Some puppies, such as Wolfie, do not suffer from this effect, and he was his usual outgoing self, who wanted to interact with the next dog who came in. Even so, there was still the potential for his mind to become anxious due to his previous experience, so monitoring the situation from start to finish was essential. With puppies who might find the situation worrying, the best thing is to create distance from the new dog, and focus your puppy's attention on something else, so that his next meeting with a new dog occurs when his mind is in a receptive state.

Chapter 6

Less is more

Wolfie has been with us for three weeks now, and is the most wonderful sweet boy, and a joy to be with. He's settled in really well, and loves being outside in the sunshine. When he's not playing, he loves to sit and watch the world go by.

He has learnt so many things already, and, as my way of teaching is part of our lives, I don't have to find time to do this, it occurs as we go through our days together. Wolfie learns very quickly, as all the time we are together is a teaching and learning experience. I, perhaps, have a little more time with Wolfie as I work from home, compared to if I went out to work, but it doesn't matter if you have a little more or less time: using Free Will Teaching your puppy is always learning when you are around.

If you are tired after work, and need to relax before doing anything active with your puppy, teach your puppy that routine. The point is that he is learning what daily life is, and his part in it. Obviously, puppies can be excitable, and usually have lots of energy, so compromises have to be made on our part. But you don't have to completely change your routine, or feel that you must be active in your teaching when you need quiet time. Puppies

Wofie loves being wherever Matt is, and is very happy to be near him, and simply watch the world go by.

also need quality quiet time, and also to learn how to wait without becoming frustrated, so build this into your routine. He can always learn that he can expend some energy and anticipation of activities with you by playing on his own, or bringing a toy to you to throw as you relax before you take him out.

As with the routine for bringing in the shopping, we have talked through lots more routines with Wolfie. He knows the names of lots of things, lots of phrases, and is progressing with context and how it all comes together in language. Wolfie is gaining confidence and awareness with this way of teaching, and is already able to regulate himself to a degree. It does all go to pot when his arousal level increases and he gets excited, however, but that's to be expected. It doesn't take him long to learn words, phrases, and context, and soon all I have to do is have a conversation with Wolfie as we go about our day, as he knows what I am talking about and where he fits in. As a result of this, impulse control and self-restraint are learnt naturally, and not as a specific and isolated exercise.

Unless we are out on the lead or there is potential danger, all of my interactions with Wolfie are hands-off. I do not physically do things for him, but use voice, body language and movements to convey what I am saying, and suggestions for what he might do.

There is a need for Wolfie to be able to follow instructions without deviation, and my approach to teaching mean that these are woven into my overall methodology, where teaching is based on increasing Wolfie's intellectual and emotional cognition. Wolfie is free to choose what he does, and, as we progress, through awareness and understanding he learns the boundaries that keep him safe and promote appropriate behaviour. This is where the 'less is more' concept comes into play: the more I manage him, the less able he is to make decisions and manage himself. The less I manage him, the more he will learn how to manage his mind, actions, and responses. I want my input to reduce and his to increase as he learns and we progress. I won't need to continue to manage him and tell him what to

do: this is only necessary while he is learning about himself and the world. As he progresses, Wolfie will become more skilled and precise at doing those things that are very specific.

It is very easy to over-manage a puppy, because we want to spend plenty of time with him, and teach him what he can and can't do, but this usually results in being overly focused on him, and trying to manage everything he does. If he doesn't experience a variety of things, he will not learn as well, and if we are constantly following him around and correcting him, he may become anxious or defensive. If not allowed to interact naturally with the environment and the things in it, he may try harder to do so, eluding us if we approach, and taking objects the moment we're not looking. His anticipation of having an object can increase, and he may become single-minded and overly-focused in this objective.

In reality, a puppy's attention span is so short that, in most cases, you can afford to wait and see what he does, rather than immediately intervene, as long as there is no danger to his safety. Puppies need to learn how to hold, let go, and do things gently, and need the opportunity to do so. Teach him how to interact with the things in your home, but don't let him have everything he can get his mouth around. And, as mentioned in chapter one, putting away those things he shouldn't get hold of is key to setting up the environment so that he can explore and learn without injury to himself or damage to your possessions.

If you over-manage him, this could also increase his desire to take things. A puppy who is always followed around is very likely to develop an obsessional approach to acquiring objects, learning, en route, to be quick about it. This prevents impulse control and self-restraint developing as they should, and often leads to him trying to elude us, whilst feeling irritation or anger, and showing possessive and guarding behaviour if he does get hold of something. Asking a puppy to relinquish something he shouldn't have whilst in this state of mind will not be successful.

The last part of this cycle is that we then

A puppy called Wolfie

try even harder to ensure our puppy does not get hold of something he shouldn't. Taking this scenario to its conclusion, some dogs will even swallow whatever they have to prevent it being taken from them. Throughout all of this run a range of emotions and motivations, each unique to the individual, the situation, and the experiences that have contributed to this type of behaviour.

I am happy to let Wolfie sniff and investigate many things he shouldn't have when he is calm and able to think, but not when in 'mad puppy' mode. If he is interested in a shoe or the remote control, I show it to him and let him investigate it. Once again, I talk him through what he is doing, and tell him 'It's Mum's' or 'It's Dad's.' 'Only smell it; don't eat it' is one of my phrases. If he tries to put his mouth around the object, I gently move it away and repeat this phrase, then offer it back so that he can have another sniff, and say the same thing again. It doesn't take long for him to understand this, although, obviously, it does take a little longer for him to be able to manage himself, and have the necessary self-restraint to leave it alone without supervision.

Self-restraint takes time to become a natural part of life, so whilst Wolfie is developing this, I manage him around things he shouldn't take, and put them away if I am not suprvising him. As he learns the phrases, I quickly progress to being at a distance from him, and can be sure that, as long as he is in a calm mood, I can be on the other side of the room, and have only to say 'Remember, just smell,' and, nine times out of ten, that's exactly what he does.

All of our conversations and guidance about what he can do are followed up by positive feedback. I may praise Wolfie, and tell him he is a very clever boy for only smelling the shoe, or say 'Well done! Let's do such-and-such." If he decides it is simply too tempting and puts his mouth around it, I say 'Oh no! That's Dad's shoe, you can't eat it. Remember, just smell.'

It is important that I give Wolfie the option to willingly come away from the object rather than take it from him, and I work in this way so that we both develop a sense of safety, reliability, and trust in each other around objects Wolfie has, be these his things or objects he should not have. My strategy is to change his focus and interest him in something else, to show him that are other things that are even better than the shoe he currently has in his mouth.

I have a range of things to try, such as finding a toy, being exciting and getting his attention, hiding so he can find me, going outside, telling him we're going to play something, or ask him if he wants his favourite food treat. I don't use these in the same order, and don't rely on one thing in preference to everything else. I teach him that a range of things I have are good, interesting, and worth getting involved with.

I do not directly address the fact that he has a shoe in his mouth, although one solution to this scenario is to teach your puppy to give up what he has in exchange for something else. This can work well for some dogs, but not always so well with those who like to hold things, or don't see a reason to give it up just because you ask him to. It is also possible that the puppy attaches a high reward value to picking up something that he shouldn't, which makes asking him to give it back harder for him to do. He may also learn that he has your attention when he has something you want, so the reward is in your response to him. If his hormones are having an influence, or when he is older and surer about what he wants, he may not be as ready to comply.

I focus on teaching Wolfie that he can disengage from one activity and move on to another; picking up the shoe is just one activity. I also build into this the necessary phrases to ensure that this activity is one that is not ongoing, but just a development stage of puppy experimentation. So, telling him 'Oh, that's Dad's,' is followed up with, 'Well done, that's not for you, remember, it's Dad's,' when he releases the shoe. I repeat this phrase whenever he shows interest in something that is not his to have, so he knows that it is not to be picked up or chewed.

Wolfie finds the couple of bamboo bushes

Wolfie explores the wooden post with this teeth: an essential part of puppy development.

were unsuccessful, as the bamboo was far too interesting, so I had my back-up plan of a little food This worked and Wolfie came away. I praised him and immediately told him what we were going to do, which helped him think about something other than the bamboo. Allowing Wolfie to chew the bamboo for any length of time would create a strong reinforcement for doing it, which I did not want. As the other strategies didn't work, food was the quickest way of achieving the desired result. However, once he'd disengaged from the chewing a couple of times using this method, I no longer wanted to use the food, or there was a risk that he may not disengage without this, meaning that his reason for doing so would be the food reward, rather than because he chose to move away.

I use food as a last resort, as this is the least effective way of distracting and refocusing attention in the long term, and it very often ends up being a lure or bribe. In the short term it is usually very effective, but if you rely on this as your main strategy, at some point many dogs will decide the food is no longer as rewarding as it was, or that what he is currently doing is much more interesting. Becoming aware of your intention very quickly changes any interest he may have in disengaging from what he is doing to becoming more sure that he wants to continue doing it. Without having a range of things to help him disengage and refocus on something else, once food becomes regarded as boring or with suspicion, you have no means of redirecting what your dog is doing.

Of course, whatever strategy I use – be it a toy, excitement, or food – I may be introducing an element that has to be present in order for Wolfie to leave the bamboo. But dogs are scavengers by nature, and food probably represents extra motivation in the short term, although it's not always a successful long term strategy. Many dogs will respond to food every single time, and that's great, but there are also many who do not, in which case other options are required.

I am very careful about using anything that is particularly enticing with a puppy as a strategy

we have at the top of the garden very interesting, and will happily stand and chew them, and I used the same phrase I used for the shoe when Wolfie first decided that chewing the bamboo was a good idea: 'That's Dad's. Come on, let's keep going' I told him, and walked a couple of steps. I was teaching him to disengage himself from an activity, so did not want to stand right by the bamboo, unless I had to. Moving changes the situation, and a squeaky toy, or an excited 'Oooh, look at this, come on, this way,' can help persuade Wolfie to leave the bamboo.

The first couple of times I tried this, however,

A puppy called Wolfie

to disengage, as it can often result in this being the only thing the pup will disengage for, which has obvious limitations. I also feel that, in this scenario, the pup does not derive a similar level of interest and enjoyment from a range of activities, as the very high value reward is all he wants.

The next time Wolfie and I go up the garden I tell him 'Keep going, that's Dad's,' as we get close to the bamboo, letting him know in advance what he should do. This also serves to keep part of his mind on listening to me, and not just on the bamboo. Many actions can be successfully interrupted to teach impulse control, self-restraint or to disengage, if these are at the front of his mind and what he is thinking about, because it is much easier to change focus if not already concentrating on and thinking about something else.

Wolfie does have a little nibble on the bamboo, but now it's time to move on with my strategy or we will be stuck in the first stage which is actively enticing him away with food.

The next step is to repeat, 'That's Dad's bamboo, come on, it's not for you, we're going to keep going.' I walk a little further away this time, and in an interested voice say: 'Wolfie, come on, that's still Dad's.' The moment Wolfie moves or looks at me I praise him. 'What a clever boy you are, let's go, then,' even if he is still near the bamboo and has not really moved. I'm praising him for being able to take his attention from the bamboo, regardless of how small a move this is.

If he goes back to chewing the bamboo, I say 'What are you like? That's not yours,' continuing to talk him through it, using my voice, and feigning interest in something else, crouching down – anything to get his attention so that he can again disengage from the bamboo. I give loads of really enthusiastic feedback, conversation, and movement to hold his interest away from the bamboo, and each time, I trust him to know more about what to do around the bamboo, so that I do a little less.

After a few times of doing this, Wolfie pretty much ignores the bamboo whenever we go up the garden, and if he does have a chew, comes

away almost at once. I keep up with my side of the conversation to guide him: at this point maintaining and reinforcing what he has learnt, rather than teaching him.

The whole process reaches this stage quickly. Sometimes we take a step or two backwards, especially when hormones begin to have an influence, but it's easy to just provide a little more input to get him through it.

Those things that prevent the smooth transition from actively teaching to maintaining are an over-reliance on a single thing to draw the puppy's attention; over-managing him and not trusting him to respond, so you end up doing the same thing for too long before you progress it; expecting him to respond immediately, when he needs a little time, and correcting him rather than helping him understand what's required so that he can do it himself. The temptation to do any or all of these things can be great, and you will be learning this as you teach your puppy. Being able to override our natural inclination to take control of a situation is essential when teaching, as we need our intellectual mind to be at the forefront in order to assess and decide our strategy for our dogs to be successful. If we act on instinct, our emotional mind will be at the forefront, preventing logical thought, and thus impairing the quality of our teaching.

When considering distraction techniques, we very often believe that what we use to distract our pup will prevent further occurrences of the unwanted behaviour, but beware of creating a routine whereby you inadvertently *reinforce* what your puppy is doing for the 'reward' on offer. Using the foregoing bamboo scenario, the strategy of having different responses to unwanted actions and a means of progression avoids this situation.

This time of year, my work is usually busy with puppies. Foundation courses are on the go and, as I work from home, puppies are arriving here on several evenings each week. I also hold one-to-one sessions during the day, so Wolfie gets to see plenty of dogs from over the garden gate as they arrive, providing him an opportunity to see a variety of dogs

Puppy foundation class.

without interacting with them. As he has been used to being left on his own, he is happy to sit in the garden whilst I am teaching.

A one-to-one session, with only one dog, makes for a quiet day, and, prior to each session, I make sure I have done plenty of things with Wolfie so that he is a little tired, rather than raring to go, which helps prevent him becoming too excited when clients arrive. Group classes are noisier, however, and Wolfie is much more excited at seeing several

puppies arrive. It is also the time that Matt comes home from work, so Wolfie is excited by this, too. He copes well, however, and doesn't bark much. Matt's job is to play with him whilst I teach in the evening.

Socialisation is interpreted by some as interaction with other dogs, but it actually refers to all types of experiences that puppies have, such as exposure to stimuli, learning about the world, and social relationships with dogs, people, and any other species the puppy may have regular contact with.

A puppy called Wolfie

Socialisation is also ongoing, as your puppy does not stop learning and developing once he reaches the end of the accepted socialisation period. What is learnt during this period is built on after it, which is why it is so important, and done in the right way, or your puppy will develop unhealthy or dysfunctional behaviour patterns, ranging from mild anxiety to extreme fear, and over-enthusiasm to mania, which are not helpful to developing social relationships and interpersonal skills.

Free Will Teaching allows an approach that ensures our puppy's interaction in terms of social relationships, exposure to stimuli, and learning about the world are constructive learning experiences that positively affect the emotional mind and his personality, supporting his development into adulthood. This approach is detailed in all of Wolfie's experiences throughout this book, but it is not necessarily noted as specific socialisation experiences. I hope the following overview is useful in this respect.

How you go about socialisation is dependent on your puppy's personality and responses to various things. Assessing Wolfie during the first few days he's with us provides information about how to proceed with his socialisation. He has gone by car to the vet in town, out for a walk along the lane, and experienced various things in his new home. From this I know that, despite being quiet all the way home from North Yorkshire, he does not like car journeys.

He shows interest in dogs and people we see when we are out, and often pulls to get to them. He does not like loud noises, and is worried by vehicles going past us, particularly large ones.

Socialisation for Wolfie begins with tailoring what we do to best deal with his responses to these things.

Car journeys
I put some of Wolfie's toys in the car, and we do things around it with the doors open, leaving Wolfie to explore the inside as best he can: he's too small to get in without help. He's not worried by this interaction – it's only when the car moves that he is –

and it's good to reinforce a positive association with all aspects of it when stationary.

I also lift Wolfie into the car and strap him in, then get in myself, and we sit and talk, or play with a toy, then get out again. I take him out in the car when he is calm and relaxed. I've noticed that going more slowly is better for him, so I drive at about three miles an hour down the lane, and stop at the first gateway we come to, where we get out and have a short walk.

Wolfie's not keen to get back in the car after our walk, so I talk him through it; tell him we are going home, and what we will do when we get there, using a reassuring voice, and again driving slowly. Once home, I get him out, tell him he's a clever boy, and to go and get a drink, find Dad, etc. We do this several times a week when I feel he is able to cope with it. I don't try to increase the distance much – it's not about how far we go, but how Wolfie copes. There are times when we need to go further, such as trips into town for vaccinations, or taking him out and about so he can experience the world, and it's not always possible to drive at three miles an hour, of course, although choosing a quieter and less busy route is helpful, as I can drive at a slower speed without holding up other road users, and pull over to let them pass.

I tell Wolfie what we are going to do when we get wherever we're going, and that he is doing really well, and is a 'lovely pudding.' We call him this a lot as he really likes it, and doing so in this situation taps into that association to help his emotional mind remain calm, and not become anxious. Note, though, that I would not be making this association if Wolfie was terrified, as he is likely to then associate the phrase with a negative emotion. When pairing associations, consider what each of the pair is doing for the mind, and what effect that pairing will have.

Loud noises and vehicles
For Wolfie to become accustomed to loud noises, and vehicles going past, he has to feel safe, so his exposure to these must be managed so that his mind is able to cope without anxiety or fear.

Village shows, and larger town shows during the summer, where there are lots of people, dogs, unusual noises and equipment, might seem like ideal places to visit in order to socialise our puppy, but consider this from Wolfie's perspective. He's not experienced very much in his short life, and is still adjusting to his new home, so going to a loud and busy show might take him so far out of his comfort zone that he wouldn't be able to cope, and would feel afraid. This, then, would not be a positive learning experience, and Wolfie may associate all the things he sees and hears there with his fear, resulting in him becoming afraid of dogs, people, or whatever objects he saw. It would also change his noise sensitivity from that of a transitional response to moving from his original home to ours (which will resolve if managed properly), to make him a noise-sensitive dog for the rest of his life.

For now, we avoid these types of events, along with the town in general at weekends when it is busy. We go out and experience new things gradually, when it is quiet, so that Wolfie is confident every step of the way.

Dogs and people

Wolfie is very interested in saying hello to the dogs and people he sees when we are out, and will pull to get to them. He needs some self-restraint in this respect, and also to be able to read others to know whether or not they want to interact.

It's my responsibility to ensure that he does not have a bad experience at this stage. He's only met a couple of dogs at the vet, so hasn't much experience of what they are like. If I don't manage the situation, it's possible he may greet several dogs who are not friendly, and who do not want to interact, and then Wolfie will have had more experience of unfriendly dogs than friendly ones. All of these experiences shape how he responds, and his developing personality, with the result that he may decide his fellow dogs are not nice, and he must protect himself. This may manifest with him being afraid of other dogs, and trying to avoid them, or he might growl or snap at them to tell them to go away.

We also have a duty of care to every dog and person we come into contact with: it's not just about Wolfie being happy to engage, but also whether or not the dog or person concerned wants to engage with *him*. As Wolfie will pull me towards people and dogs he wants to greet, we start from the point of being at a distance, so that he doesn't get close to them when he does this. I use the language he has learnt at home, and talk him through it. I use relevant phrases such as 'Let's go,' 'This way,' and 'Carefully,' and add in 'Keep going' when I don't want to stop. As we go past people, and it becomes obvious whether they want to stroke Wolfie or ignore him, I tell him 'Yes, we'll say hi,' or 'No, not this time.' In this way, Wolfie can begin to read the body language of those we come across, and know that if they show no interest in him, he should carry on.

Where possible, we remain at a distance to make this choice easy for Wolfie, although often we are walking close to others on the street, so I teach him as we go, encouraging him to keep going if others don't want to say hello. We do the same for dogs, except that we do not walk as close to them as we do to people, and ensure there is enough room by waiting in a wider part of the path for them to go by first, or crossing the road, so Wolfie does not say hello unless the situation is right for it.

Already, Wolfie is bigger than many dogs we see, and is an excitable puppy, so other dogs are not necessarily going to appreciate him getting into their space without being invited to do so. So we work on being calm when he sees a dog, and I say 'Carefully with little ones' when they are smaller than him, and 'Wait; see if they want to say Hi,' when Wolfie says he wants to interact. I read the other dog's body language, and avoid him if the signals say he does not want to interact, and only do so when their carers confirm their dog is happy to do so, and my assessment of the dog's body language agrees with this.

Not everyone is able to correctly interpret body language, which means that some carers are unaware that their dog is uncomfortable. I don't want Wolfie to be on the receiving end of a telling-off by

A puppy called Wolfie

a dog, nor to put another dog in a position where this happens, so, if I feel, despite assurances to the contrary, that it would not be right to let Wolfie interact, I simply say 'Thanks, but we're in training; he's a little excitable to be able to say Hi at the moment,' and carry on by. When greetings do happen, they are kept short, so there's not enough time for either dogs' mood to change, and Wolfie also learns to disengage after saying Hi.

I always err on the side of caution in this instance, and we move away from a dog or person sooner than we perhaps may need to. But whilst Wolfie is young and still learning, this is the safest way of ensuring his mood does not change to one of anxiety.

When it comes to interpreting body language, puppies are not necessarily automatically competent at this. There's a need to learn social manners, for a start. Often, puppies are concentrating on their feelings and what they want to do, and are not aware of what another dog is saying, or not able to understand it, even if they are.

I teach Wolfie about interaction with dogs the same way I do as with people. If a dog ignores him, he carries on; if a dog is wagging his tail in a friendly manner, we stay and see where the conversation goes. If the dog invites Wolfie, we get closer; if he doesn't we stay away. I'm teaching Wolfie to read the initial signs of whether or not to approach another dog, and what his emotional state should be. I also teach him how to disengage and walk away, so that he has an option to leave if he becomes uncomfortable.

Essentially, I'm introducing a framework, within which Wolfie can have a conversation with another dog, I don't need to teach him how to play bow or sniff and be sniffed in return, as these things happen naturally as he interacts, and he develops his communication skills. If I was to teach Wolfie which movements to respond with when he sees another dog, it would be disastrous, as conversations do not comprise set movements; it's necessary to read each other and respond accordingly, depending on how he feels. Teaching Wolfie particular actions

would result in a conversation that was orchestrated, leading to misinterpretation, or suppression of Wolfie's emotional state.

Until Wolfie learns to read body language and adjust accordingly himself, when he engages in conversations with other dogs, my job is to tell him to watch his arousal level so that he doesn't get too excitable, and when to disengage if either he or the other dog is no longer enjoying the communication,

An additional risk to your puppy is that you cannot control the behaviour or movement of a dog who is off-lead. We do not regularly visit a park with Wolfie as we have our own land on which to walk and exercise him, so we don't know the dogs who use the park. Also, most of the parks around us open onto busy roads, which is not safe for a puppy learning recall, or even for an adult dog, as it takes only one instance of not being able to resist a chase, and he may end up on the road. Because of this, we are careful to only visit parks that have an on-lead policy, or the beach when it is very quiet, and we can see other dogs from a distance, which enables us to have the time to walk away if we do not think it a good idea for an off-lead dog to interact with Wolfie.

As Wolfie's experiences with meeting other dogs increase, we become more relaxed about going to places where there are off-lead dogs. If Wolfie shows distress about off-lead dogs running up to him, we will take things slower, and encounter off-lead dogs only when he is ready to do so.

Our lifestyle was different with our previous dog, Indie, the Great Dane. We lived very close to a very large park that was well away from busy roads, and Indie went to the park every day, going off-lead after just a few visits. Recall was learnt when we were there, so the risk of meeting unfriendly, off-lead dogs had to be minimized by always visiting the park on the same days and at the same times. People often walk their dogs on a regular and reliable basis, which gave Indie the opportunity to meet the same dogs each time we were there. We got to know who he liked and which dogs were friendly, and, by chatting to others, which days and times to avoid the park. By the time we let Indie off-lead, he was already used to the dogs around him, and we knew he was safe.

When considering socialisation, it's not necessarily what or how much a puppy experiences (providing there are adequate varied and positive experiences), but how he feels and responds to those experiences. It's also worth noting that it's not only fear responses that indicate a puppy is not coping well, as over-arousal and manic behaviour is the result of a puppy who is not happy. Every puppy is different, and needs an approach tailored specifically to him. New stimuli that does not result in a bad experience, which he is happy about and can choose to investigate or move away from, provides Wolfie with a store of good memories to draw on when the sensitive period ends, giving him the tools to cope with whatever happens in life, and promoting emotional resilience.

Whilst editing the original draft of this book, a couple of experiences highlight how socialisation is ongoing, and that there will always be something new your dog has no previous experience of. Wolfie is now two years old, and Remy, who is introduced later in the book, is now a year old. Last week we went to the park and saw a collection of storm troopers milling about, who were obviously part of an event. A couple of days later we went to the beach to find several children buried up to their necks in the sand! Neither Wolfie nor Remy had ever seen anything like this, and, from their perspectives, people dressed head to foot in storm trooper suits do not look like people; neither is it usual for dogs to see laughing and talking heads sticking out of the sand: two scenarios that were certainly not part of our dogs' socialisation experiences. Both Wolfie and Remy showed interest in investigating the storm troopers, but just looked at and then ignored the kids, and we carried on with our walk.

In order to have strong coping strategies, and a healthy, confident mind, it's not necessary (nor practicable) for a puppy to experience everything he may encounter by the time he is twelve weeks old, but he does need to know how to deal with *unusual* things, be self-confident, and not afraid of anything

that is different ... also how to assess whether this is something to engage with, ignore, or move away from. Knowing the difference between something unusual and a potentially threatening encounter is an essential part of puppy development and learning during the sensitive period, which will enable a dog to accurately assess and respond to an unusual situation later in life.

WOLFIE'S DIARY

June 25
Day 21 with us: 11 weeks and six days old

AM

6.20:	Breakfast. Play directed at us, bitey – 5/10. Easier to manage as he's begun waiting for us to play with him, rather than just losing the plot and diving in with his teeth. The only problem is that we can't eat breakfast whilst he is doing this!
7.40:	Settled down. Play – 4/10, mooch about, whining – needed more breakfast
10.00:	Sleeping
11.35:	Awake, mooching, a little play, more play, biting

PM

12.10:	Lunch, mooching about
12.30:	Whining, doesn't know what to do with himself. A little playing, more lunch, tried to relax, but couldn't
1.15pm:	Finally grew too tired and went to sleep

So far, Wolfie is –

• learning self-reliance; to enjoy his own company, and self-amusement. I can trust him to regulate his moods as best he can. He's asking for what he wants, too, as we've noticed what he does when he wants a particular thing, and he knows what elicits our response

- regulating motivation and drive himself, and understanding his needs (is he hungry or not?)

- making choices

- having cuddles, but only when he is calm, and not for long or he loses the plot and becomes over-excited and bitey. Biting at 5/10 now, and frequency has reduced, too

- greeting people – approaching, with tail wagging in a friendly manner – no hesitation now. We ask that people wait for him to come to them, and, if he engages, they put out their hand

With Wolfie's early morning playtime more focused on us, now, rather than his toys, this does interrupt our breakfast. I could take him outside and leave him to play on his own, which is the easy option for me, but prefer a small interruption at breakfast so that I can help him through this period, and teach him to be around us, but not expect us to play when we are unable to.

This strategy also eliminates the potential problem of Wolfie deciding to play with something he shouldn't if left unsupervised in the garden for any length of time. Also, if I simply take him outside when he tries to interact with us at a time that's not convenient, he's likely to associate playing with us with being put outside, and will eventually try and avoid being taken outside as he does not want to be shut out on his own (understandably). And there's also a chance that he will continue to regard breakfast-time as playtime as he grows older, making it even more difficult to break this association.

This is another phase that Wolfie is going through whilst learning and developing. Going forwards a couple of months, his body rhythm changes and he is not as awake at this time of the morning. I use this time as an opportunity to continue Wolfie's education, because I have no intention of shutting him outside as it will make him sad. So, I interrupt my breakfast to redirect Wolfie to his toys, eat a little more breakfast, and then repeat the process. Voice feedback I provide backs up this course of action, and he begins to understand the phrases, and what is and isn't a good thing to do when I am eating breakfast.

So far, Wolfie has –

- had 12 visitors, including a baby
- slept through saxophone lessons (!)
- seen milk truck and tractors
- met Molly, the dog next door
- not barked at the doorbell
- greeted (and was fine with) people coming into the house via the front door, and back door via the garden
- visited various towns and parks

If Wolfie had barked at the doorbell, I would have talked him through it so that he knew what was going on. A really good strategy, here, is to ask: 'Listen! What can you hear?' as Wolfie quickly gets the idea that in order to listen he has to be quiet. The quiet only last for a couple of seconds to start with, but work from there, and follow it up with, phrases such as 'Well, let's see what's going on: are you coming with me?' 'Ah, I see it's a delivery, well we'd better see what it is.' Teaching Wolfie to be attentive in order to learn the routine means that he becomes more focused on what's going on, rather than just barking or becoming over-excited.

Recall
We have begun recall work in our field. This is a much larger area than the garden, and the horses adjoin it, so there are plenty of things to engage Wolfie.

We build on the recall work we have already done involving games to establish that we are both part of the walk. My next step in teaching recall is to use directional cues to tell Wolfie what I am doing, and what he might do. Using the language

Off you go, I'll follow you ...

... now walk with me ...

Let's go this way: you follow me.

A puppy called Wolfie

he already knows from what I've taught him around the home and garden, I apply this to being out in the field. As Wolfie races away when I open the gate to the field, I say 'Off you go, then! I'll follow you.' (He's enthusiastic and running fast, so I am usually behind him.) I'm not worried about where he goes as it's a secure field, but I tell him where I am going. 'Wolfie, let's go over to the gate' I shout, and walk towards the gate.

At this stage he will come when he is ready: although he knows what a gate is, he is far too excited to take any notice of me. When he stops to look for me, or pauses, I call 'There you are, come on over to the gate.' He gets to the gate in his own time, and I reinforce his decision to do so with praise as I am happy to see him, and we play a game of ball, or I say, 'Well, what shall we do next?' and engage his mind in conversation.

I use all the phrases he already knows that are applicable to this situation, and add in new ones for him to learn. 'I'll follow you,' and 'You follow me' are things I say when coming out of the house, going to and from the car with the shopping, or in the garden, and also when we are off-lead on the field. If I am in front of Wolfie, I tell him where I am going, and then say 'You follow me.' When he is in front, I tell him to carry on and I'll follow him. If we are walking together I say 'Walk with me.' I do not walk around after him, though, but might go off in a different direction, or walk adjacent to him as he is on one side of the field and I am on the other.

The next step is for me to avoid any proximity to Wolfie, standing still and calling directions to him. This builds his ability to respond when I am further away, or he is not going in the direction I want him to, or I'm not yet at the point at which I want to meet him.

I'm developing our sense of being together on the walk, even if I am on the other side of the field, and soon he begins to check in with me to see where I am, and if I have anything to say. I always respond to this with 'Hello, Wolfie, there you are/ let's do this/keep going/wait for me,' or whatever is relevant. As we progress, he begins checking in

with me when he wants to run, and, when I open the gate, instead of simply running off, he often walks with me, or looks at me, to which I respond, 'Go on, then, off you go.'

The same thing happens when Wolfie hears Matt's car coming down the lane on his way home from work. Wolfie looks at me and I say, 'Yes, you're right, that's Dad: go and find him, then' and off he goes. From this point, it doesn't matter where in the field I am or where Wolfie is, as we have established that our conversation and relationship is a normal part of our walk.

We do all the things we did originally in the garden out in the field: we play, and Wolfie chases balls and Frisbee, although he rarely retrieves them. I also use Wolfie's favourite chew, which is something I give him simply because he is lovely. Going to him, I would ask Wolfie if he'd like a chew. Once he'd become used to this, I asked him if he wanted one when he was at a distance from me, and he came to me to get it. He doesn't get this chew very often, so it remains something he really enjoys. And as there is no requirement from Wolfie other than to come and get it, it works as a fantastic recall, tool.

Wolfie is not overly toy-motivated, but, if he was, I would also have a special toy that comes out when he is off-lead; again, this should be something exciting enough to compete with being off-lead, which he will come to me for. We also play a game of 'come back to me,' when we interact and have fun, and then I tell him 'Off you go!', and he runs off. I am making myself something that Wolfie wants to come back in preference to whatever else is going on or about, by letting him know that the fun is here, with mc.

Wolfie is a sight hound, so, if something catches his attention, he's off after it. At this early stage in his life, I cannot rely on him listening to me, if he is to be off-lead, he must to be under control. He simply cannot go running up to another dog if we do not know whether the dog is happy for Wolfie to do so. As Wolfie grows, there's also the risk that people and dogs might be concerned about his size

Resting in the field after a morning's teaching session.

– if he were to actually run *into* an adult, child or dog – the impact would be fairly significant.

All these considerations mean that our recall is practised in our fields. I know of some owners who take their dogs onto open land, such as Exmoor, to let them off-lead, but this is also potentially problematic because of the horses, deer, sheep and cows who roam there. I've been told that Wolfie will never have a reliable recall because he is a sight hound, and, whilst he is young and learning impulse control and self-restraint, I would have to agree that if he saw something in the distance on Exmoor, say, he would be off, and would end up a long way away! So, this rules out open land for us, at least until his recall is reliable in new environments. As Wolfie progresses, our bond develops and he becomes less impulsive: he can be off-lead as long as the situation is managed properly.

When Indie was a puppy we lived in a built-up area with a very large park, where we taught him recall, beginning with letting Indie off-lead when it was very quiet, and any other dogs were a good distance away. He'd be off-lead for only 30 seconds or so to begin with, then Matt and I would stand a short distance apart and call him from one to the other, clipping on his lead again when we had finished. As time went by, Indie was off-lead a little longer each day.

On-lead we played hide-and-seek: I would stand behind a tree, and Matt and Indie would find me. We used voice cues for directional information, and Indie's off-lead time increased further. We added in the games that I've been playing with Wolfie: Indie's favourite toy was a Frisbee – this was more interesting than anything else.

When Indie came back to play games with us, we also got him used to having his lead clipped on. We've not done this with Wolfie, as he is in our

A puppy called Wolfie

fields, and as he prefers to come right back and lean on us as we are standing in the field, it is easy to hold on to him. With Indie, we were in a park, so this was an essential part of the routine. Clipping his lead on and off when Indie came back to us did not always happen, as I wanted to avoid a situation where clipping on his lead before we played became a necessary part of the routine, which would reduce the value for Indie of coming back to me.

We also played retrieve with the Frisbee, when Indie was obviously off-lead, providing an opportunity for him to learn to stand and wait, attention on the Frisbee, when he was off-lead. We began at a distance from other dogs on the park whilst we established a bond between us, with Indie meeting other dogs only when he was on-lead. After the first few weeks we gradually got closer to other dogs when playing our games, and as part of his walk. Indie's off-lead time was temporarily reduced, then, so that he didn't get so excited and involved in a game that he couldn't listen and come back to us. As he became used to being around dogs, his off-lead time increased again.

Sometimes we had to go to him when he found it hard to stop playing with another dog; sometimes we walked away, telling him where we were going, expecting him to follow, although it was necessary, sometimes, to make this option more enticing by adding in the Frisbee as an acceptable alternative. By working gradually, and making every activity in the park interesting and engaging, Indie became very reliable. He was able to come away from dogs, did not try to avoid us, and was happy going along with our general directions on walks.

Success is down to putting in the time, and managing your expectations. Going back to Wolfie's recall, I have worked on him responding to my side of the conversation so far, but have not done anything about teaching him to do this *quickly*. Expecting a puppy to immediately run to you the moment you call is unrealistic, generally, so, first you teach, and then you refine for those abilities you want or need in a given situation.

An example of this is when I called Wolfie to come to the gate on the yard. He didn't, so I walked around the barn to check where he was ... turning back, I saw that he *was* waiting at a gate, but not the one I meant! I had made the error of assuming Wolfie would go to a particular gate, so hadn't specified which one this was. Wolfie did do as I asked, but, as I had not provided clear direction about which gate, he decided for himself, which was a brilliant response that demonstrates he's already beginning to problem-solve.

Only you know what stage you and your puppy have reached, and what he is capable of, so someone else's expectations may not be relevant or accurate to your situation. Having practised our recall for a few weeks, we were out one day and I called Wolfie to 'Come this way,' but he did not respond. Observing this, someone commented about Wolfie's apparent refusal to do as I asked in a derisory way, but the point is that Wolfie *did* come, only not immediately, as he needed time to process the request. It is good practice to wait for your dog to give a response, rather than immediately repeat your request. I knew Wolfie was listening to me, and understood what I had asked him to do: there was no point repeating myself.

By waiting for Wolfie to respond, I am doing two things. I am making it easy for him to succeed, as he is still young and learning so needs time to respond, and I am giving him the choice to decide whether he can and will respond, which is a really important part of Free Will Teaching. Wolfie will either a) do what I ask, b) stand and look at me, c) ignore me, d) begin to respond but then return to what he was doing. All of these options tell me something about how Wolfie is feeling, what his preference is, and where his motivation lies at that time, which, in turn, provides the information I need to adjust my response to further the conversation, and work towards recall being more reliable.

It may be that Wolfie was scenting and didn't really hear me, so I *do* need to repeat myself, or it may be that he really doesn't want to go the way I'm asking him to, especially if he is enjoying being in the field and I am asking him to go back to the gate.

If this is the case, I need to engage his mind in what our next activity will be so that he can disengage with the present one, and *want* to move on to the next. Or it might be that he has seen something of interest and has focused on this, in which case I need to help him disengage, but I also want to see what has captured his attention and have a conversation about that. If he is watching someone walk along the lane, for example, a conversation about that being normal/ignoring them and carrying on helps to prevent him over-focusing or obsession. By basing my response on Wolfie's, I'm ensuring that we don't get stuck in a situation whereby I call/he doesn't come/I call again, etc.

WOLFIE'S DIARY
June 27
Day 23 with us: 12 weeks and one day old

NOTE
Wolfie is now the size of a six-month-old Labrador, but is still only 12 weeks old ...

PROGRESS
Wolfie is now greeting strangers without hesitation, and has met the puppies in my puppy class, and got on really well with them. His impulse control is coming along brilliantly. He is restraining himself from chasing Chilli the farm cat, even though it has become harder for him to do that. Chilli is now sufficiently comfortable with Wolfie that she is trying to interact, does not feel the need to vacate the area if he comes running, and is generally present where he is. Chilli is varying between getting closer and investigating Wolfie, and moving away and giving appeasement signals. She's not quite sure whether or not she wants to get close. On the surface it seems as if the situation has deteriorated, because Wolfie is focusing more on Chilli as she doesn't

run away from him, and he is getting closer and therefore very excited because of this. This is a progression of their relationship, and is exactly what I would expect to happen as they get to know one another. Wolfie's excitement needs managing, and his self-restraint developing, but I have not had to step in other than to remind him with a voice cue to be careful, and distract him when Chilli has been daft enough to sit in a position she cannot retreat from unless she goes right past him! At least she hasn't tried to run past him – I doubt he'd be able to restrain himself – each time I've distracted Wolfie to enable Chilli to leave whilst he isn't looking.

Wolfie now knows 'kiss' very well, and this is a very good alternative to mouthing/biting our hands and feet, as it means lick or just touch with his nose; either is fine with me. His mad half-hour play, lunge, bite routine is still a work-in-progress, and he is still trying to play like this with us, as well as his toys. He is teething, so his teeth are hurting him, and his impulse control is least strong in this area: not good, considering his increasing size and strength! We are at the point where he can interrupt himself and sit, wait, or find a toy, when we ask him to, unless he's become too manic, and then there's no hope! These times are much less frequent and briefer, however, although we still have to leave him to it and not be around him.

Overall, Wolfie is happy, easy-going, able to manage himself, not get into mischief, tell us when he's hungry, wants to play, and wants a cuddle. The only things he needs guidance with, still, are his interactions with Chilli, and his mad half-hour.

He's also developing his awareness and preferences, and I've begun teaching him how to make a choice, and decide what he wants to do. He is responding to the language I've taught him, and picking up more words and phrases, and those he knows well can be repeated less often, and moved on to a maintenance level, rather than teaching, as I continue to teach him new ones.

TEACHING CHOICE
I begin by asking Wolfie whether he wants to do one

A puppy called Wolfie

Getting to know Chilli the cat.

I have to repeat this little routine a couple of times as he's just learning this concept. If he chooses a direction, I say 'Okay, then, let's go ...' but if he doesn't, I choose for him, so he can learn how choice works. It doesn't take long before he understands how to make decisions, and chooses himself where he wants to go.

Note: Don't expect your puppy to always go straight away from standing still to walking in the direction he wants to go, because he's often deciding this whilst remaining still. It isn't until another choice is offered, and you take a step in the other direction that he will move.

I can apply choice to many things, and progress it from this basic level of choosing between two specific things. Talking about this reminds me of the Yorkshire pudding incident! We'd been cooking a roast, and the Yorkshire puddings were dished up on our plates. Wolfie was mooching about in the kitchen, and we weren't taking much notice of him. Looking round, I spotted Wolfie delicately picking up one of the Yorkshire puddings from a plate (by this point, Wolfie was able to reach the kitchen counter quite easily). Although an understandable response would be to exclaim at this, my approach was to ask Wolfie 'Oh, are you hungry, did that look yummy? Well, eat it all up, then.'

When he'd finished eating, Wolfie returned to the counter, heading for the other Yorkshire there. 'You can't take that; wait and see if there's one for you,' I told him. Wolfie sniffed at the Yorkshire pudding, and I said, 'Hold on, let's see if there's another for you, then.' I got one out of the oven and gave it to him, saying, 'That's all there is: off you go with it.'

Relating this story to a friend, I was asked whether taking this approach was simply teaching Wolfie to take what he wanted, but I haven't taught him to do that: he did it on his own with no input from me. Wolfie is a young puppy, and to have the self-restraint necessary to ignore something that smelt

of two things. 'Shall we go to the field or up the hill?' If he is unsure about which he'd like to do, I take a few steps in one direction, asking 'Do you want to go up the hill?' I wait a few seconds, then walk in the other direction, asking 'Do you want to go to the field?'

so yummy was beyond him. Although I didn't expect him to take the food, I had left it somewhere he could reach it, so the situation was of my doing. I have taught Wolfie to make his own decisions, and how I interact with him means he feels confident enough to do so, without any fear of consequences, which is so important for an effective learning environment, and development of his self-worth. What happened was a result of Wolfie's continuing education, which he's still in the early stages of. By responding as I did, I can use the episode to continue to teach Wolfie how to manage himself around food.

Finally, reprimanding Wolfie for this incident is not productive feedback, and doesn't teach him anything. It shuts down the conversation, whereas my response allowed it to continue and progress his understanding of what to do when food is within reach.

In any case, there were more Yorkshire puddings, so no one went without, and we discovered they are one of Wolfie's favourite foods, so now we make sure there is always one for him, too!

VISIT HUBBLE AND HATTIE ON THE WEB:
WWW.HUBBLEANDHATTIE.COM • WWW.HUBBLEANDHATTIE.BLOGSPOT.CO.UK • DETAILS OF ALL BOOKS
• SPECIAL OFFERS • NEWSLETTER • NEW BOOK NEWS

Chapter 7
Learning about the world

Wolfie has been going for a walk along the lane for a while now, and his lead walking is coming along really well. He is more inclined to sit down and choose not to move for some time, rather than rush about, pulling me all over the place. For those of you with dogs who do pull like a train, you will read how I deal with this with Remy in the relevant chapter. Unlike Wolfie, Remy has no intention of even slowing, let alone stopping!

The worst thing I can do when Wolfie decides not to move is to bribe him with food, because, in the short term, this will not change his desire to stay put, he's not motivated to move, and he's simply taking the opportunity to have food if it's available. Pretty soon he will become suspicious of the food, knowing it's intended to get him to do something he doesn't want to, and will ignore it, as it will not be sufficiently motivational. Of course, some dogs will do anything for food, however many times it's used in this way, in which case, you have a solution.

The first thing I do is ascertain *why* Wolfie has stopped and is refusing to continue. Is he happy and content? Anxious? Tired? Do his legs hurt? Or does he not want to go home? Most people are familiar with their off-lead dogs not coming back to them at the end of the walk, as they don't want the fun to end; the same happens when dogs are on-lead, if they don't want to go home and would rather stay out. I could use many of the words and phrases

On walks, Wolfie spends more time lying down than he does walking!

that Wolfie already knows to motivate him to do something, but what I actually do depends on why he does not want to move.

Choice comes into this. I can suggest a course of action based on what I think is reason for his reluctance to move, which addresses that reason and motivates Wolfie. If I think he is tired, or he has growing pains and his legs hurt, I can suggest a rest, then a few more steps, and then rest again. If he doesn't want to go home and I have time, I can suggest we go a little further; if I don't have time, I can provide motivation for what we can do when we get home. If he is anxious we can move away from the source of his anxiety, towards safety, whilst distracting him and helping him cope by telling him what we are seeing, and will see next. If Wolfie does not respond to my first option, I suggest others to him.

Wolfie's default strategy when he is scared is to flee, but, as he gets older, becomes more self-confident, and his knowledge of the world grows, this will happen less often. His strategy is fine when we are at home, and he runs back to the house, but not so good when we are out on a walk, and Wolfie tries to run away from cars and tractors.

When it is not safe or appropriate for him to run and we have to stay still, Wolfie needs an alternative strategy that will enable him to cope with the situation and manage his flee instinct. I also have to manage his flee instinct at times when we are able to escape from what is causing him anxiety. In these instances, I need to prevent his anxiety from escalating and triggering his fear and subsequent instinct to flee.

All Wolfie's responses are on a scale of mild to strong. For example, if he's just a little scared he will run only a short distance, his mind will quickly settle, and he won't feel ongoing fear. However, if he becomes completely terrified, Wolfie will run as if his life depends on it (and will do so for longer), will show additional fear signs, such as avoidance, growling, or snapping if something gets too close, and will be totally panicked. It will take him a fair amount of time to return to normal, and the after-effects may leave him jumpy and wary for longer still.

Whatever I do, it's important I ensure that Wolfie's emotional state remains below his panic threshold, and mild fear does not escalate, or I run the risk of this becoming a long term issue. However, denying him the option to run will increase his fear, because forcing a dog to confront what it is that makes him fearful will make things worse. This is what's known as an exposure technique – sometimes called flooding – which, if done at all, should be used only in human therapy, where the client is fully aware of what is about to happen, has learned the necessary coping strategies to get through it, and is able to experience it without overloading their emotional mind, so can analyse their feelings and make progress. For Wolfie, countermeasures are required to offset the increase in fear he will feel when he doesn't have the option of running away.

I need to be in front of the situation, because if strategies to help Wolfie cope are not in place by the time the car or tractor reaches us, he will be too scared to gain any benefit from these. Luckily, I can hear when a vehicle is coming along the lane, so can put my strategy in place before it gets to us.

I begin by timing our walks to when traffic is light. The lanes are small around here, and not hugely busy, but we do see tractors, horseboxes, and large vehicles. The milk lorry visits surrounding dairy farms, and comes along our lane at the same time each day, so I avoid walking Wolfie there at this time: there will be plenty of opportunity for him to learn that he is fine when large, noisy vehicles pass him, but not right at the start.

We time our walks to when we are least likely to meet tractors and other large vehicles, so that I can begin teaching Wolfie to cope with light traffic, such as cars, and move on to more scary vehicles when he is ready.

One of the things I can do when I hear a vehicle coming is move to a distance sufficiently far away for Wolfie to feel okay. If this is not possible, we go into the nearest gateway or similar where the lane widens, so we are not as close to the vehicle when

A puppy called Wolfie

it passes us. Of course, this does mean that we are actually running away, as I want to get in position ahead of the vehicle, but there's a fine line between Wolfie regarding this as running in response to the noise, or running as part of a game we are playing.

How I act has an effect on Wolfie, how he regards the situation, and the level of anxiety he may experience. Avoiding something that our dog doesn't like, rather than putting him in a situation he finds scary, may backfire, inasmuch as doing this may become associated with the scary thing, which can lead to anticipation, and our dog being more fearful than he should.

Avoidance does not progress his coping ability, so he remains fearful, but there are some circumstances where this is the best ongoing strategy. For example, an elderly dog who is losing his sight or hearing, and who finds going out stressful, is likely to prefer to stay in his garden or on very familiar quiet routes. As his condition is only going to worsen over time, avoidance is a sensible strategy for his quality of life.

My usual routine is to do different things with Wolfie on our walk. We might run, turn around and go the way we came, take a detour, do some tricks, or sit and watch the world go by, as well as those activities that Wolfie does on his own, such as investigating, sniffing, and following a scent. This approach has many benefits, because it –

- keeps me involved with the walk
- keeps Wolfie engaged with me
- helps with off-lead work and recall
- helps manage his arousal level
- helps avoid obsessive activities
- maintains Wolfie's relaxed, happy state of mind

I can engage Wolfie in any or all of the above activities when I hear a car approaching, and none will be specifically associated with the oncoming vehicle. From my point of view, it would be easy to panic if I didn't know what to do, but, because these activities are familiar to Wolfie, I can use them to engage him, which means I am concentrating on

Wolfie and what we are doing, my body language and voice tone normal, rather than anticipating this stressful event. Wolfie's attention is diverted away from the oncoming vehicle, so he is not anticipating it either. Of course, he will still find the situation scary – he's young, and still learning – but by talking to him reassuringly, and distracting his attention when necessary and refocusing him, the emotion he feels can dissipate, and he does not dwell on his fear as he hears the vehicle noise fade.

Wolfie has been enjoying weekly walks with his friend, Dina, a Romanian rescue dog. His walk with the lovely Dina this week was much improved on last week, as he realised that he could sniff about and do his own thing, rather than doggedly (excuse the pun!) follow her. We also worked on being calm, for when he starts going over the top, and I want him to rebalance and continue on, which helps when we pass I don't want him to stop and investigate, like horse poo, and also a little relay work to allow him to be either in front or behind whoever he's walking with, and not have to stop when they do.

When dogs are in a familiar group, and this includes people as well as other dogs, it's often the case that they walk in a particular position within the group, and are reluctant to leave it. Some dogs like to be in front, some like to keep up with the others, and some like to see what each dog who stops is sniffing. All normal behaviour, but it makes life so much easier if your dog is versatile and does not have to do exactly the same thing every time, and easier for a dog to be relaxed and comfortable with changes. Wolfie's ability to change where he is in the group works well with Chilli the cat, too, who comes with us for a walk most days. As cats have a tendency to do, Chilli will drape herself on the floor at any opportunity, so the ability to go past her is essential.

WOLFIE'S DIARY
July 2
Day 28 with us: 12 weeks and six days old

Wolfie loves his walks with Dina and their respective Dads!

AM

11.35: Manic – 8/10. Very bitey, not wanting to go out as torrential rain (very sensible), so we stayed in. This didn't help, however, as my presence is the reinforcement for Wolfie's mania, and if I leave him he calms down. He's too young to do this with me about when he's in such an aroused state, and circumstances have to change for arousal to dissipate. So, work was on hold whilst I did things in other rooms to give Wolfie the opportunity to calm himself so that we could spend some time together.

When Wolfie becomes manic with an activity, instead of finding resolution and satisfaction by engaging in it, his mind continues trying to achieve, not realising that it already has, reinforcing the mania and making being calm very difficult. A change in

A puppy called Wolfie

circumstance to break this loop is often needed, as this is not a healthy state of mind, and the transition from mania to a calm state can take a little time. Watch for signs from your dog that tell you he is beginning to calm down – a sigh, shake off (where a dog physically shakes in an effort to change the focus of his emotional mind), visibly relaxing his body, rather than looking tense. Don't resume engaging with him too soon or this may set off the mania again.

DEALING WITH MOUTHING

All puppies mouth and bite: it's part of their development, and helps them learn bite inhibition. Wolfie is no exception, and when he becomes over-excited, he gets very bitey. I have a toy with me all the time, and if he starts biting me or the furniture, I give him the toy, which, because he's a young puppy, still, does work, although his attention span is short, and he does not want to calmly sit and chew a toy, he wants to keep exploring with his teeth. I engage with Wolfie when he does this, telling him what is and isn't a toy, using my voice as feedback to his decisions, and also use it as an opportunity to teach bite inhibition, as long as he is not manic. If he bites me, I say 'Careful, that's mum, have a toy instead' each time he does. I repeat this phrase, and add others, such as 'Oh no, don't bite me, have your toy.' As we progress, Wolfie's mouth becomes softer until the point at which he goes to bite me but then chooses not to. It's a simple progression, then, to his not putting his teeth on me at all as he does not try to engage with me with his mouth, and chooses a toy instead.

It is really important to teach good bite inhibition so that, as a young puppy, he is not afraid to explore with his teeth, which shows him his own strength and how to control it. If a puppy is never allowed to mouth, the possibility exists that he will hold back until he no longer can, and then have no control over his bite. A dog is far less likely to cause injury if he has learned to control his bite action, and to walk away and find a toy. If he is reprimanded for mouthing, he will not have learned this ability. This does not mean that I encourage Wolfie to mouth: I am simply making the most of this stage in his life when he is exploring with his teeth and learning how to interact. If he becomes too excitable, I keep my hands well out of his way, as he won't be able to learn when in this state; nor is he really aware of how hard he may be biting. The whole learning experience should be completed within a few weeks when he is still a young puppy, and is not an ongoing exercise. Wolfie is taught how to feel what his mouth is doing, how to control his strength, and how to make the decision to find an alternative to mouth or bite.

Sometimes, a loud, high-pitched noise is used to stop a puppy biting, because that's the noise that siblings make when young and trying out their teeth on each other. This may work, but often does not. One problem is that your puppy gets used to the noise, and then will ignore it, so it becomes less effective. This is an attempt to stop a puppy biting, that doesn't teach the puppy how to do this. It can be useful in some situations, and can be a strong interrupter, but it is not teaching the puppy bite inhibition. A noise like this can also fuel mania, as it can be quite exciting and stimulating for the mind.

When working with over-excitable dogs, I often see owners matching what their dog is doing, as they've been told that they must be more exciting than the dog to get through to him. But couple this activity with a high-pitched voice, and it's easy to see that all they are doing is stimulating their dog! I ask owners to do the exact opposite by calming their body language and their voice so as not to fuel their dog's mania.

INVESTIGATORY EXPERIENCES

When Wolfie becomes manic I have a number of things I can try to help his mind calm down. We do not engage in teaching bite inhibition when Wolfie is in this state of mind, and my hands and the rest of me are well away from him. Tone of voice, movements and actions can all contribute to escalating his current state of mind, or help to dissipate the emotions so that Wolfie can return to a

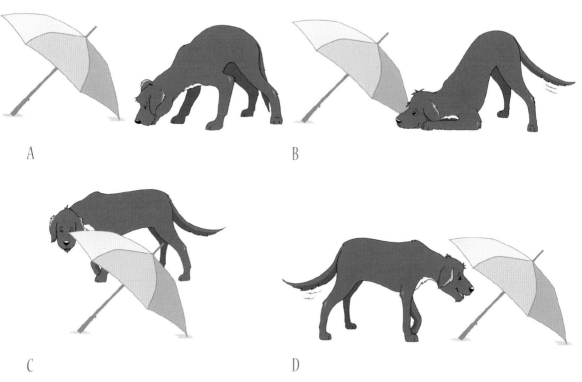

A

B

C

D

(Courtesy Mighty Dog Graphics)

calm state. What I do depends on the situation, and I may change activity, minimise my responses, or remove myself. I use a very slow, calm tone of voice if he is very manic, and a slightly more interesting voice and deliberate body language if I think distracting and redirecting him will calm the mania and help him focus on something else. I continue with teaching language whilst this is going on, so he can begin to think through his emotions, and be aware of what is going on. This is teaching him to regulate his emotional mind. If he is aware of what he is doing, and able to be in control of his mind rather than be swept away by it, Wolfie will be safer, more reliable, and less extreme if things do go wrong and his emotional mind takes over.

When Wolfie – and, indeed many puppies – investigate new things, you often see this sequence –

A When he first sees a new object, he's a bit wary, but cautiously gets closer to it

B If he stays near it, you may see a play bow/tail wag ...

C ... and then he backs away, still assessing it

D If he thinks all is fine, he investigates again

This is an important learning sequence. There is conflict in the stages, in that he wants to investigate, but is also unsure about doing so. Wolfie is learning that he is safe, and that nothing happens to him when he investigates, and can process the experience which goes towards future coping strategies and emotional resilience.

How I contribute makes a difference to

A puppy called Wolfie

Wolfie's experience. His first response is to be wary, and he goes between taking a couple of steps towards the new object and then taking a step back. I do not encourage him to go closer and investigate: if he stays where he is, I can reassure him that everything is fine; if he turns away and does not want to continue his investigation, we move away, and I say something like 'Don't worry, it's just a [whatever it is], we'll have a look another time.' If I encourage him when he is wary I am most likely to cause a negative association with the object, and any anxiety he feels may then be associated with it, or even investigating in general.

When Wolfie goes back to investigate, and shows play-type movements, he is most likely demonstrating appeasement gestures to convey that he is not a threat, and this behaviour also serves to help him remain calm. The lack of response from an inanimate object then causes him to step back again, whilst he reassesses the situation. He returns to it for a final investigation, having decided it is fine, before moving on.

If Wolfie goes through this sequence at his own pace, he takes away from the encounter the fact that he was fine, and can manage unease and anxiety in a new situation, which builds his confidence. It is so important that these types of experiences are supported by me in the right way for emotional resilience to develop, and the ability to adapt to life becomes second nature to him.

WOLFIE'S DIARY
July 3
Day 29 with us: 13 weeks old

NOTES
We've just come back from the vet for Wolfie's third and final vaccination, and he had quite an experience this time. He saw another new vet – so now he's seen three – and had lots of cuddles from the staff. He has grown and is a whopping 20.45kg (45.08lb) – I did notice the difference picking him up to put him in the car. A ramp is the next priority, I think!

Wolfie saw a muzzled dog who was not comfortable around others, but he was really good and walked past: the dog didn't grumble, and the owner was happy. There was also a little terrier, quite barky when on her mum's knee, although on the floor she had a waggy tail, and said hello to Wolfie. Then there was a large Collie, who Wolfie didn't say hello to, although both looked interested.

He didn't try to get to the cat in her basket, although he was lying on the floor, casting sneaky glances at her! By the time we were called into the consulting room, we had to walk past three dogs in close proximity, but Wolfie coped brilliantly. As we came out of the consulting room, a growling, lunging dog came in; we just kept our distance, and walked on past. Wolfie did really well – neither scared, nor offering a response.

I thought Wolfie might have had enough by then, but, no, so we walked down the road a little, then back to the car, but he didn't want to get in! This was great, as we were parked in one of the roads in town, with shops, people and cars all about. On our last visit to the vet we remained in that environment for only a few minutes, but this time we went all the way up to the end of the road. Wolfie was more relaxed (though not sure about the traffic), and wanted to say hello to everyone he met. As you can imagine, he was sound asleep by the time we got home.

Life is so lovely with Wolfie, and we have settled well into our daily routine well. Learning and new experiences are all taken at Wolfie's pace, and designed for optimum success and development. We assess how Wolfie will cope with going to different places, and each time we go out it provides more information about how he is coping, and how to proceed.

We are now walking along the lane once

or twice a day, at Wolfie's pace, and if he wants to go a little further we do, but always mindful that we have to cover the same distance going back, so if I think we've gone far enough, we'll turn around. Giant breeds grow very quickly, and Wolfie does have growing pains (Panosteitis), making his legs hurt. He whines and doesn't want to do much. When this happens we usually stay at home, playing or having slow off-lead walks in the field. If he wants to go along the lane we do, but for a very short distance only. We also give his legs a massage, which is very beneficial.

Wolfie had a scare on the hill by the pond this morning. A big log was hidden in the long grass and I nearly fell over it, so moved it out of the way, which made Wolfie jump, as he obviously was not expecting a large tree branch to suddenly appear. He then went through the sequence that puppies often do when they see new stimuli, described earlier. He cautiously approached the log, backed away, went back, play bowed, barked, moved back to assess, then went back to it for a proper investigation.

He's found his voice and it is brilliant. Such a lovely rich tone, he's been howling at his toy that makes a long squeak. He also joins in when Matt plays the saxophone, which is hilarious – his pitch is spot-on!

WOLFIE'S DIARY
July 9
Day 35 with us: 13 weeks and six days old

NOTES
Wolfie-boy has grown again – I'm sure he's gained a couple of inches whilst asleep this afternoon!

Wolfie is not a retriever, and 'fetch' has simply not happened. He gives me a toy, or jumps about as I have one ready to throw, then runs after it, but, once I have thrown all of the toys, I have to pick them all up with Wolfie happily finding the flapping of my trouser legs more interesting than the toys! However, our play has really improved since Wolfie

realised that he could fetch the toys himself, and does not have to be glued to my leg as I do this – great news for my trousers.

Throughout all of our play times I've added in lots of words and phrases: 'Pick it up,' 'It's yours,' 'Now it's mine,' 'Are you watching?' 'Where did it go?' 'Can I see?' [he lets go then I throw it], 'I've got it,' 'You've got it.' 'Bring it back' and 'fetch it' are now included as he has realised he can carry a toy to me.

Using lots of different words/phrases for the same thing gives me many options if one word or phrase doesn't work when it comes to catching his interest and redirecting him, and he's insistent that I am more fun than his toys! Thankfully, this hardly happens at all, now, though he is still an excitable puppy.

When we get up in the mornings Wolfie has cuddles and tummy rubs, instead of being over-excited at seeing us, and wanting to play, which is great as my breakfast is no longer interrupted, He loves cuddles and sitting on the settee, although he's not quite big enough to climb up himself, and hasn't worked out how to jump up, so Matt's been helping him. So far he's tried lots of different foods, and loves roast dinner days. He's eating what we are eating, apart from those foods that are poisonous/not suitable, and is thriving.

RECALL PROMPTS
So many of the things we do with our puppy can be used as part of our recall strategy: the names of things and places, and phrases that direct his movement, such as 'this way,' 'other side,' 'follow me.' Games we play like hide-and-seek, running together, chasing a toy, bringing it back. Calling him in from the garden, or a different room in the house.

Wolfie has a favourite food treat that I give him every so often, just because I love him, so I call his name from a distance, and, when he looks at

A puppy called Wolfie

me, ask if he wants his special treat, and he always comes to me for this. I want to create the idea that I am worth coming to when I call him, as it is always rewarding in one way or another. By asking Wolfie if he wants his treat, to play, or to do something with me, I am providing him with the necessary motivation to come to me, and now he associates me with his favourite treat, toys, reward, and excitement.

I've taught Wolfie 'wait' and 'no further,' both of which act as an emergency stop when out. He understands what I am saying when I tell him what we are going to do, which provides motivation fro him to disengage with a current activity and move on to something else.

As we progress, Wolfie automatically begins checking in with me when he is off-lead, as I am an important part of our walks. When he does this, I have a number of responses, including 'wait for me,' 'off you go,' 'I'll follow you,' and 'meet you at the pond,' depending on how excited he is. I add in 'don't go too far' when he checks in with me when off-lead to maintain a proximity with him. If he gets a little ahead I ask him to wait for me. He's still young and learning so I match my conversation and requests to what I think he is capable of.

All of these things, which are part of other aspects of life and learning, are also instrumental in a robust recall strategy. Different situations require different recall options, and sometimes Wolfie does not recall, so I need an alternative. If I use the things he already knows it makes it easier for Wolfie to recall, and I always have options if he finds it difficult.

I also choose when to let him off the lead and when to recall him to avoid problems. If I think something is too tempting for him to ignore, he stays on-lead. If I know he cannot recall when he gets too close to a particular thing, I recall before we reach that point.

WOLFIE'S DIARY
July 24
Day 50 with us: 16 weeks old

NOTES

He's been with us for 7 weeks now, and is 16 weeks old today.

Lead walking is going well; he's good at walking with us, and the times he sits on the floor and doesn't want to move are fewer – just as well because, at one point I was spending a very long time going not very far!! He loves running, and, between playing in the fields and going out, we're getting plenty of exercise. Great for my appetite! He's really progressing with playing without trying to bite us, and now he's got the idea that he can move away, he's really enjoying running after toys we throw. Mad half-hours are manageable, and fun, not manic. He hasn't quite mastered eye/mouth co-ordination yet: he sees a thrown toy as it flies towards him but looks confused when it falls on the ground! He's met more horses, and an entire herd of cows said hello the other day – he wasn't overly sure of their intentions, though.

We've been out and about in the town, and he's now not trying to say Hi to everyone who passes us, only those who stop to speak to him. He had his first encounter with a dog who growled, barked and lunged at him all in the blink of an eye; thankfully, at a little distance, and he was okay; just walked on.

His latest weigh in at the vet has him at 28.9kg (63.7lb), so he's getting bigger, and is now too heavy for me to pick up and put in the car. He's learning more and more language, so is managing himself really well. He had a visit from a friend who said he was really calm for a puppy, which prompted two thoughts: one, what a nice compliment; he is doing so well at balancing his behaviour, and two: he was actually very excited, and if he had been any more active I would have asked him to calm down. It's interesting how perceptions can be so different, as my friend's perception of an excitable puppy is, to me, actually one who is over-excited, without impulse control.

Off to puppy school

Wolfie starts puppy class with me on Monday, with Matt escorting him the vast distance from house to exercise yard! I have six puppies booked in, so it will be interesting to see how he copes when I'm teaching, and being around other dogs for an hour.

He has not toileted in the house for the last five weeks, and he's only been with for seven, so that's brilliant. I stopped checking whether he needed to go out in the night two weeks ago, as he hasn't needed to go out for ages. He's usually asleep when I've checked him, but, if not, he gives me a smiley face and settles back down. He even went out in torrential rain without any fuss this morning!

He had his first taste of homemade steak pie and mash last night – yummy! And he had a new car experience, when he travelled in style in our classic XJS. Doesn't he add some class!

It's Monday and time for Wolfie to begin puppy classes. A well-run class is a super experience for both dog and carer, and my foundation course lasts six weeks, with usually between four and six puppies on each course. I do a small amount of clicker training to demonstrate its correct use, and I do this for sit, down, and wait cues. The majority of the course is about reading canine body language, teaching spoken language, the pup learning impulse control and self-restraint via self-regulation of the emotional mind, how to have a productive conversation, and strategies for resolving issues, situations, or anything that crops up. I address lead walking, off-lead, routines at home, socialisation, and introductions and interactions between dogs and people. I also include a little trick work as this is great fun for puppy and carer, and provides the inspiration to take this further, if desired, or to consider another activity with their dog.

Wolfie really enjoyed his first class, albeit he was a little confused to begin with about why he couldn't stand with me, although he soon got used to

Wolfie – complete with car harness – travels in style!

listening to Matt. Attending a class like mine allows puppies to learn and practise social skills in a secure and managed environment, without pups being at risk of altercation, fearful during interaction, or doing something they don't want to.

The beginning of the course focuses on the pup being around other dogs and people, but still listening to their carer, and we learn strategies for meet-and-greet, and for walking past without stopping.

As the course progresses, the puppies become better at managing their excitement levels, any anxiety, and reading each others' body language. It's important to teach an over-excited puppy to be calm when he greets a dog and not jump all over him, ignoring the good manners necessary to ensure that the other dog is receptive. As the weeks pass and the puppies get to know each other, they develop their own style of initial greeting within the group. They may be more forthright and quicker to initiate play with those they really like, and who like them, and more careful and quieter with those whose response is not so obviously welcoming.

It's a joy to see how they develop: the exuberant ones learning how to stay calm; the nervous ones become more confident, and how each adjusts their behaviour when in conversation with each other. By the time the course comes to an end, carers and puppies are good at recognising and understanding canine body language, with carer and puppy working in harmony when they meet other dogs. The puppies still need guidance as they continue meeting dogs outside of class, as it is easy for them to become over-excited. But with strategies learnt in class to address this, their self-restraint and management of their emotional mind progresses.

Wolfie's self-restraint around food is also developing nicely, even though he can reach the kitchen counter, and could help himself to food near the edge. We've been progressing self-restraint since the very first time he put his head in the fridge when I opened it, and he now has a good idea of what is for him and what isn't when I am getting food out of the fridge, and when it is left on the counter.

Wolfie enjoys puppy class.

He asks rather than takes, and tells me if he is interested in something he hasn't tried.

HOT CHILLI

Chilli has decided that Wolfie is worth playing with, and has begun playing the hide, seek and ambush game. This involves her hiding (not very well, I have to say), running at Wolfie and ambushing him when he gets close, then running away at top speed. If Wolfie doesn't follow her she either repeats the sequence or sits and looks at him until he does something, then she moves. It is great fun, but a bit much for Wolfie to cope with, unfortunately, and he soon becomes over-excited. I manage this by checking where Chilli is hiding, and, if in an area where she cannot get out of Wolfie's way if he *does* chase her, I intervene by distracting Chilli beforehand, and we have calm time instead.

Sometimes, I tell Wolfie where Chilli is, and ask if he can see her so that his excitement level rises more gradually than if she springs the game on him. As he is waiting for her to begin the game, I tell him 'Carefully with Chilli, wait for her.' Although anticipation can escalate excitement, Wolfie is doing very well at managing his emotional mind, and not escalating much until he is in the middle of a game or run, so, guidance from me, together with already being able to manage his anticipation to some extent, helps Wolfie. If he goes over the top, I change activities and help him calm his emotions.

We play a 'gotcha' game where I say 'I'm going to get you,' and he runs away, tail wagging happily. He's not very good at keeping away, however, and, when he comes close enough I touch him and say, 'Gotcha,' which happens many times. This makes his tail wag even more, as this is the bit he likes best, so he doesn't try to run very far.

Another game we play is with a toy, which we each hold on to. If he tugs the toy I say 'It's yours,' and if I tug it, I say 'It's mine,' and we go between it being his and mine, always with a gentle tug. When he comes back to me with it, I say 'Bring it back,' and then, 'Aha, it's mine,' as I hold it and the game continues.

WOLFIE'S DIARY
August 3
Two months with us: 17 weeks and 3 days old

NOTES
Some lovely Wolfie facts –

- he loves roast duck and lamb

- he has a couple of pieces of apple to finish after his meals – which he really likes!

- he has gone up two sizes in his harness

In the last 7 weeks, he has eaten 14kg (30.86lb) of dry biscuits, along with many potatoes, bread, sausages, vegetables and roast meats. Oh, and we all had steak for dinner at the weekend – that made him very happy!

He has five holes where baby teeth used to be, so is a little gummy! Speaking of which, who remembers the Gummy Bears cartoon? Wolfie has also become very bouncy, so I reckon he's been drinking gummy berry juice!

- he's only manic bitey when he is very tired or very hungry now (hooray), so easily resolved!

- he loves going out for a walk; he wags his tail lots when we ask him if he wants to go out

- he's really enjoying his walks with Dina, his Romanian doggy friend

- he loves chasing butterflies

- he loves running then sitting in the grass in the sun

And he played with one of the dogs next door yesterday, and spent the next ten minutes outside hoping he would come back out ...

Wolfie loves to chase bees, which is not a good idea, so I've been teaching him 'Mind the bees.' I say this every time he shows interest in a bee, or one comes close enough that he might. I distract him to focus on something else, and the bee is left to bumble about without attention from a Wolfhound. Sometimes he can't restrain himself, and, as with everything, this is a work-in-progress. Wolfie is still learning, so I will continue with this and the many other things he is learning until he can manage himself without help.

Wolfie is also getting plenty of practise at puppy class. It's a busy year as I have courses starting every couple of weeks, so Wolfie joins each new one. At the moment he's attending class twice a week, but there is always the opportunity for him to return to the house and garden if he finds it too much, but he's enjoying it at the moment.

Car journeys are gradually getting better, and he is mostly comfortable, though sometimes whines and does not like it. We are still progressing this; I am still driving relatively slowly to minimise his upset,

A puppy called Wolfie

though we are going further now, which is great progress. Wolfie has acclimatised to the car quite quickly because he was only ever anxious about it, and not scared, or terrified of it. I have ensured that each journey is within his capabilities by assessing his emotional state before deciding to take him out. If we have a scheduled appointment, such as at the vet, I make sure we have done some activities before we go so that Wolfie is quieter and more relaxed. I also make sure he hasn't just eaten: he's never yet been car-sick, so I don't want to take any chances.

😊 *Teaching tip*
If a teaching strategy isn't working, change it. Additionally, a particular strategy does not necessarily continue to be the right one as your puppy develops; often, you need to adjust or progress this for whatever development stage your puppy is undergoing.

WOLFIE'S DIARY
August 6
Two months with us: 17 weeks and six days old

NOTES
The settee ate Wolfie in the night ...
  Well, it got to his shoulders, and then I rescued him. Wolfie's favourite sleeping position is on his back with his legs stretched out. I can only assume that moving about in his sleep resulted in him ending up under the settee, and when he tried to move there wasn't enough room, so he was stuck. Or the settee really did fancy him as a midnight snack ...

Wolfie is progressing really well with walking along the lane, and sitting down and not wanting to move is becoming a much less frequent occurrence. He's also getting better at coping with cars and tractors we meet in the lane, so the natural progression is that, as long as there's not something really big and noisy coming, we do not have to stand at a distance. This does mean that cars now pass closer to us, so I have begun teaching Wolfie 'stay close' when we need to stay still to let traffic pass. We move to the outside edge of the road and I crouch down and hold the back of Wolfie's harness with one hand, placing the other on his chest. As the cars get so close it's vital that Wolfie does not suddenly lunge, and my holding him in this way prevents this whilst he learns. If he'd seemed too worried when we first tried this I would have gone back to the previous step and stayed at a distance from the cars. As it is, Wolfie is a little worried, but copes well, and does not try to run. I do not notice any flee instinct, and he is not concerned once the vehicle has gone past. This strategy is going really well, and Wolfie is now automatically moving to the edge of the road when he hears approaching traffic, staying close and sitting in advance of the car passing us.

  Our 'steady' cue is now pretty well perfect, as we've been practising this every time we go for a run along the lane, and Wolfie has got really good at keeping the same pace, so I don't need to stop any more. Obviously, he is now bigger, stronger, and faster than he was when we began this a couple of months ago. He also loves running, so his motivation to get faster is strong. Although he really wants to speed up, he doesn't, however, and has found a way of managing his enthusiasm. His solution? Instead of getting faster and lengthening his stride, he goes higher in the air, and runs with a more bouncy gait. This is often referred to as handicapping during play between dogs, when they match their activity to who they are playing with. I haven't taught Wolfie to do this when we run, he's done it of his accord. From the expression on his face, he is definitely enjoying himself.

Our 'steady' cue is now pretty well perfect.

A puppy called Wolfie

I have taught him to apply 'steady' to whatever pace we are going, so if we are running down a steep hill, I can ask him to be steady to account for my slower pace. I have not actively taught Wolfie to run at different speeds, steady is the concept, and he is able to apply that to the different speeds we walk and run at, because, once he understands that steady means maintain a pace, it is immaterial what that pace is.

WOLFIE'S DIARY
August 15
Two-and-a-half months with us: 19 weeks and one day old

NOTES

Our first trip to Dulverton today, a really busy town in tourist season, so plenty going on. We walked all around the town and saw lots of different people and dogs. Wolfie said Hi to a lovely Labrador, and a group of terriers. He was great walking past everyone without trying to say hello.

We walked down to the river where there were plenty of dogs playing and running around, and some came to say hello. We also saw a Jack Russell whose body language said 'please don't come any closer,' so we didn't interact with him.

Wolfie had his first ice cream, clotted cream flavour, which he thought was delicious. Everybody said how lovely he was. It was a bit of a sensory overload, but he was fine with it, and didn't become over-aroused, or show any sign that he wasn't enjoying it: he was interested and attentive the whole time. Totally worn out, he was fast asleep by the time we got home.

AND SO TO BED ...

Wolfie is an outdoor kind of boy, and now that we are well into summer, he spends most of his time outside. When not playing or mooching about he loves to sit in the long grass and watch the world go by. The only problem with this is that, over the last few weeks, he has been increasingly reluctant to come in at bedtime. I am sure he would happily sleep outside all night if he could.

The hot weather means it is still nice outside at bedtime, and often cooler than inside. We're trying to cook quick dinners in the evening so that the oven is not on much, and the kitchen/TV room that Wolfie lives in cools down quickly. Wolfie is very sure he cannot come in if he is too hot.

Bedtime now needs a strategy. If we go out and tell Wolfie it's time to come in, he wanders off up the garden! Sometimes he will stand and let us go to him, give him a cuddle, and ask him to come inside, on which occasions he does. But if he is in a more playful mood, he wags his tail at us and trots further away, and we can't help but laugh.

We use a range of things to entice Wolfie inside. If he is in when it is nearly bedtime, we shut the door rather than risk him going out (should he need to toilet at this point, he will ask to go out). We may offer him something nice to eat. We might go out on the yard for a quick game, and then ask him to come in with us. We might try to catch him and then run away, which usually results in him following us, unless he's sure he doesn't want to come in, in which case we won't play that game. Sometimes, I go in the opposite direction to him and then 'find' him, which usually results in a waggy tail and a cuddle, and I can guide him inside.

We always offer Wolfie some tasty food when he does come in, so that there is something nice to be inside for. He gets lots of praise, and we sit with him for a while before we go to bed, so he's not immediately left on his own.

If it looks like we have no chance of getting him in, we have occasionally closed the back door for a while, and find that he does want to come in when we re-open it a little time later. When this doesn't happen, we might make a noise, play with a toy, bring a box into the area, anything to catch his interest so he comes in.

Whilst we need to help him decide to come in of his own accord, we must ensure that we do not excite Wolfie in the process, as he will be even less likely to want to come inside, and more likely to want to play rather than sleep, whether inside or out. Although I am using games to get his attention, I am doing so in a completely different way to when we are actually playing. All of my movements are small, quiet, and matter-of-fact, compared to the exaggerated postures I adopt when we are playing. My voice is calm and quiet, with a hint of humour so that Wolfie knows I am happy and engaging with him; just enough to catch his interest without sending him into play mode. If he doesn't respond to one thing, I turn away and try something else. If I keep trying the same thing without success, chances are my movements and voice will increase and become louder, which will make Wolfie more excited, and want to run away from me to play more of this game.

Once I'm with him or have his attention, I talk softly to him, telling him he's a lovely boy, and let's go inside for something yummy. I often leave Matt inside and ask Wolfie to find his Dad, as this is good motivation for him to come in. Once inside I stop whatever I was doing to entice him in and change to calming things, such as a cuddle or massage, whilst telling him it's time for bed.

We manage to get Wolfie inside relatively quickly most days, but occasionally it takes a bit longer: we just have to be patient.

Chapter 8

Terrible teens

WOLFIE'S DIARY
August 19
Two-and-a-half months with us: 19 weeks and five days old

NOTES
Wolfie has seriously lost the plot today, and has gone backwards by weeks. He can't walk without pulling all over the place, is sitting down and refusing to move, and chewing his lead. In fact, these things are worse than they've ever been: they weren't really anything more than a minor interruption before, but he's really embraced them today ...

He can't seem to play; he's gone right back to biting me and ignoring his toys, and is completely brainless ... We've had no calm mooching, playing, or just watching the world go by: it's been either manic awake, or crashed out ... I think his mind has left the building!

HORMONAL INFLUENCE
It is very clear that Wolfie's first major hormonal phase has begun. Often called the teenage period, or likened to the terrible twos, commonly used to describe children of that age when their brain goes through a development stage, the signs are

obvious. However, there are differences to be seen between puppies at this stage. Testosterone is one of the hormones that come into play, and how much is produced, how much it affects arousal levels, and how each puppy deals with how he feels is individually determined. Some puppies remain fairly balanced and calm, some experience a very intense reaction, and some will be at a point between the two extremes.

Wolfie is a high-arousal puppy, who goes very quickly from a typically excited puppy to over-arousal, when he doesn't know what he's doing, can't calm down, and can't listen. He is learning to think through his emotions and interrupt himself when in this state, with me helping by talking him through it and redirecting him. But if it gets to a point where nothing helps, and he can't interrupt himself, I leave him to play on his own so his mind can calm down, as my presence goes partway toward fuelling his over-arousal.

Now that Wolfie is in his first hormonal phase, these issues are exacerbated. Hormones affect the emotional mind, amplifying emotions, arousal level and actions. With a high-arousal puppy, the hormonal phase intensifies these reactions, and Wolfie is then driven by his emotional mind when anything stimulates his arousal level sufficiently: interaction, play, and, as he's a sight hound, movement. Often he is fine if it's just one thing, but if it goes on for too long, or several things happen, his arousal level goes sky-high. This condition is referred to as trigger stacking: any stimulus that

During his first hormonal phase, Wolfie is constantly on high alert, as his arousal level rises ...

causes an emotional response, whether good or bad, is a trigger, and stacking refers to a number of triggers occurring at the same time, or subsequent to each other. The number of triggers that take a dog into over-arousal is individual to each animal, and stacking can also occur with just one trigger if this is ongoing, and causes a continual increase in arousal level. Any dog can be high-arousal, although some breeds are more predisposed to this.

Wolfie is a normal puppy who plays, grabs clothing or hands, jumps up when he gets excited, and explores the world in various ways, one of which is using his teeth to investigate and hold things. Many puppies jump and bite when they go over the top, and Wolfie is the same: his focus is on me, not his toys, once he tips over into mania, and the result is a much more intense expression of these behaviours. He has no idea what he's doing; neither can he stop. I want to make it very clear that Wolfie is not trying to bite me, and is in no way aggressive. He is a young puppy who is not yet able to manage his emotional mind.

Many people experience this behaviour with their puppies, and it's hard enough work managing it when a puppy is normal size. If the pup is a giant breed, this presents extra considerations. Wolfie was 28.9kg (63.7lb) at his last weight check about four weeks ago, so is already a substantial size and weight, which makes dealing with this behaviour a little more difficult than working with a smaller dog.

Being in a state of over-arousal is dysfunctional as there is no resolution, no joy, or satisfaction: Wolfie is frustrated and trying to achieve something, but his emotional state makes this impossible. When Wolfie loses control, his focus is on me,. This is common for many dogs, though they may focus on other dogs or something in the environment, such as digging, or biting and ripping soft furnishings. I have implemented safety measures as there a bigger risk to me due to his lack of bite inhibition, size and strength, but safety measures should be in place, whatever size of puppy. These will not only keep me safe, but also interrupt Wolfie's manic behaviour, which is an

A puppy called Wolfie

important part of teaching Wolfie to manage his emotional mind, come down from over-arousal, and eventually prevent his mind from becoming so aroused in the first place.

The things I have taught Wolfie so far are going to be a huge help when working through this period. As he knows so many words and phrases, I can do so much with just my voice. For example, I can ask him to find a toy, go to a specific location (such as the gate or pond), tell him 'I'll follow you,' 'Wait there,' 'Off you go outside,' 'I'll be back in a minute,' etc. Timing is important, because the more aroused his mind, is the harder it will be for him to listen, so I work like this with my voice when he is still able to think. This manages Wolfie's arousal level for a good part of the day, which means we can be together, and I need only separate myself from Wolfie for short periods.

I always carry a toy with me when we are in the house and garden, and a bucket of toys when we are in the field. When Wolfie becomes over-aroused, I use my voice primarily to get through to him, accompanied by a back-up of toys and bucket, to redirect him whilst he regains control of his mind. Loose-fitting clothes and gloves are essential when he's not able to listen. There are times when I have no other choice than to be separate from Wolfie, as my absence is the change that allows his mind to calm. But, as much as I can, I stay with him to talk him through this phase, and help him calm his mind so that I do not need to remove myself from the situation on an ongoing basis.

It's quite easy to separate myself from Wolfie when we're inside, as I can quickly and easily get to a door, although this is a last resort, and not something I do often. I keep a toy handy so that

... especially when he's outside.

when he tries to bite, I can put that in his mouth so that we are not connected whilst I am leaving the room, and his focus is on the toy, rather than me.

Outside, it's a lot harder to separate us, as usually distance is involved. If Wolfie is in a manic state continuing to jump and bite, I need to resolve this as quickly as possible, so have had to change where we go when outside. If Wolfie receives sufficient stimulation when we go out he remains in control, but if he becomes bored, his behaviour escalates and he directs this at me. This is a huge problem when we are on-lead walking along the lane, for example, as he is too big for me to be able to hold the end of his lead away from my body to create enough distance that he can't reach me. And we can't separate until we're back at the house, which may take some time. This is not a safe situation.

Walks along the lane are boring, familiar, and nothing much happens, and there is no outlet for his mania, so these have been suspended until Wolfie can manage his mind, and have been replaced with driving into and walking around town several evenings a week when Matt gets home from work. A little nervous in case he loses the plot – it doesn't look good to an observer – I take a toy, just in case, but it seems we've got the balance right between there being enough stimulation to keep his interest, and not so busy that he goes into mania.

When we are in the garden and field I keep close to a door or gate, and let Wolfie explore on his own. When I move about, I use whatever is in the garden, such as bushes, or the garden table and chairs, to stand by, so there is something between or next to us that can take his focus from me. I can also place toys or food there, directing his attention towards receiving something nice that does not involve me. This is where the language I have taught him has really helped, as I ask him to find what I've put there, go to the other side of an object, or go ahead of me, so that he has a purpose to keep his mind occupied, and he is not walking next to me. I may tell him to go to the pond or the gate and I'll meet him there when I want to take him further than

the back garden. If Wolfie becomes manic at any point I can open the gate so that one of us can go through.

Everything I do is intended to keep Wolfie below the threshold. If he goes into mania and I remove myself from the situation almost immediately Wolfie quickly calms down, but this is not always an option, and its efficacy is limited, inasmuch as my return causes his arousal level to rise again. I need to teach him how to regulate himself when I am present or we'll always be in the situation of not being able to even walk around the garden, as I have to remove myself if Wolfie goes over the top.

Wolfie *will* learn to manage his emotional mind and control his arousal level, despite the influence of hormones, as this phase is transitory, and his hormone level will drop, eventually. Wolfie will experience his second hormone surge in just a few months, and this will be more intense as it's part of reaching sexual maturity, and very unsettling. It is imperative that when Wolfie experiences this second surge he has already learnt how to manage his emotional mind, or his behaviour will be extremely difficult to cope with, and there is huge potential for dysfunctional emotions and behaviours to take hold and be carried through to adulthood.

Bucket tactics

So, my bucket strategy comes into play here. I use this when a dog is directing their behaviour – be this over-excited, mania, or active defence – toward a person, and someone needs be in the same area as the dog to teach him how to redirect to something else, and learn to manage his behaviour himself. When I am in the home or garden I can separate myself from Wolfie by one of us being inside and one outside, but I cannot do this if we are in the field. So I walk around the perimeter of the field, so that there is always a fence for me to stand against, and I use the bucket as a barrier between Wolfie and me, and as a tool to redirect him.

I put a few toys and balls in the bucket and carry it with me when we go out on walks across the fields, as this gives me something to work with so

A puppy called Wolfie

A

B

C

D

(Courtesy Mighty Dog Graphics)

that I can remain with Wolfie. We can be out walking calmly, or having a play, when he starts getting over-excited. Sometimes, I can use my voice and engage him in a conversation, give him something to focus on, with suggestions like 'Let's go this way and see the sheep,' or engage him in a game with a toy or ball from the bucket when we are off-lead in the field. However, his mind will still often escalate and take him into mania, and this is when he will focus on me, jump up, and try to nip or grab my clothes, unable to focus on anything else.

This is when the bucket *really* comes into play. I turn the bucket towards him as he's jumping at me (A), and say 'Find a toy.' (B) The bucket provides a barrier between us, and, instead of grabbing me, Wolfie is presented with his toys. The first few times I tried this, all he did was put his head in the bucket, and continue to jump (C), so, as soon as I can, I take something from the bucket to try and get him to focus on this (D). If this is not successful, I again show him the bucket and say 'Find a toy.' If Wolfie dips his head into the bucket, I give him positive feedback in a calm tone so as not to increase his arousal level.

At this stage, whether or not he selects a toy is immaterial, as I am simply teaching him to redirect his focus on the bucket rather than on me, so when he lifts his head I say, 'Come on, let's go this way.' It's tempting to just stay where you are once your puppy has refocused like this, as the fear is that moving might set him off again. That *may* happen, but unless you progress the situation by moving, the mania will continue, as his mind is still trying to achieve something, and not succeeding. Any change provides an opportunity to get through to him.

The bucket always comes with us, and I teach Wolfie to redirect to this. I also take the time to understand what mood he is in, what stimulation his mind can cope with, and what is likely to trigger an escalation to mania. If it is windy, there will be lots of insects that Wolfie will find stimulating, and if Wolfie is in the spike part of his hormone cycle, he is going to escalate far quicker than if he is in the growth phase, and it is a calm and quiet day. I can reduce

the number of manic episodes if I choose activities to help him stay within normal excitement levels. On manic days, we play games and stay near the house so that I can easily remove myself from the situation. On calm days, we walk in the field with the bucket of balls.

The detail I have described here is for a puppy in over-arousal due to excitement and hormones, if I use this strategy for dogs displaying active defence, the detail would be different to allow for the difference in motivation.

I am also rotating the toys in the bucket, and adding in a new one every few days. A new toy increases excitement, and if Wolfie was not high-arousal and in a hormonal phase, we would be able to play tug, fetch and other games, as we usually do, being mindful that he didn't become manic. However, as Wolfie's mind is taking him into mania too easily, new toys are introduced into the bucket as a way of providing more stimulation, excitement, and the pleasure of a new toy. As with any puppy, familiar toys become boring in time, and Wolfie doesn't need to miss out on new toys just because they may send his mind over the top. They also keep his mind on the bucket as a source of fun and exciting things, which helps prevent him focusing on me.

THE JOYS OF RUNNING

Whether I am with him or on the other side of the gate, I talk Wolfie through his mania,and the more I do this, the easier it is for him to listen, and start to respond. Wolfie loves running, so when the bucket and chasing balls are simply not working I encourage him to run to expend his excess energy. I've already been using the phrases 'Go for a run,' and 'That's a good run' when he is running, so use this strategy as an alternative to the bucket.

It takes a little time to get through to him. Sometimes he does run when I suggest it, and sometimes I use a toy to start him running and encourage him to continue – I say 'Keep going' if he is running towards me so he carries on past. After Wolfie has finished running, he usually lies down, but is not yet calm – I can tell from his body, which he

A puppy called Wolfie

is still alert and tense, rather than tired and relaxed. The first couple of times this happened I didn't spot this, and once he'd stopped running I thought it safe to go to him, and, unfortunately, my closeness reignited his mania. Lesson learnt; since then I wait to see his body visibly relax before I go to him. As this is happening I talk him through it with phrases such as 'That was a nice run,' 'Aren't you a lovely boy' 'Time to relax now.' Once I see his body relax, I match my body language and breathing to his as I approach him, again telling him 'Time to relax.' We then begin a conversation about what to do next, or simply sit and relax for a while longer.

WOLFIE'S DIARY
August 28
Three months with us: 21 weeks old

NOTES
Had a lovely morning by the pond, chasing dragonflies and saying Hi to the horses.

Wolfie-boy has been a teenager for ten days now, and things have settled down.

I've made adjustments to his diet and routine to compensate for this phase, and it's having a good effect. I've also been reminding him of all the things he already knows, so he can think through his emotional mind and not be swept away by it. It would have been really difficult if I hadn't already put a huge amount of teaching in place, but as I have we are mostly sailing through choppy waters, with the odd capsize!

Physically, Wolfie's face is broadening; you can see him beginning to change from those lovely puppy features into a very handsome dog (I shouldn't say so myself, but he is, just look at him!).

His voice is becoming deeper, and his little boy bits are now not quite so little ... He is sleeping more, and he's having another growth spurt: he has sore legs.

And, despite his mind being all over the place, he is trying really hard to work through

this phase. He's remaining balanced and able to think, successfully overriding his emotional mind, allowing his intellectual mind to make decisions for a good portion of the time. All puppies go through this hormonal phase, when they are somewhere around 4.5-6 months old. Knowing how to manage their behaviour through this difficult time helps them through this phase, coming out the other side happy and well-balanced.

Observing Wolfie in this phase, I can easily see the hormone cycle (refer to chapter 5 for details). Each part of it lasts 3-4 days, so the whole cycle is around 10-12 days. Knowing the timing, I can predict how Wolfie is going to be each day and adjust our activities accordingly. The bucket is always with us, as although I have implemented measures to minimise the hormonal effect, they still influence Wolfie's mind and thinking. When his mind can't cope, he reverts almost immediately to mania, so all safety strategies remain in place.

The most difficult part of the day is before bedtime, as Wolfie is finding it really difficult to achieve a calm state of mind so that he can sleep. Over-tiredness does not help the current situation, as it makes him less able to calm down and more easily frustrated. Trying to calm Wolfie inside the house just does not work and, on several occasions, he's still been on the go at 9.30pm, and we've ended up going to bed in the hope that he will eventually settle (he has, but this is not a good situation). So, I have begun taking him outside to play with toys from the bucket at around 8pm, and this seems to be working. We stay outside for 10-30 minutes, until he's expended his energy and he tells me he doesn't want to play any more, when we go in and I settle him. It's still quite late by the time he's gone to sleep, but it is so much easier this way. Once his hormonal phase passes, Wolfie won't have so much excess energy, and I expect bedtime to be easier and quieter.

Wolfie is also starving much of the time, which is working very well for using diet to help maintain a more even brain chemistry. He was having 4-5 meals a day when he arrived with us, which has settled at four for a while. Eating smaller amounts minimises the changes that occur in brain chemistry due to being hungry or after eating, so I have added small portions of mashed potato in-between his usual meals. As a slow release carbohydrate, the potato helps to keep brain chemistry at a more even level (other slow release carbohydrates do this, too, but Wolfie really likes mash).

I've made changes to other ingredients in his diet that also help maintain brain chemistry levels. This is very effective, and complements the other things I have implemented to help Wolfie through this phase. As Wolfie eats a home-cooked diet, it is easy for me to make changes. Each dog is an individual, and what suits one may not suit another, so there are many things to consider when deciding what your puppy will eat, and so many different opinions. Whatever approach you decide on, get professional advice to ensure that you provide a balanced nutritional diet that is right for your puppy.

WHAT'S YOURS IS MINE ...

Wolfie is doing really well with not taking things not intended for him. At this stage we are still being very tidy in the house, and making sure that things are not left out to tempt him, but sometimes we forget and, as time goes by, and Wolfie doesn't show much more interest than sniffing these things, we become more relaxed. This is a natural progression, and development of Wolfie's reliability. Well, until he decided that he would take the tea towel that hangs from the oven door into the garden!

I've never moved tea towels out of his way: we use them often, and Wolfie has not previously shown any interest in them, but, as I'm standing in the kitchen, Wolfie picks up the tea towel with his mouth, and, with his tail high and a happy spring to his step, takes it outside. My reaction? 'Pudding, what a cheeky boy you are!' I say with a laugh.

Unless Wolfie has something that is dangerous, I do not need to hurry to retrieve what he has, as I do not want to him to decide that he has to run away, begin ripping what he has taken, or eat it before I get to him. He may well begin to rip the towel anyway, as he's a puppy, and although tearing toys is not his focus, he does do this sometimes. But if I am immediately after him, and he does want to rip the towel, he will learn that he has to begin straight away, before the towel, or whatever, is taken from him ... if I take my time, so will he.

I find something yummy for him to eat, and grab a couple of his favourite toys before heading out to the garden. I have no intention of making this a negative experience, so, keeping a distance so that he doesn't move away from me, I ask in an excited voice 'Wolfie I've got your toy, do you want to come with me?' whilst squeaking the toy. Wolfie gets up and approaches, his attention on me, and we wander away from the tea towel.

When he is engaged with his toy, I walk over and pick up the towel. Wolfie comes running, and I say, 'Silly boy, that's not for you' and take the towel inside, hanging it on the oven door whilst distracting Wolfie by saying 'Let's go and find your toy,' and 'Would you like one of these yummy treats? This ensures his focus is on the good things I am providing, rather than the tea towel, but if he goes to it again, I tell him it's not for him and he leaves it alone.

If my toy strategy had not worked, I could have tried dropping some of his favourite treats nearby whilst he was outside with the towel, and retrieved it whilst he was eating them, or I could have got out his harness to go for a walk. Really, whatever works to divert his attention from the tea towel is preferable to chasing him around to get it back!

Had my attention been on Wolfie, I would have seen what was in his mind, and distracted him before he took the tea towel, but this was actually a good thing as it provided Wolfie with an important learning experience. The sense of having done something for and by himself gave him huge satisfaction, as was obvious from his body language.

A puppy called Wolfie

This is an important part of puppy development, trying something on his own, without any input from me, and succeeding, and gave Wolfie confidence that, in the future, he can try and will achieve. It also made him very happy and boosted his sense of fun! If he's always prevented from being playful and having fun, his sense of enjoyment will suffer. He's only a puppy, and these things happen, so better to go with the flow and allow him to learn and develop from it than dampen his spirit. There's a big difference between allowing Wolfie to explore boundaries in a safe and controlled way and leaving him to help himself to anything he likes. I manage our environment, and there's nothing he can get hold of that would be a big problem. It is also a good learning experience for him to know that if he has something he shouldn't, it's usual for me to take it back.

The tea towel incident doesn't happen again, as it had lost interest for Wolfie, although he does go on to have Matt's shoe, the odd sock, etc, that have been left out. My response was the same, though, and the situation is easily resolved without creating a focus on the item. In time, we will be able to leave anything about and know that he will not take what is not for him.

Business and pleasure

My working time is split between seeing clients and the computer. When I see clients Wolfie is left on his own, but I am here and around him the rest of the time. These might seem ideal circumstances, but there are difficulties, just different ones to those I might have if I went out to work. It does mean I have more time with Wolfie, but I do still need to work, so although I am here most of the time, he has to be able to do things on his own.

A downside to our situation is that we don't have a set routine, and what I do and when I do it varies each day. I used to go out to work, so my previous dogs learnt our daily routine, and knew what was happening, and when, but Wolfie hasn't got that. Lunchtime, or taking a phone call require that Wolfie is able to amuse himself, but as these

activities are variable, Wolfie is not in a routine of settling down or playing on his own at specific times. As he is still a puppy, this lack of routine means that he is not always able to just sit and wait for me to be ready to do something. As he gets older, changes in routine won't matter, as he will be able to adjust, but, for now, I have to time activities like these to when he is likely to be ready for a sleep or to sit quietly.

There is some routine to our day, of course – we have breakfast, play, go for a walk, and then Wolfie is usually ready for a snooze – so I arrange to see clients, make phone calls, etc, for when I think he is most likely to be settling down. When lunchtime is depends on what work I have on that day, so, again, there's no set time for this, which means it is easier to eat when Wolfie is not desperate to play or do something. Of course, I could do things when it suits me rather than Wolfie, in which case I may be going out just as he is having a mad half-hour, which would not be good for the furniture – or him. I could shut him outside to play on his own when I want to have lunch, but, being a puppy, he is likely to quickly become bored and resort to digging the garden, or chewing the garden chairs. I adjust each day to compensate for our lack of routine

Wolfie's diary
August 29
Three months with us: 21 weeks old

Notes

We took Wolfie into South Molton with us this morning. It's summer, a nice day (Yes, really – it wasn't raining), and tourist season, so the town was quite busy. We visited our vet to say Hi, and have a weigh-in. Wolfie is now 40kg (88lb) – no wonder his legs hurt when he has a growth spurt like this. Wolfie had loads of cuddles.

His lead walking is coming on really well, and he no longer feels the need to take the initiative and say Hi to everyone he passes, but waits to be asked. He met a really lovely Lab x Staffie who wanted to play, and although Wolfie was three times the size of him, he was nice and not bouncy!

He had loads more cuddles, and is becoming something of a local figure. Wolfhounds are not common here, and people are really interested to meet him.

Wolfie's also now able to sit *with* us instead of always wanting to sit *on* us when we are on the settee – well, as long as he's not feeling excitable, as then he tries to get on our knee. Which would be fine, if he wasn't in hormone mode and bitey – it's not easy to persuade a 40kg (88lb) puppy to get off without mishap! However, his teenage phase is going smoothly, with only the odd manic moments indoors. He's doing well with trying to be calm when he meets the horses over the boundary fence next door, and they follow him along the fence!

After leaving Wolfie on his own whilst I went out, I return home to find that the sofa is scattered across the room, with seats and back panels all over the floor. Wolfie looks delighted! To deal with this I will need to use my distract, diffuse, and refocus strategy, which is a fantastic way to help redirect the many emotions and motivations a dog has, change his perceptions, and resolve behavioural issues – anxiety and fear amongst them.

Distract, diffuse, and refocus

• ignore your instinct to address the situation directly

• distract your puppy and get his attention

• diffuse his excitement/calm arousal level by talking him through the situation

• refocus his attention on something else

• if steps 2, 3 or 4 are unsuccessful, remove your puppy from the source of the excitement/arousal, or he will refocus on what he was doing

On this occasion, Wolfie is calm, so I piece together the sofa whilst talking to him. I say, 'Oh dear, I see the settee exploded, well, never mind, let's put it back together.' As he gets his little nose involved, I say 'Yes, just watch, it goes there, right, let's get the next bit.' When the sofa is whole again, we move on to doing something else.

The sofa is thus dismantled on a couple more occasions – one time when I'd been out in the garden for just a few minutes – and, on this occasion, because Wolfie was in a fairly high state of arousal, it made much more sense to engage him with a toy outside, and then leave him there whilst I put the sofa back together. How I choose to deal with a situation like this is based on Wolfie's ability to do what I ask. If his arousal level is very high, he is much less able to listen to me, so I distract, diffuse and refocus. If his arousal level is up but manageable, I distract and diffuse, without needing to refocus, as he is fine to be with me. If he is calm, there is no need for any of these steps. When it came to teaching Wolfie not to chew the bamboo, for example, there was no arousal, so I simply distracted and refocused him. There is no need to diffuse unless an emotion he is feeling requires this. So many of the things we've done when teaching Wolfie have a basis in distract and refocus, with diffuse added when he is excited or aroused.

Sometimes, this strategy will work better if it is in context with what your puppy is doing. This is often the case where there is excitement, arousal, and a strong motivation to do something specific. Look at what the motivation is. If chewing the sofa, for example, a chew toy is a good alternative to offer, as playing fetch may not satisfy the motivation to chew. If the motivation is eating – trying to get food, say – then asking him to play with a toy may not be that successful, but doing something that involves food rewards may meet his motivation.

As with so many things, practise is essential to achieve the desired result. I use this strategy when Wolfie is over-excited and doesn't know what to do with himself, is getting too manic with play, or when he does something that he shouldn't. Teaching

A puppy called Wolfie

Wolfie when he is calm means I do not need to match an alternative activity to his motivation. His self restraint is progressing really well, and, as we have worked on lots of activities with similar reward values, he can easily disengage and refocus on something else. Sometimes he needs a little extra encouragement, but not often.

(☺) *Teaching Tip*
If you focus on something in particular, so, too, will your puppy.

WOLFIE'S DIARY

September 26
Three months and three weeks with us: Five months and three weeks old

NOTES

Wolfie has had an epiphany: he's realised that he can stop himself from biting me when he loses the plot and doesn't know what to do with himself. Yippee! When his arousal levels go up and he becomes frustrated, as the only moving object he has to interact with, I am the obvious target for venting that frustration. He'll use toys, or branches of trees as a way of venting and calming himself when he's on his own, but not when I am about. This is normal behaviour for a young puppy, but it has rather more impact when the puppy in question is the size of and has the strength of an adult male German Shepherd. Hence, the constant presence of the bucket when we go out.

Having taught Wolfie to focus on the toys in the bucket rather than me until he calms down, we have now progressed to him being able to calm down in 10-15 seconds. On Thursday, he went one better, however. Four times on our morning walk across the field, Wolfie ran to me and began to engage, but stopped himself before he touched me.

It was as if a light bulb had gone on in his head, and he realised that he could *choose* what he wanted to do! This was even more impressive for the fact that Wolfie had watched my horses enjoying a morning run, which really raised his arousal level. Wolfie continued interrupting himself to remain calm all day, even when Matt came home from work, which usually makes him over-excited. He was happy, balanced, calm, and engaging. Great progress from my little pudding!

When the mind goes into over-arousal and becomes manic, it cannot find resolution, which leads to frustration, and then to trying harder to find resolution. Coming down from over-arousal can be distressing for a dog, and result in negative emotions and mood. This vicious cycle has to be interrupted so that the mind can find a way to calm itself, which becomes easier to achieve the more it happens. Awareness and control over the mind prevents this happening in the first place, and Wolfie has been trying really hard to manage himself and bring down his arousal level, to the point where he goes into over-arousal far less often, and is able to calm down in 20-30 seconds.

Running has been a big contributory factor in this, and I've associated the phrase 'Go for a run' with when Wolfie is running, and have encouraged him to run when he's over-aroused by throwing a toy from the bucket. Gradually, he's been more and more able to do as I suggest, by interrupting the chain of events sooner and taking himself for a run. Running diffuses his state of over-arousal, and, as it's an activity that Wolfie finds immensely pleasurable, it also deals with any feelings of frustration he has, leaving him with positive emotions and a sense of contentment.

The above diary entry records how Wolfie has now managed to control his emotional mind, and not let it go into a state of over-arousal. He has worked through this for the last two months, and this is the beginning of the end of this issue. It will take some time, yet, but he will get better at regulating his mind, and in another month or so his hormone levels will drop and become stable, until he goes through his second hormonal phase as an adolescent.

It is so important for Wolfie to learn to regulate and manage his mind during this stage in his life, as his second hormonal phase in a few months will involve testosterone levels being at their highest, signalling sexual maturity. We are likely to see social relationship issues, obsessive and repetitive behaviours, increased independence, and higher levels of over-arousal and mania. He's likely to be less responsive, less able to think through his emotional state, and some puppy issues that he has moved on from – such as chewing the sofa – may resurface. Now he knows how to regulate himself, he will manage these difficulties better, which has a direct impact on his ability to get through this phase.

If Wolfie were to go through this phase without having learnt to regulate himself, it would be a very difficult period for both him and us. Sadly, many puppies are either given up or neutered at this stage as they are just too hard to manage ...

VISIT HUBBLE AND HATTIE ON THE WEB:
WWW.HUBBLEANDHATTIE.COM • WWW.HUBBLEANDHATTIE.BLOGSPOT.CO.UK • DETAILS OF ALL BOOKS
• SPECIAL OFFERS • NEWSLETTER • NEW BOOK NEWS

111

Chapter 9
A teenager – again!

WOLFIE'S DIARY
November 3
Four months and three weeks with us: 7 months old

NOTES

Wolfie is 7 months old today. The vet gave him an adolescent check-up last night, and he was such a little pudding. He said Hi to everyone, and most people got a kiss, too! He now weighs 58kg (127.8lb), and looks like a proper big boy. He's almost reached the height of Indie (our Great Dane, who we lost earlier this year), which is ahead of how tall Indie was at 7 months.

Wolfie's really enjoying playing tag with us, hide, seek and ambush with Chilli, the cat, and standing as far out on the reeds in the pond as he can without falling in!

He has a lovely point developing when he sees game, and is automatically checking in with us when off-lead. His self-restraint is coming on really well, and impulse control is pretty much sussed, other than when off-lead, and he sees something he wants to chase. Being a youngster, he does still go over the top and get bitey occasionally, but far less often than he used to, and his ability to manage his emotions is progressing well. Wolfie has fitted into our lives so well, and he makes us very happy.

He loves galloping around, pouncing on and playing with toys, and at the moment he seems to have forgotten he is a sight hound, and is really developing his scenting skills. He's found loads of pheasants recently, and his usual routine is to flush the bird, run a little way after him, and then check in with me. I say something like 'Good check in, off you go, then,' and he does. The rest of our off-lead work is coming along well, and I am now doing a fair amount of distance work with him, using my voice, and he is responding really well most of the time. There are occasions where he's too interested or excited to respond, but that is easily resolved by adjusting what I am doing to help him. It may be asking for something else, getting closer, going to him, or talking him through it, and then suggesting we do something together, rather than leaving him to follow me.

FINDING HIS VOICE

Wolfie's knowledge has taken a big leap forward, he's a clever boy, and things have clicked easily.

He half-fell in the pond the other day. Sitting on the bank, he moved position, and the back half of him disappeared! He wasn't worried and stayed where he was – I pulled him out as I'm not at all sure he'd be so complacent if the rest of him went in!

Wolfie uses different barks to signify different things, and we have: happy play bark, I heard something bark, I'm not sure about that bark, and something is not right bark. It is so important to understand Wolfie's language through his voice as well as his body, and being able to interpret both of these ways of communication means I can get to know him and understand him better. Just as sometimes we say one thing with our voice and another with our body language, so, too, do dogs, and if there is conflict in how they are feeling there will be conflict in the language. Being able to see this leads to a better understanding of Wolfie and the nuances of his feelings, emotions, and language.

Our boy is pretty well-balanced all the time, now. He's at the tail end of his first hormone phase, so it's less intense, though still possible to recognise the stages –

- hormone spike November 22

- hormonal behaviour abates November 26; now in growth period and tired

- reduced testosterone, withdrawal phase November 30

Wolfie can interrupt and think through his emotions and arousal level without too much effort – other than for the odd moment or two.

WOLFIE'S DIARY
November 24
Five-and-a-half months with us: 7 months and 3 weeks old

AM

6.00:	Up and mooching
6.20:	Asleep
7.30:	Up, walk, play, mooch, relax
8.30:	Run in field, breakfast
9.30:	Relax, sleep
11.45:	Awake, mooch, watch horses

PM

12.15:	Walk
1.20:	Lunch, relax

3.30:	Awake, mooch, play
4.50:	Dinner, relaxing
5.30:	Out, vet check and walk
7.30:	Home, play, more dinner, play
8.20:	Sleep

Things are much more relaxed in the evenings now that Wolfie has got through the stage where he couldn't get his mind to calm down at bedtime.

A WORRYING TIME ...

It's now December, and Wolfie is eight months old and a joy to live with. His first hormonal period is just behind him, and his sunny personality, and calm, happy approach to life takes precedence now that his testosterone level has dropped. He is engaging, content, and in control of his mind. However, we do have a small worry ... Wolfie has a lump on his foot, so a trip to the vet was needed, and today he is going in for surgery to have the lump removed. We arrive at the vet with Wolfie happy and enthusiastic, as usual – I think he's trying to convince them to hire him as each time we go in, he trots behind the reception desk!

We go into the consulting room with one of the veterinary nurses, and she runs through what will happen. Ensuring that things go smoothly for Wolfie entailed giving the nurse important information about Wolfie that will help those looking after him, keeping him as relaxed as possible during this new experience –

- he knows language, so talk to him, tell him what to do and he will understand

- if he backs away, he's not being difficult, he's just unsure and out of his comfort zone. Give him a couple of minutes to adjust

- please don't bring Wolfie into the reception

area when we come to collect him if other dogs are present. His emotional mind is precarious and impressionable at this age, and, as he may be feeling the after-effects of the procedure, there's a risk that he may not view interaction with another dog from his usual perspective, which increases the potential for any such experience to be less than ideal

The veterinary nurse was brilliant, and knew exactly what I was talking about. As she led Wolfie from the room, she said, 'Come on, Wolfie, let's go this way,' and he happily followed with a waggy tail! Having this information makes it possible for everyone involved to interact with Wolfie in a way that is familiar to him, which will make him feel safer.

Thankfully, surgery went well, and the lump has gone to be analysed. What a relief that everything went well: there's always a risk, not only with sedation and the procedure, but also with how a dog copes emotionally with the experience. I've taught Wolfie to be confident within himself, and to understand language, which sets him up for success

in whatever situation he might find himself. He's home now, and still very groggy. He has a boot to keep his bandages dry, and the biggest buster collar I've ever seen. Hopefully, we won't need to use that, as he'll barely fit through the door with it on!

Wolfie is not allowed to play, run, or do anything off-lead, which could be a huge problem. As a youngster of just nine months, he still needs to expend a lot of energy, and if he doesn't do this by running, he'll do it with play, but that means jumping and pouncing, and he can't do these, either.

Having taught Wolfie impulse control, self-restraint, how to regulate his mind and manage himself in different situations, I am now almost completely hands-off, and Wolfie is guided by my voice and body language ... this is what will enable us to get through this period of inactivity easily and successfully.

Wolfie is predictable first thing in the morning. We have gone past the stage of him being excitable and wanting to play, and now he likes to go outside, have a slow mooch around, and then settle on the grass whilst we have breakfast and get ready

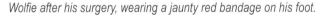

Wolfie after his surgery, wearing a jaunty red bandage on his foot.

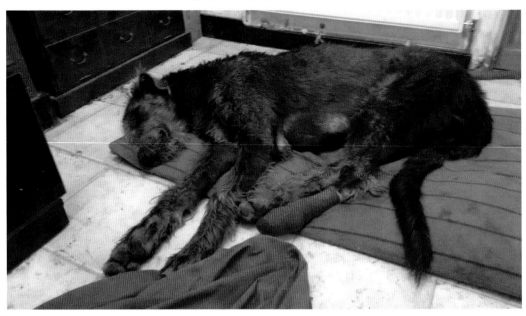

for work. It's the morning after his operation, and I can let him out as usual and trust that he will be calm and quiet – there is no need to put a lead on him and sit with him in the garden. As we go about our usual morning routine, I keep checking on Wolfie, but, as usual, he has a slow wander and settles down.

As the first day progresses, I add in additional phrases to help him manage himself. 'Mind your foot,' I say, and 'Be careful with your feet' as he goes outside. We vary between him being on- and off-lead throughout the day. If he's likely to become excited the lead goes on so that I can manage his movements. I talk him through everything, remaining calm, and reminding him to be careful with his foot. When he wants to run or play, I tell him 'Not yet, mind your foot, steady up the hill with Mum.' We're having some gentle games of tug, and engaging Wolfie's mind with some targeting (touching various items with his nose). His wound is right on that part of his foot where it pulls when he moves, and practising sits, downs, etc, involves too much movement at the wound site, so we're keeping to cues that allow him to remain standing or laying down.

As the days progress Wolfie becomes better at managing himself and understanding that he can't run about, which means he is off-lead more often, although I remain with him ready to intervene if he becomes excited. This is easy to determine as I watch what he's doing and his body language, so am aware of when this is likely to happen, and can provide distraction by talking to him as I approach and clip on the lead. I focus on engaging his mind so that he interrupts what he was about to do. This would not have been possible when he was in the first hormonal phase, and unable to regulate his mind, but, as this has passed, his hormone level has dropped and is stable; his mind much better balanced.

I am able to trust him off-lead for much of the time, and 'Mind your foot' results in him lifting it and bunny-hopping on three legs! We had a lovely few hours out yesterday – some walking, and lots of watching the world go by.

By far the most difficult aspect to manage has been keeping the bandage clean and dry. It's December in North Devon, and we live on a farm. It rains most of the time, and there is mud everywhere. The only way of keeping the bandage clean and dry when we go outside is to put Wolfie's foot in a plastic bag, and pull his boot over that. However, this is not a satisfactory solution, as the plastic bag makes his foot sweat, so the wound is wet within the bandaging, which is not at all good for his wound or foot. Going without the plastic bag resolves this, but means his bandage will get wet and muddy outside. The only real solution is to keep Wolfie inside all the time, but he simply cannot sit in the house all day doing nothing: he'll get bored and, without any exercise to expend his energy, his arousal level will rise. We do not use the plastic bag as this is the worst thing for his recovering foot. Instead, we use the boot, which protects him from the mud and change the bandages more often as his foot becomes wet.

WOLFIE'S DIARY
December 12
Six-and-a-quarter months with us: 8 months and two weeks old

NOTES

Wolfie went for another check-up on his foot last night, and it's doing very well. The bandaging is now off so that the wound can scab. Some stitches were removed, and we have another appointment on Monday for a couple more to be taken out.

As usual, Wolfie was a little pudding, and stood eating a chew whilst the vet tended to his foot. He's now wearing one of my socks when we go out, just to keep the mud off. The most important news is that the lump was not malignant, but a calcified mass. This *can* indicate Cushings Disease, so, despite there being only a very slim chance of Wolfie having it, they checked for this, too, and the result came back negative. The most likely cause of the

A puppy called Wolfie

lump is trauma to the foot, which makes sense as, when he was a little puppy, he had no idea what his legs were doing, and did bang his feet a few times, running around. Thank goodness he's okay, and healthy.

A couple of times Wolfie has taken the spare sock that we keep in the car, and run up the garden with it. Historically, we've never chased Wolfie if he's taken something that is not his to take, and instead have played games that introduced him to the idea of exchanging objects, by distracting him from whatever it is he has, and refocusing him on something else, or tossing some tasty food or toy nearby, and retrieving the object as he leaves it. We're now at the point that if Wolfie takes something the pleasure for him is in doing that, rather than keeping it or running off with it, and often the object is quickly discarded or left on the ground. Should he decide to hold on to it, I go to him and ask 'What have you got? That's mum's,' and he lets go of it and walks away with a waggy tail. I no longer need a distraction or alternative.

Chilli is continuing to entice Wolfie to play, and whenever we wander up the garden, there she is, hiding behind a tree, waiting to ambush him. Her timing is not good, given that Wolfie is so restricted in what he can do due to his foot, and he's doing really well with checking himself after an initial couple of steps in response to Chilli's play invite. This is great as it means I'm not being pulled about when he is on-lead, and neither am I having to chase after him when he is off-lead. I am keeping an eye out for Chilli, and ensuring that Wolfie is either on-lead or close to me to prevent him becoming excited, and attempting to run at great speed around the garden.

As the weeks progress and his wound heals, Wolfie can begin to do a little more. We still have to be careful where he puts his feet, and what movements he makes with his foot so as not to

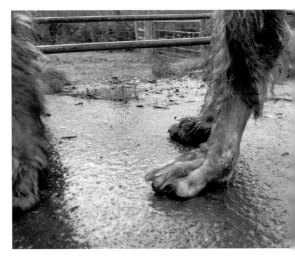

Wolfie's foot is healing well ...

open the wound, but, by Christmas this has healed sufficiently for this to be less of a concern. He's still wearing a sock for some protection when we are out.

Wolfie is now regulating his own routine very well. He's not as hungry, and his meals have reduced in number, as he has told us he doesn't need to eat that often. He tells us when he needs to

...and he wears a sock over his injury now that the bandage is off.

settle or sleep, so is not becoming over-tired now, either. His mind has developed and is again better balanced.

As it is the Christmas holidays, Matt has some time off work, which is exciting for Wolfie. He loves us both, I know, but is becoming something of a Daddy's boy. Wolfie helps with whatever Matt is doing around the house, and they go for long walks along the lanes together.

Because of this excitement, Wolfie's arousal level is a little higher, so he's less in control of his mind, and a little more bitey; unable to apply self-restraint when he's involved in something exciting.

We've gone backwards with the bucket a little, and sometimes he can't wait for me to throw a ball, but begins jumping up, although he is doing well with mostly staying within his own space rather than trying to interact with me. He's also managing to come back down very quickly, and regain control of his emotional mind.

This is just a small step backward, which is to be expected as he is developing his regulating skills.

Teaching Tip

We have reached the point where Wolfie is reliable and calm, and our input is needed less as he regulates himself. However, when there are retrograde steps like this, we need to return to providing more input so that he can remember how to get through this, and regain control of his mind.

Wolfie's diary
January 4
7 months with us: Nine months old

Notes
Final foot check at the vet. There was a Spaniel in the reception room when we arrived, who said Hi to Wolfie. Not long after, a Golden Retriever came out of a consulting room and also said Hi. Then two young Labradors came in, and we had a mix of five dogs and puppies, all calm and with good social manners. It was a lovely experience for Wolfie – he is really happy when he meets other dogs. He wagged his tail and offered a play bow, his body language telling me he wanted to be active and play, so I told him we'd play later and just to say Hi for now. He was very good and didn't pursue this. I then said, 'Come on, let's sit down,' and Wolfie walked over to a chair and parked his bum on it, making everyone laugh.

He was great with the vet for his foot check, settling quickly on the floor and lifting his foot. The wound is completely healed, so now it's just a case of his hair growing back.

Wolfie has also decided that he's a big boy now, who doesn't need to have lots of naps during the day. His decision was strongly influenced by Matt being home over Christmas, doing lots of things that Wolfie could help with, and he's consequently gone from a morning and afternoon nap, with bedtime at around 8.30pm, to one nap in the middle of the day, and bedtime at around 7pm. Sometimes, Wolfie goes through the entire day without a proper nap. He might have a little doze, but is up as soon as he hears anything going on.

This is a natural transition as a puppy grows older and does not require as much sleep. It won't last long, however, as his body will soon regulate itself, and Wolfie will move on to a more adult sleeping pattern, that includes proper restorative dozing or sleep during the day, as his body and mind requires it.

Wolfie is also continuing to progress balancing his emotions and not going over the top. He's really good at containing himself around the horses now, instead of leaping about and becoming

A puppy called Wolfie

Wolfie feels he is a big boy now, and all grown up!

over-excited. He even received big snuggles from them yesterday! We've been developing our communication skills, and Wolfie is very good at telling me what he wants and needs. I've also been teaching him to apply things in different contexts, so he is becoming good at problem-solving.

A SECOND DOG, PERHAPS?

We've known for a little while that Wolfie would like a doggy companion. He's not content to just see friends when we are out, and whines when they leave. At home, he spends a fair amount of time waiting for Molly to appear next door, and, when she does, prefers spending time near rather than doing anything with me. He is really sociable and needs

company. Although it's too soon to add another dog to our family, we have begun looking. Wolfie has yet to go through his second hormonal phase, so it's not a sensible option to have a puppy now, even if we were to find one. In any case, we need time to research the right companion for Wolfie.

We go through the same process as that used when choosing Wolfie, and make a short list of possible breeds. Now, though, we have additional questions –

● Are we quite sure that Wolfie wants to live with another dog?
The answer to this is a very definite 'yes.' Wolfie is reluctant to leave his canine friends when he sees them, and is very happy when other dogs visit us here, at home. He waits every day to see if Molly next door is out in the garden, and runs to the fence when he hears her bark

● What age of dog will work best?
Wolfie is still a puppy, so we want a youngster to grow up alongside him

● What size, energy level, and activity preferences will be a good match?
Wolfie likes to be active and play, so a dog who does not want or need more than minimal exercise is not for us. Wolfie also likes to sit and watch the world go by, so a dog who wants to be on the go all the time is also the wrong fit. A dog who is not so interested in the company of people and dogs is not the right choice, either.

We want a dog who can run and play with Wolfie. We like big dogs, so a very small dog doesn't seem right for us. However, another Wolfhound, or very large dog, is not right for us, either, as it will be me who is on the other end of the lead, whilst Matt has Wolfie's lead. A smaller dog is decided on; one who is not too big or strong for me to hold on to

● What kind of dog will compliment Wolfie's personality?
Wolfie is an open, friendly boy who's great with other

dogs, as he reads their signals very well, and the conversation between him and whoever he meets is mutually enjoyable. We expect dogs to automatically understand each others' body language and respond appropriately, but, whilst they *do* understand that of those they know, it's not always easy to interpret the body language of a stranger.

Think about a friend who you know well, and how only subtle body language is necessary to tell you how they're feeling. Then look at a stranger. I expect you can interpret some signs, but, as you don't actually know that person, you can only guess at the reasons for the signs you see, and neither do you know how he or she will respond if you interact with them. Your own emotional state influences how you view things, and there is also impulse control to consider.

There is a lot more to dogs communicating successfully than simply expecting them to get on with it. Teaching Wolfie to read the body language and signals of other canines well enough to respond in an appropriate way allows him to feel secure and comfortable around other dogs. If an approaching dog displays signals that tell Wolfie he is not coping, Wolfie simply turns away. We would like this same easygoing personality in our new dog.

There is also another consideration. As an animal behaviourist, I am well-placed to take on a dog who has issues, and there is always a desire to help a dog in need. However, I have to look after my own emotional resilience, too.

I have previously taken on an extremely reactive rescue dog, sorely in need of a home, and have always been drawn to and had challenging breeds. Most of my work involves canine reactivity and aggression.

Now that I am older, the work involved in this – and being aware and vigilant all of the time – is more than I can manage, emotionally and physically. I am still in the midst of this emotionally draining lifestyle with my work, so would like a more relaxed life with my own dogs.

Taking all of these things into account, we

make the decision to once again look for a pedigree puppy from a very good breeder.

This time round our short list requires a little more thought, as it does not include any of the giant or large breeds we might normally consider. We don't want to dismiss a breed because we have only a basic understanding of it, so begin by looking at each breed in terms of size, and whether we like the look of them. Next, we look at breed traits and personality in depth, dropping any from the list that are not the right fit. We have a number of reasons for deciding against a breed once we have done our research, but find that we have decided against every breed on our short list! So, we start again, and the result is the same with our second list!

We've exhausted two short lists because the breeds we thought might be right for us turned out not to be after we'd done our research. Now, we're down to those breeds that we would not ordinarily consider, but, if we had not spent time looking into each breed, we may have already decided on one, and missed out on the breed we do eventually choose. It's just as well we've begun looking now, as this process has taken some time! Everything happens for a reason ...

WOLFIE'S DIARY
January 23
Seven months and three weeks with us: nine-and-a-half months old

NOTES
Wolfie is now nine-and-a-half months old, and reached a milestone last night, with the onset of his second major hormone phase, which signifies the adolescent stage of brain development and sexual maturity.

Wolfie became amorous for the first time, and the recipient of his affection was me, demonstrated by him being very soppy, and lots of kisses and nose-pushes! We went through about

A puppy called Wolfie

twenty minutes of him not knowing what to do with himself, more kisses for me, and general aimless wandering about, before he sat on the settee and said 'Woo, woo, woooo,' in an 'I don't know what to do' way! I managed to persuade him that, since he'd been up for hours and really was very tired, it might be a good idea if he went to bed.

He's still soppy this morning, and has enjoyed a huge run in the field, so is having a morning snooze before we go out this afternoon.

HORMONES STRIKE AGAIN!

As with the first hormonal phase, testosterone levels increase (to their highest level in this phase) and affect Wolfie's emotional mind, making him easily excitable, unable to listen or concentrate, more unpredictable, and unreliable. It's as though everything he's learnt so far has gone out the window, and he hasn't a clue! Given that Wolfie is a high-arousal puppy, I would expect this phase to have a strong effect on his emotional mind and his ability to regulate himself, and how well he copes with it depends on him and us. We have taught Wolfie to think through his emotions and arousal level to regulate his emotional mind, which he practised doing throughout his first hormonal phase. If he was not equipped with these skills, he could well be swept away by his emotional mind during this second phase, and managing him would be very difficult.

We've had a couple of lovely weekends, taking Wolfie to Tiverton park twice, and meeting some lovely dogs, including a Labradoodle puppy who was very sweet, and wanted to play with Wolfie. Wolfie's had loads of Dad-time, playing the broom game and running as fast as he can.

The increased hormonal influence means that Wolfie does not want to sleep: daytime naps are an hour to two hours at most, and even then he's not sound asleep. He's managing his emotions really well: no mania at all, he interrupts himself, or remembers if we ask him to. He is also telling us what might help him settle when he doesn't know what to do with himself . He had such a huge run yesterday he completely wore himself out, and flopped on the settee. I looked at him, and noticed he was gently steaming ...

As the hormonal phase progresses, testosterone levels continues to increase and impact Wolfie's emotional mind. He's still self-regulating, and we've not had any high-arousal episodes, although other behaviour has resurfaced, as Wolfie reverts to doing things he hasn't since he was a puppy, such as chewing, pulling sleeves, trying to eat Matt's shoes. We worked on and resolved these issues ages ago, but Wolfie is revisiting them. We also find that Wolfie's impulse control, self-restraint, and ability to recall all regress, as he finds it harder to manage his mind.

This is often the most difficult and frustrating period for both owner and puppy. We know that our puppy has learnt how to behave appropriately and what is not his to chew, and he no longer jumps up, or bites clothing. We've spent time and energy teaching him impulse control, self-restraint and a solid recall. So, why, when he has learnt all of these things, does he behave like a young puppy who knows nothing? From our puppy's point of view, he's having to cope with a surge of hormones that interrupt his thought processes, make him excitable, and make it difficult to relax. He doesn't know what to do with himself, and is not thinking properly, so reverts to going through his repertoire of actions and responses in the hope that something will help him.

When faced with a puppy who seems to have forgotten all that we have taught him, the patience and time we had when teaching him as a young puppy is not always easy to find again. We had to make compromises in order to spend time teaching our puppy, and, as he has learnt, the need to manage him decreased, as we established our understanding of each other, with an expectation of reliable actions and responses.

It's not surprising, then, that frustration and annoyance may result when our usual approaches

Wolfie's rising hormone levels have caused him to forget his self-restraint.

Wolfie does not act as he normally would, I must ensure that I manage my own emotional mind and not become frustrated. Thankfully, I'm not impulsive, so it's not in my nature to get cross, shout and tell off Wolfie. My default is to stop and think about how to manage the situation. Frustration increases when it's not possible to achieve something, so stopping and thinking arrests this process, keeping the intellectual mind at the forefront, and enabling progress without becoming more frustrated.

MANAGING HIS HORMONES

We need to remind Wolfie of what he knows, and make it easy for him to respond by going back a couple of steps to an easier version of this. Wolfie is struggling to think through the hormonal influence he's experiencing, so this helps him do so. Once he has realised that he can think and has practised it, it becomes easier for him to keep his intellectual mind at the forefront, and he mostly returns to managing himself well.

As this hormonal phase also denotes sexual maturity, a reliable recall remains difficult for a while, particularly when there are female dogs around, and keeping your puppy on-lead, or on a long line when appropriate may be essential during this time. We also manage Wolfie more around horses. Lots of horses go along the lane which runs alongside our fields, and, being a sight hound, Wolfie will chase them. He can't get to them, being on this side of the fence, but I do not want him to chase the horses and scare them. Up until now, his impulse control has been really good, and, often, he can stop himself from chasing in the first place. If not, his self-restraint kicks in as I ask him to be careful, slow down, etc, and he stops at a distance from the horses.

This is no longer happening, however, and Wolfie is unable to stop himself chasing. I can hear the horses as they come along the lane, so I adjust to help Wolfie. I usually keep the gates between fields open, so that Wolfie has a clear run through

and routine elicit different responses or no response at all from our puppy. Our natural reaction to this might be unhelpful responses, such as telling our pup 'No, don't do that!' 'What are you doing?' etc, but these are not constructive. Similarly, if we don't receive the expected response after trying a second time, we may try something different. This approach is good when teaching something new, but should be used very carefully at this stage in our puppy's life, because we are not teaching our puppy something new, and it will take him longer to learn this than to remember the response he already knows.

We've set up Wolfie to get through this phase as easily as possible by teaching him how to regulate his mind, but this only gets him so far, and he still needs help and support from us in order to keep his emotions and arousal level under control. When them, but now I keep them closed so that, should he chase, he can only go so far. It also means that I can check whether horses are coming along the lane before I open the gate to the next field. If Wolfie is not running or playing, he's usually wandering about fairly close to me, so when I hear a horse, I ask him to come to me or say 'Wait there,' and I go to him. I started off by standing at his side and leaning down to place my hands at the top of his legs by his chest. Talking to him whilst I did that was enough to help him manage his desire to chase, and it wasn't long before all I had to do was place my hand on Wolfie's other side, as he stood next to me and leant against my legs.

When he is in the hormone spike part of the cycle, however, I hold him with both hands as he struggles not to run, though is managing himself well, otherwise. If he wanted to move away from me I wouldn't be able to stop him without anything to hold on to, so if unable to manage himself with only my light touch, I would put on his harness so that I could hold on tightly. If that was the case, I would also be managing him more closely when in the field, and engaging him in activities that help take his mind off chasing, as he'd not be learning anything if all I did was simply hang onto his harness as he struggled to get away and chase.

Doing this does not change his desire to chase, of course, nor teach him how to manage his mind and impulse. Wolfie needs to remember that he can disengage, manage his impulse so he doesn't chase, and use self-restraint to continue not to chase.

Learning to regulate the emotional mind is essential for healthy brain function, and choosing those activities that Wolfie's mind is able to cope with during this phase is essential, as this is also the adolescent phase, where significant brain development and changes occur. An ongoing lack of self-regulation results in a lack of impulse control and self-restraint, leading to poor decision-making when seeking rewards, an interest in novel stimuli, and increased risk of dysfunctional and obsessional behaviour in adulthood. This is further influenced by the neurological changes and sensitivity of the mind at this stage.

THE ADOLESCENT BRAIN

Adolescence and early adulthood are probably the most important development stages in a puppy's brain after the first weeks of the sensitive period. Brain plasticity (the brain's ability to change throughout life) was thought to cease at puberty, but studies have shown that this is not so. Whilst sensory and motor processing stabilises during the sensitive period, executive decision-making, judgement and impulse control, amongst other processes, stabilise later. This has an impact on how emotional information from the amygdala (a part of the brain responsible for detecting fear and preparing for emergency events) is processed. Social cognition also continues to develop, with specific aspects relating to the adolescent phase of life. During this phase the brain circuits of motivation and reward become particularly sensitive to developing addictions, obsessions, and dysfunctional behaviour patterns, in part due to poor judgement and lack of impulse control.

During the adolescent phase and into early adulthood, brain processes continue to develop, stabilise and mature. Up to this point, the brain retains everything our puppy has learnt, and every single emotion, response, action, and experience has its own synaptic connection. Using the analogy of a rose bush, from the moment our puppy is born (A), he learns, and his rose bush has grown with every experience (B), and now has an abundance of branches, leaves, and flowers (C). As the brain matures it goes through a process called synaptic pruning, where the brain decides which parts of the rose bush are necessary for the animal's continued survival, and to achieve a balance between learning new things, and using existing information to navigate life. This process develops some parts of the rose bush to maturity – with sensory and motor processing amongst the first – and also discards those parts which are not useful (D).

How the brain does this depends on many

factors, including what our pup experiences during the adolescent phase. Remaining with the rose bush analogy, those branches that are used more often become stronger, and are retained by the brain. Those branches that are used less often or not at all are marked by a protein which, when detected, attract cells that bond to it and the branch is pruned, or destroyed. In short, then, and simply, the function of synaptic pruning is to remove those synaptic connections (branches) that are of no use to the brain, in order to make way for new connections that move the brain towards a more complex and sophisticated understanding of the world, from both a cognitive and perceptual perspective.

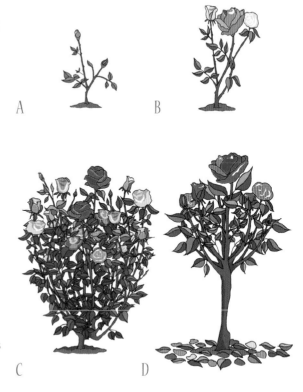

Because brain plasticity is still current, how we handle this stage in our puppy's life has a significant influence on the development and expression of his adult mind and personality.

When it comes to negative experiences, a puppy who finds himself suddenly in changed circumstances during the adolescent phase may become anxious or scared. The emotions, responses and actions he feels and uses at this time are those 'branches' that the brain reinforces as pertinent to survival. Which 'branches' the brain uses inform our pup's perception of events, and a previously confident puppy may now become anxious.

Social cognitive development has a heightened sensitivity to rejection at this time, so negative encounters with other dogs can result in an increased probability of our pup becoming less comfortable around them. Motivational drives increase, resulting in increased risk-taking and a desire to experience more adult-like activities. Inhibitory circuits are immature at this time, and these stabilise synaptic function and neural circuit activity, regulating motivation, repetitive actions, over-attachment and risk-taking. Not yet capable of regulating the increase in motivational drive present during this phase, the brain is therefore at risk of developing addictions, obsessions, and a desire for novel experiences.

Neutering during the adolescent phase can have significant detrimental effects on our pup's personality and social capabilities, as well as the development of a strong, resilient adult brain.

Of course, the foregoing is a simplified account of what happens, and there are many complex processes working within the brain during this time, unique to the individual. The personality and experiences of each individual also influences and informs the brain's perceptual standpoint, and how it works. Some dogs breeze through life in general, some find it extremely difficult, and others are somewhere in-between.

We have the opportunity to positively affect our puppy's brain at this time by doing everything we can to help, such as –

- ensuring our puppy receives plenty of positive (from his viewpoint) experiences
- ensuring our puppy does not have significant

negative experiences that would exacerbate fear and anxiety

• ensuring that our relationship with our puppy does not change because it is difficult for us to cope with the adolescent hormonal phase

Our love, care, understanding and tolerance are required in order to guide him through this period, and allow him to maintain the same emotional feelings for us that he's always had.

When we are caring and tolerant his mind will respond with similar emotions, and will determine how he behaves towards us. If we change how we are with him, and become frustrated and intolerant, his mind will generate fewer feelings of love and contentment towards us, with anxiety and wariness more evident, and also informing how he feels and behaves towards us. This situation should certainly be avoided, as we do not want the brain to reinforce negative emotions and feelings.

VISIT HUBBLE AND HATTIE ON THE WEB:
WWW.HUBBLEANDHATTIE.COM • WWW.HUBBLEANDHATTIE.BLOGSPOT.CO.UK • DETAILS OF ALL BOOKS
• SPECIAL OFFERS • NEWSLETTER • NEW BOOK NEWS

Chapter 10
A question of balance ...

We've been taking Wolfie to the beach at Exmouth. It's quiet at this time of the year, and dogs are able to walk its length, without the restrictions imposed during tourist season. This is Wolfie's favourite place: he absolutely loves meeting other dogs and people, walking and running on the sand with Matt. It's one of my favourite places, too: my Mum's family come from Exmouth, and we used to visit the area over the summer when I was a child.

We usually spend a few hours on the beach with Wolfie, walking and relaxing, and it is here that he has the minimum self-restraint. As soon as he sees the sea he becomes excited, and can't wait to get out of the car. Matt has been dragged toward the sand on several occasions due to Wolfie's enthusiasm to get there.

We talk Wolfie through the routine of what has to happen before we can go onto the beach – boring things like buying a car park ticket, putting on our wellies, and making sure we have everything we need. Wolfie does a little jump, and pulls Matt towards the beach, trying to tell him to hurry up. We

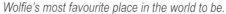
Wolfie's most favourite place in the world to be.

are making progress, though. When we first came here, Matt had to go straight onto the sand whilst I did the boring bits as Wolfie simply could not wait. Now, although still desperate to get there, he is beginning to self-regulate. The more often we go the better Wolfie becomes at waiting for us to go through the routine, prior to going on the beach, and teaching him to think through this excitement helps him to manage his anticipation, and keep his emotions under control.

Wolfie will always be excited by his favourite place for years to come, and I always want that to be the case, even once he's learnt how to manage his feelings.

Molly is next door's Spaniel puppy – about the same age as Wolfie – so they both arrived in the same week. Wolfie desperately wants to be on the same side of the fence as her, and is not content to only see her when she is in the garden.

Molly is a very sociable puppy, but very barky. Wolfie looks for her whenever he is out, and it is obvious he wants her company. However, whenever Molly sees Wolfie and me she barks and barks, and the only way to get her to stop is to take Wolfie inside. As she lives next door to us, they should at least be able to see each other without Molly feeling the need to bark constantly, so every time they are both in the garden I talk Wolfie through what he's doing to teach him to listen to her, rather than be an excited puppy running about.

As Wolfie begins to listen and read Molly, he adjusts what he does in response to what she does. I use my body language, voice, and where I am standing to promote a sense of calmness and safety, working indirectly without any obvious outward signs, to help both of them become comfortable with each other.

We've been progressing things, and gradually Molly's bark has changed from a constant *woof, woof, woof*, whilst coming up to the fence then jumping back, to inquisitive barks and brief silences whilst she waits to see what response she gets.

Wolfie is so good, and stands quietly, waiting for her, not barking back, and not setting her off

barking again. Recently, their interactions have got to the point where Molly comes out and barks for Wolfie, he goes to see her, and they have a play, but Molly still has bouts of barking.

This morning there has been a breakthrough! Molly barked only a little, mostly talking to Wolfie, not just *woof, woof*, and Wolfie responded by running a little more than usual. They have now been running and playing up and down the fence line for the last half-hour, tails wagging, play bowing and running off, then back, without barking. A sneaky peak at them reveals both lying down by the fence next to each other!

WOLFIE'S DIARY
February 7
8 months with us: ten months old

NOTES
Wolfie has been undergoing another growth phase: he's very sleepy, doesn't have much energy, and looks like he needs to grow into his legs and tail , so I expect he'll get a little taller. We've also been pursuing some different activities.

We've had a go at scent work, which has been interesting. Wolfie's nose is pretty good, and he swaps between scenting and looking for the hidden items ... I'm going to need some bigger boxes so that he cannot as easily look over the top of them! We've also had a go at agility which was hilarious. As Wolfie usually follows Matt around, it made sense for Matt to do this with him, but Matt ended up doing the course whilst Wolfie stood and looked on with an expression that clearly said I don't see the point of this! He needs some motivation to have a go, obviously – Wolfie, not Matt!

Matt and Wolfie have joined the improver's course I have been running, which is lovely, as it's a group of adolescents that Wolfie did the puppy course with last year. All the puppies know one another, and are also entire (not neutered) adolescents, so we have male/female dynamics going on. My handsome Wolfie has made quite an impression on the girls – they all love him!

multiple dogs can live peaceably together, and form strong friendships.

Just as importantly, if we were to introduce a puppy now, how might he react to Wolfie when he becomes over-aroused, and how would Wolfie respond? The best relationships are based on

Puppy improver's class goes to town.

Knowing that Wolfie wants canine company at home, and knowing when the time is right to make this happen are two different things. Wolfie really struggled with his arousal level and first hormonal phase, and was not able to manage his mind well enough to regulate himself. At that point in his life, the addition of another dog would have been far too much for any of us to cope with. Wolfie needs to be able to manage himself well enough to live with another dog without me needing to resort to physical intervention on a regular basis. Of course, there are certain situations where this is unavoidable, but I do not want us to experience these when all we need do is wait a while. Besides, Wolfie is an Irish Wolfhound, and is quickly becoming bigger and stronger than me! Although, size and strength is not the issue, we must do our best to create an environment where

complete trust, so starting from a point whereby an existing dog is not yet emotionally balanced, and not receptive to new situations is not ideal, as there's an increased possibility of creating misunderstandings and associations that are not conducive to a good friendship. The end result of this may be that two dogs never achieve the relationship you would like them to have, or a breakdown in the friendship further down the line. There are many situations and circumstances in which dogs do not have a favourable view of other dogs, and a dog who has issues with other dogs can greatly benefit from living with a canine companion, and the support that such a relationship provides. These situations are completely different to Wolfie's, so we assess matters from his perspective to decide when the time is right for him.

A puppy called Wolfie

THE TIME IS RIGHT

By now it's late February and Wolfie is managing his second hormonal phase really well, and regulating himself in all situations. If he becomes over-excited it takes him only a few seconds to calm down and get control of his emotions. We've been working on this since he was a little puppy, and he's really got it sussed now. He is happy, content, and relaxed; there's no frustration, or displacement behaviours, he just checks himself when his mind goes into emotional mode, and so remains a lovely, happy enthusiastic puppy, without loss of his intellectual mind. I am so impressed with how he manages himself, and how he is such a happy boy. This tells us that the time is right, now, to bring another puppy into our home. Wolfie will continue to develop his mind, and, by the time a puppy is ready to join us, he will be a little older and even better balanced.

After all of our research we have finally decided on a breed – a French Barbet, better known as the French Water Dog, although it is a very versatile breed, competent in a range of activities (abilities include herding, retrieving (in and out of water), scenting, flushing game, and guarding) – with a good work drive and love of learning. The breed is good with other dogs and people, and has a happy disposition. These dogs are not for everyone, though, as they possess a powerful instinct, and need plenty of mental and physical stimulation. Typically of us, we have chosen another rare breed ... not that many Irish Wolfhounds are born in England, and there are few breeders ... there are even fewer French Barbets! The next step is to research breeders and make contact with them.

WOLFIE'S DIARY

February 17
8 months and one week with us: ten months and one week old

NOTES

The quad bike's due for a service today, so as Matt got it out ready, Wolfie was treated to an impromptu run at 7.20 this morning. He loves running more than anything.

Once Matt had left for work we had a nice walk through the crunchy, frosty fields. However, the quad bike is now being serviced, and Wolfie can hear it, so is convinced that Dad must be home, and has spent the last 20 minutes whining in the garden, wanting to be let through to the exercise yard.

Wolfie, is Dad's boy, and he loves going out with the quad bike, so it's taken a little time for him to accept that he cannot go out to the yard to see what's going on. I'm sure the man working on the quad bike does not need Wolfie's help! I've talked Wolfie through it, and finally he has resigned himself to waiting, lying in the garden next to the gate ...

It's now teatime and we're playing ball in the yard when Wolfie thinks he can hear Matt's car. My clever boy doesn't stay where he is until the car he hears comes down the lane, but runs a few steps up the garden, turns to ask me if he can go (fantastic checking in); I say 'Yes,' and he carries on.

Halfway up the garden he again checks in with me, then runs all the way to the top, through the gate and into the field to see along the lane, and whether it is Matt arriving home. Unfortunately, although the car sounds very similar to Matt's, it's not him.

We stay and have a good run in the field until we do hear Matt's car, and Wolfie races home to meet him.

PUPPY TALES

It's the middle of March and we have some puppy news. We have found a lovely Barbet breeder – Karen Surrall of Awelymor Italian Spinoni and French Barbet. Initially exchanging info about each other via email, we have a long phone call to see if we are right for one of her puppies, and I'm thrilled to say that, yes, Karen feels we will be suitable guardians. Fate must have brought us together, because her girl, Anouk, is due to be mated the following week, and our names are down for one of her puppies. This is perfect timing as it will be around the end of July that the puppies will be ready to leave home, which gives us another four months to continue teaching Wolfie and making sure all is ready for our new pup.

My little pudding Wolfie now weighs 69.8kg (153.9lb), 10kg (22lb) heavier than when he was last weighed in November. His growth is slowing, but he's really developing in other ways. Being well balanced and managing his emotions when he is excited or feeling amorous are now very reliable, which is brilliant, given that he's only 11-and-a-half months old. We do have the occasional episode where control of his arousal level escapes him and he bites, but it's a gentle hold only before he realises what he's doing and lets go.

We had a visitor today, and Wolfie was bouncing six inches off the ground on his front feet, and being rather enthusiastic with his nose! He calmed down after a minute or so, and then went in for the well known Wolfhound 'lean on someone's legs' in the hope of a cuddle. This is a huge improvement, as previously he's leapt so high in the air that it's shocked my horse, Star, as Wolfie's body was the same height as her head ... Maybe we should consider a career in show-jumping for Wolfie?

Wolfie is doing really well at applying context to a situation, and has become pretty good at pointing, and not only in the sense of pointing at pheasants in the field. If I ask him if he wants to go for a walk, and the answer is 'yes,' he points at my gloves with his nose. If he wants to go out and I haven't asked, he also points at my gloves, and, if they're not handy, he points at his bucket of balls!

Yesterday, Wolfie let Matt know he wanted to set off on his evening walk, by first nosing him, and then going to the utility door, and pointing at that with his nose. When Matt didn't respond initially, Wolfie repeated his actions. Matt opened the door into the utility room, asking 'What do you want?' whereupon Wolfie entered the room and nosed his harness.

Another day, hearing a car pull up outside, Wolfie firstly went to the yard to have a look, then came back inside and pointed to the front door. A few seconds later the doorbell rang! My clever boy is so cool – although he did run off up the garden with a sock the other day, too ...

At this stage in Wolfie's life we are progressing many things to increase his understanding and awareness, and continuing to build on his sense of context. Horses live at the property next door, and in the summer they spend time in the grassed areas right next to us. Last summer I taught Wolfie to be calm when the horses were out, and to not become excitable. The horses have not been out over the winter, but have been the last few days because of the warm weather, and yesterday a mare and foal were in the field. This was a new experience for Wolfie (who is only a little bigger than the foal), and he was lovely and calm, but also inquisitive, causing the mare some concern. I spent a few minutes with Wolfie, telling him how to be around the two horses, and then brought him out of our field.

Mare and foal are back out today, and Wolfie went out into the field as usual, and proceeded to have a conversation with the mare. He watched her, and every time she nodded her head or swished her tail, he moved back, taking a step forward again as she resettled. As their understanding of each grew, the mare relaxed, and her foal nosed Wolfie through the fence. It was so amazing to see. Of course, I was there to supervise, should this be needed, and we did not stay long.

Birthday boy!

It's April 3, and Wolfie's birthday – he's a year old – and we're off to the beach: Wolfie's favourite place.

Wolfie loves the excitement of all the things going on at the beach, and meets lovely dogs with whom he can play. He gets loads of cuddles from other beach-goers, and has a lot of fun walking and sitting on the sand.

Wolfie has a little splash in the sea, but is not really sure about the waves. Besides, why would a Wolfhound want to get his paws wet? It's much nicer on the sand, plus it doesn't sneak up on you. By the time we get home Wolfie is very tired, but does

Happy first birthday, Wolfie!

manage to eat a lovely birthday dinner before he falls asleep.

Wolfie's first year has been wonderful; he is such a perfect boy, loving and playful, and enjoying life. Watching him progress and master his emotional mind has been so rewarding, and has resulted in a well-balanced, confident boy who is happy, engaging and outgoing.

Following Wolfie's birthday celebrations, we have something else to celebrate: an email from Karen telling us that Anouk is in pup, and expecting a litter toward the end of May.

My puppy classes are beginning to get busy again now that spring is here and the weather is better, and Wolfie continues to join in the odd class when he is interested, and is also enjoying some of the workshops I am running. We go out somewhere every week – usually at the weekend – to the beach, into town, or one of the surrounding villages. Matt takes him for a walk along the lanes by us for Dad-and-Wolfie time, which Wolfie really enjoys.

PUPPY PREP

Time passes quickly; our days are full of love and fun with Wolfie, with lots of progressions and new things to learn. We review all of the language Wolfie knows to assess whether there's anything essential he needs to learn before the new puppy arrives. Wolfie will be managing himself around the pup, so ensuring he has the relevant language and understanding is paramount.

We run through the important things. Wolfie knows how to be careful with little ones; this is something we say when we are out and he meets small dogs, and his response to this is to lie down, which is not something we've taught him to do: he's decided himself that this is a good idea. It works well, and more often than not they approach to say hi and interact with him. Wolfie understands that 'carefully' means he has to manage his body and move with care, and is able to apply this in other contexts, too, such as when it's slippery underfoot, or when he had an injured paw.

Wolfie knows how to disengage from one activity or focus and do something else. Teaching him to understand that many activities have a high reward value, and stopping one does not mean the end of fun or engagement of his mind, also means that Wolfie is not obsessive. This will be very useful when the puppy arrives, as he will not want Wolfie following him around all the time, and Wolfie will more easily turn his attention away from him because of this.

Another important factor is what Wolfie does when he becomes excited. I initially taught him to put his head in a bucket and pick up a toy, but this was mostly to redirect his focus from me when he went into over-arousal. Whilst he likes playing with toys, he's not a retriever, and this game does not interest him as much as running does. Redirecting Wolfie with the bucket of toys is no longer necessary, and, instead, he goes for a run to expend excess energy and emotion. His motivation to run is that it makes him happy, rather than using it as a way of bringing down his arousal level. These are important behaviours for facilitating positive interactions between Wolfie and the puppy, along with all the other skills Wolfie has acquired to help puppy settle in and the two of them become friends.

Anouk's puppies are born ...

... and are soon four weeks old, and ready to visit!

(Both images courtesy Karen Surrall)

VISITING TIME!

Before we know it, Anouk's puppies have been born and are soon four weeks old, and we are off to Wales to visit them. Wolfie is coming with us, as it's a long journey, and we can't leave him at home on his own. We've seen photos of the litter, from which we have chosen Mr Red (named for the colour of his collar) as our favourite. Now we will see if Mr Red likes us, and if he is the right personality for our family – we're so excited!

After driving for three-and-a-half hours we are there. It's nice that Karen is able to meet Wolfie and see his personality, as this gives her more information to go on when advising which puppy is the one for us. Matt and Wolfie go off for a walk whilst I go inside to meet the puppies. Their dam, Anouk, is friendly, and so beautiful. The puppies are seriously cute! Lovely little black balls of wavy hair, they are engaging and delightful – I could take all of them home!

Spending time with the puppies, and chatting to Karen, Mr Red's personality confirms that he is the right one to come and live with us and Wolfie. Taking my turn with Wolfie whilst Matt meets the puppies, it seems that, when he sat on the floor with them, Mr Red immediately approached and sat on his knee –

another sign that this was the perfect puppy for us. Wolfie has a brother!

Our journey home is full of excitement and plans to make sure everything will be ready when we pick up Mr Red in a few weeks' time. At the moment he is tiny, and although he'll be about twice the size when we collect him, it is very clear that the puppy-proofing we did for Wolfie is not going to be any use. Mr Red is small enough to get through many more gaps, so some additional work is needed to keep him safe. We also have to think of a name, and, as he is French, we are focusing on Gallic names at the moment.

One consideration is possible resource-guarding with the boys. Wolfhounds are not resource-guarders by nature, but any dog may guard resources, given the right circumstances. Wolfie has never done this with us, and we have done everything possible to ensure he feels safe when we are around his resources and favourite things. Now, we must ensure that our boys do not feel the need to defend resources from each other.

There are plenty of toys out in the house and garden, and Wolfie does not show any kind of possessive, guarding or hiding behaviour with them, so we will leave these out, for now. This means that there is nothing new for Wolfie to get excited about, and Mr Red will see that toys lying about is usual, when he arrives. We'll be watching and closely supervising any interactions with toys to see how they act, and whether we need to intervene. What we do not want is a disagreement over a toy, which may damage their fledgling friendship.

At mealtimes Wolfie and Mr Red will be in separate areas. Eating another dog's food, chew, or bone can elicit an instant and strong defensive response from the dog whose food it is. Some dogs will just walk away, not wanting the confrontation, but the potential is there for an altercation if food is not managed around multiple dogs.

Generally, there's less guarding around water, although some dogs will guard their water bowls. Ensuring that there are several options for drinking is a good idea, therefore.

Sleeping arrangements are considered next. Being awakened suddenly can cause a sleeping dog to respond defensively, and some dogs do not like to be disturbed when awake and in their bed either. We also have another issue: Mr Red was about 3.5kg (7.7lb) at four weeks old, so is likely to be around 7kg (15lb) when we collect him ... Wolfie is 70kg (154lb). This is a huge size difference, and should Wolfie roll over onto him in the night, he may well squash Mr Red, causing injury or even death. Our solution is to erect a stair gate between our living areas: Wolfie in one and Mr Red in the other, until it is safe for them to be together, always assuming that they will be comfortable sharing sleeping space.

The first few weeks that the dogs are together are critical for developing an open, trusting relationship, and we must be prepared to manage everything so that, should there be even a hint of discord, we can intervene.

We know that Wolfie will be very able to manage himself and his arousal level when Mr Red arrives. He continues to progress, and develop his self-regulation, understanding, and learning.

Gentle mentor

Wolfie has such a gentle way with other dogs, and always puts them at ease. I have clients with dogs who do not cope around other canines, and the sight of Wolfie – who is so much bigger than most dogs – could well make these fragile dogs feel anxious. Wolfie is usually in the garden when I see clients,

and they park on the drive with the yard between them and Wolfie. Wolfie usually stands in the garden by a leafy tree there to watch arrivals, so is not always noticed. Clients bypass the yard and arrive in the exercise yard via a gate a little further from the garden, which means there's quite a distance between them and Wolfie. Once on the exercise yard it's no longer possible to see Wolfie unless from the gate that opens onto the other side of the yard.

Wolfie does sometimes give the occasional bark, and sometimes the dogs I am working with explore around the gate to the yard, so are aware of Wolfie, and may have seen him. On many occasions the dogs choose to remain and look at him, appearing calm and comfortable, and not at all anxious about Wolfie's size, and there'll be a tail wag, which is not the usual response the owner sees when other dogs are around. Wolfie gives off reassuring vibes that convey his lack of threat, which helps other dogs feel safe and comfortable around him. He always responds to their body language by adjusting his to minimise any anxiety, and he never responds if the dog reacts to him in an adverse way.

This is the type of personality that professionals look for when they want a stooge dog: a working dog who helps the professional resolve dog-to-dog anxiety and fear issues within a tailored programme. If the dog I am working with shows all the signs of feeling comfortable, and wants to see Wolfie, I may take him onto the yard for a positive experience of being near another dog.

My Wolfie's lovely, gentle character is really going to help Mr Red settle into his new home!

Chapter 11

One becomes two

It's mid-July and Wolfie is now fifteen months old. Our new puppy is ready to join our family, and we make a second journey to Wales to pick up nine-week-old Mr Red. Once again, Wolfie comes with us, providing a good opportunity for the two dogs to see each other during the journey home.

Although this situation is right in our case, it may not be with other dogs. Both dogs should be in a calm and receptive state of mind when they first see each other, so that their initial impression is one of positive emotions. Wolfie hasn't felt worried about travelling in the car for some time, now, but, if he was an anxious car traveller, we would not expect him to manage such a long journey, because he would most likely be an emotional wreck at the end of it, which is not a good state of mind, generally, and certainly not when meeting a new dog.

Having just left his mum and siblings, the puppy is bound to feel anxious, and possibly even fearful, so first meetings are timed for when these negative emotions are at their lowest. If you are in this situation, watch how a new pup responds generally, and let his body language and actions be your guide to when he is most receptive to meeting other dogs and animals in the family.

Once we arrive, Matt and Wolfie go for a walk whilst I go inside, spend time with the puppies, and sort out the paperwork. They have grown well in the four weeks since we last saw them, and are gorgeous and so cute. As I clearly need enough time to cuddle them all, Matt and Wolfie will have to keep walking! Two names that we really like are Monty and Remy, and, as I sit with Mr Red, I think about which will best suit him.

Matt and Wolfie finish their walk, and Wolfie sits in the car whilst Matt joins us. As we say goodbye, Karen asks if we have thought of a name? I've decided that Remy suits him best, and Matt agrees: Karen thinks it really suits him, too. Mr Red now officially becomes Remy!

We've decided that I will drive home, whilst Matt sits with Remy on his knee. With the seats laid flat, Wolfie has the back half of the car in which to lie down. As we get in, Wolfie and Remy look at each other. Wolfie wags his tail and moves his head forward to get a better look. 'This is Remy, your brother,' we say. 'Remy, meet Wolfie, your new brother.' The boys are not close enough to actually greet each other but can look, and, from the moment we get in the car, Remy wants to look at Wolfie. Every time Matt tries to move himself or Remy so that they are more comfortable, Remy finds a position from where he can see Wolfie. After a while, Wolfie settles down for a snooze, with his face turned towards Remy.

Three-and-a-half hours later, we are home. We definitely need a cup of tea, but not as much as when we drove for seven-and-a-half hours bringing Wolfie home!

Well, hello! First greeting

First things first: the boys need to get out of the car, so we open the boot for Wolfie and he jumps out, has a drink, and stretches his legs. Wolfie is still

A puppy called Wolfie

The boys begin to get to know one another ...

wearing his harness, but is free to wander where he will. Next, we take Remy from the car, and let him have a wander in the yard. He has on his harness and lead in case we need to halt his progress – this is not necessary for Wolfie as he will do this himself by listening to what we say to him. Had he not been as calm and careful around Remy, he would have been wearing his lead, however.

Wolfie stands looking at Remy, his tail gently wagging. Remy looks up, wags *his* tail, and goes over to Wolfie. We stay with them, telling Wolfie to be very careful as Remy is only little. They sniff noses, say Hi, and we use our voices to help Wolfie remain calm, and to reassure Remy. Slowly, we wander around the garden, ensuring that Wolfie does not become too interested in or close to Remy, to allow Remy to explore his new home.

After a while we all sit in the garden, and spend the rest of the day supervising the two of them, helping Remy to investigate his new surroundings, and ensuring that both boys feel safe and comfortable, keeping everything calm so that they do not rush each other, or get too close and find they don't know how to move away. It is only day one, and things could very easily go wrong if either of them felt unsure or were startled by the other.

A potentially difficult time is when they come back together after having their separate meals, and we are very careful to supervise them, and talk them through what is happening as they do this. Remy doesn't know much, but his understanding of language will soon increase, and meanwhile we are relying on Wolfie to manage himself with voice guidance from us.

Wolfie is fantastic, and is calm and quiet with Remy all day. Remy is also quite calm, and a little inquisitive, wanting to interact with Wolfie. It's quite a big deal for Remy to see such a giant-sized dog; Wolfie must look enormous to Remy at the moment. Remy still has on his harness and lead, in case we need to get hold of him when he's wandering about, but he's fine being guided by Wolfie, who is very calm. When Wolfie is lying down, Remy is interacting with him – sniffing, using his paws – and when he attempts to get too close and stands on Wolfie, we use our hands to guide him to follow, or to prevent him going further whilst we distract him, teaching him the relevant language at the same time. We tell Remy 'Careful, don't stand on Wolfie,' or 'That's enough, come this way' if Remy is not giving Wolfie a break.

Remy likes to sniff Wolfie's nose, but I make

... and relax together with Matt.

sure he doesn't do that for too long, guiding him away and backing up the actions with the phrase 'Mind Wolfie, he's finished' if Wolfie turns his head away, and then refocusing Remy's attention on doing something else. It's important to remember that we need to use the same distract, diffuse, and refocus strategy that we did with Wolfie: simply telling Remy to leave Wolfie without giving him something else to do increases the chances that he will return to interacting with Wolfie. I only need to use the diffuse part of the strategy if Remy has become too excited, and I'm unable to redirect him to playing with a toy, or running about, because his focus is on interacting with Wolfie. Happily, this is not the case on our first day as both boys are calm and relaxed.

Having a new puppy means there's a very definite risk of ignoring Wolfie, who needs just as much attention and reassurance as does Remy. Wolfie is behaving perfectly, but we must ensure that he is happy in his mind, and does not feel left out. So Wolfie gets lots of love and praise, which gives pleasure and acts as reinforcement to managing himself.

ROUTINE AND MANAGEMENT

We do not have set routines, generally, so meals are not always at the same time, which means Wolfie is fine, whatever time we feed him. If we did have a more structured routine, we would try to keep to this, as changes in routine can cause anxiety and upset,

A puppy called Wolfie

Remy begins to explore his new home.

and we want to ensure that Wolfie's attitude remains positive. Wolfie has a chew after his dinner, but Remy is too young for one, so gets some 'Mum-time' in one part of our living area, whilst Wolfie is the other side of the stairgate sitting with Matt and eating his chew. There is the potential for argument if Remy approaches Wolfie whilst he still has his chew, so we check that Wolfie has eaten all of it before Remy comes back into this part of the room. We also make sure that Wolfie is fine with Remy coming close so

soon after he has finished, as some dogs need a couple of minutes after eating before they are happy for another to be in their personal space. Wolfie shows no sign of being uncomfortable with Remy, or that he is unreceptive to interacting with him. Remy wanders up to Wolfie, who licks his nose, and they are happy in each other's company.

After a lovely and successful day, it's time for bed. As the two boys have each other for company, albeit safely settled in separate areas, we go to bed rather than sleep with them. Wolfie doesn't need to get up for the toilet in the night, of course, so we decide that, unless Remy wakes and barks, we will not disturb them to take him out. Wolfie is an outdoors boy, and, given the chance, would happily sleep outside in the summer. I am fairly sure that if I get up to take Remy out in the night, Wolfie will want to go out, too ... and not want to come back in. If Remy sleeps through, I can avoid this situation, otherwise I shall have to manage two dogs outside in the middle of the night. Of course, I could go out with Remy only, but I'd rather not because, at this very early stage in their relationship, Wolfie may feel left out, and if he wakes up as we go out, he's likely to want a wee.

As it is, both boys sleep all night, and we get up to a nice, dry floor. If Remy does wee in the night, we'll change strategy, but, for now, we don't have to get up in the night, which I'm quite pleased about!

FIRST VISIT TO THE VET

It's day two, and we are off to the vet for Remy's first vaccination. Wolfie comes with us: he and Matt can go for a walk whilst I take Remy into the vet. Remy was very quiet in the car when we brought him home yesterday, and, like Wolfie when he came home, it seems he's not sure about car journeys. He whines and struggles to settle down, and is sick when we're almost there. There's not much to come up, as we made the appointment for a few hours after breakfast, but it seems that our new boy suffers from car sickness.

After cleaning up and having a drink, I walk slowly to the vet, Remy in my arms. He is much easier to carry than Wolfie as he's so much lighter! Going inside, Remy receives plenty of cuddles, and looks at a couple of dogs as he sits on my knee. The vet is lovely, and Remy has more cuddles, a health check, and is weighed – 7.16kg (15.78), half of Wolfie's weight at this age: no wonder he's easier to carry!

By the time the vet vaccinates him, Remy is falling asleep on the table, and he sleeps all the way home, without being sick.

REMY'S DIARY
July 25
Day 3 with us: Nine weeks and one day old

AM

5.20:	Awake and mad puppy mode – Matt is on duty!
6.20:	I get up and take over. Play in garden. Play with Wolfie. Remy in garden while I play with Wolfie in the yard. Remy and Wolfie together again; had quite an exciting play. Stopped as getting too much. Remy in house, I play with Wolfie to expend leftover frustration and release restraint of having to manage his excitement
8.00:	Breakfast, then asleep
9.10:	Relaxing, snoozing

PM

12.20:	Awake. Play on settee, play outside, play with Wolfie, really good play bows, stopping when Wolfie does, showing tummy, both reciprocating. Left Remy in garden and played with Wolfie in yard, then both boys played together again
1.15:	Lunch. Wolfie having a snooze. Remy mad play on his own
2.03:	Relaxing
3.10:	Dinner, play
3.45:	Sleep
4.15:	Awake, play
5.15:	Relaxing
6.00:	Play with Wolfie, more interaction and closeness
7.00:	More dinner, play, walk, mad half-hour
9.20:	Asleep

A puppy called Wolfie

As we did when Wolfie arrived, we've taken time off work to be with Wolfie and Remy the first two weeks. We're on day three, and each day has followed the same routine. Wolfie is calm and quiet around Remy. Remy is exploring and becoming more familiar with his new home; gaining confidence. He is also quite calm, taking his lead from Wolfie, who he follows around like a shadow. There is no doubt Remy wants to be with Wolfie, and, if he goes out of sight, wags his tail when Wolfie comes back into view. Not that this happens very often at the moment, as Remy is more likely to be next to Wolfie than anywhere else!

Time flies

A whole week has gone by already. Having spent much of my time with Wolfie whilst he was a young puppy, teaching, playing and developing his mind and skills, he is now completely trustworthy and able to manage himself, enabling me to begin a number of projects. Now, though, I am back to having no time to myself as I supervise and monitor Wolfie and Remy to ensure that nothing damages their new friendship.

Both boys are off-lead around the house, and free to wander as they choose. Either or both have on their harnesses, though, depending on what we are doing, and whether I think I may need to hold onto one of them. Wolfie has been really gentle and restrained in his play with Remy, reigning in his excitement, and being careful: it's almost as if he's moving in slow motion when he plays with this tiny puppy. Wolfie knows a huge amount of language, and although many words and phrases are easily applied to different contexts, there will still be some things we need to teach him in relation to his interactions with Remy. For now, though, teaching is more concentrated on Remy, so that he, too, can understand language and manage himself around Wolfie.

Being so controlled when playing with Remy, Wolfie has excess energy and emotion that needs release. Now we are a week in, Remy is much more confident, becoming over-excited, and going into mad puppy mode, as he can't yet control his arousal levels. At this early stage we disperse excess energy and excitement by giving them their own time. With Wolfie, this means encouraging him to go for a run. He already knows this, as we used it as part of teaching him to manage his arousal level, so saying it only a couple of times prompts Wolfie to think, 'Ah, yes, what a good idea,' and off he runs. Whilst he is busy running, I do something with Remy, so that Wolfie has his own time. I do not want Remy chasing after Wolfie until he is comfortable seeing such a large dog going full speed. As it is, Remy sees a fast approaching Wolfhound and moves to safety next to the fence – sensible boy – and watches as Wolfie tears around having a great time.

If Wolfie is calm and Remy becomes over-excited I teach him to play with me, not Wolfie. I redirect whichever dog is the first to become too excited, and, in this way, both learn that playing together does not get out of control and become manic. As they progress and grow, they will begin to regulate themselves in this situation (as Wolfie already knows how to in other situations), so that play is always play, and arousal levels don't go over the top, which can change perceptions, and lead to argument.

Remy's night-time diary

July 26
Had an awful night. Remy is not sleeping through, and I was up three times. He needed a wee and a drink the first time, but really he just wants to be with Wolfie. He's taking a long time to settle again, so each time I stayed with him on the settee until he was properly asleep, then put him back in the kitchen.

July 27
Up three times again. Remy settled the first time, but struggled after that. He's taking a good hour to fall asleep enough not to wake when I go back to bed,

and then he's awake one-and-a-half to two hours later. As I am spending as much time with Remy as I am in bed, I might as well stay with him for the night, and perhaps begin to get them both comfortable about sharing the same space overnight.

As Wolfie's and Remy's friendship has been developing this week, night-times have been deteriorating. Instead of sleeping through as he was doing, Remy has been sleeping less and less each night. He settles down well enough, and I don't go to bed until he is asleep, but he is waking up, whining and barking. I go and settle him, once again waiting for him to go back to sleep before I leave. By day five Remy is very sure he cannot sleep at night, managing to settle for only about an hour-and-a-half each time I go to him.

Happy bedfellows

This cannot go on, we both need sleep, and I know what the problem is. Remy is in one half of the room, and Wolfie is in the other. My boys are forming such a strong friendship that Remy does not want to be on his own in his side of the room. There's only one solution: open up the room so that they are not separated. This does come with a risk, of course. Wolfie is so big that Remy would be squashed if he were to lay on him. I also don't know how Wolfie will react should Remy decide to crawl over him whilst Wolfie is sleeping. So far, Wolfie has been perfect with Remy, and there's no sign that he is anything other than happy ... but, still, this is risky ...

On the evening of day three I open up the room, and say goodnight to Matt, who goes to bed. It falls to me to sleep with the boys to ensure they are safe as I am the lighter sleeper. It seems that this is the right decision, as both boys settle for bed with contented sighs, Remy curled at the bottom of Wolfie's bed near his back legs. Wolfie turns over a couple of times in the night, and each time Remy wakes and moves to avoid Wolfie's legs, then settles back to sleep. The following night Remy has progressed to actually laying on Wolfie's legs, moving when Wolfie does.

An unfortunate downside to this happy situation is that, on the odd occasion Remy needs to go out for a wee in the night, Wolfie also gets

Remy wants to sleep with Wolfie.

A puppy called Wolfie

up to go out. He doesn't need a wee – he's slept through the night since he was tiny – but is taking the opportunity to go outside in the hope of sleeping there, just as he wanted to do last summer. It's the middle of the night, and I do not want Remy to regard this as a sensible time to go out, or decide to play. Wolfie is older now and less inclined to run up the garden, so I leave him for a few minutes before asking him to come in to be with Remy. There is only one occasion when this doesn't work, when Wolfie clearly has no intention of coming in. As I am sleeping on the settee, I leave the door open, expecting Wolfie to soon follow, though wake a little later to find he's still outside. I get up and he comes straight in when I look out the door.

I spend a week on the settee to be sure they're fine, but my first night back in bed is not as restful as it should be, as I am only half-asleep, alert enough to wake if I hear anything. I also get up to check on them several times. I continue this for a few days, and then, finally, I sleep properly. The boys are much happier being together, neither wakes up to go out in the night, and they both have happy faces and waggy tails in the morning.

Remy is a brave boy, and has settled really well, happy to explore his new environment with or without Wolfie. Remy is a very bouncy, enthusiastic puppy when he's playing and tearing around the garden, and Wolfie has remained calm and careful. To show such self-restraint at 15 months of age is fantastic. Our boys are doing everything together, and, from the moment we brought them home, Remy has followed Wolfie around, looking up to his big brother. Remy climbs on Wolfie when he is laying down, and pulls Wolfie's tail (which is the only bit he can reach when Wolfie is standing up) when he wants to play, They run around the garden, wander up the hill, and sit together when they are quiet.

Whereas Wolfie was content to be left on his own on occasion, Remy is not happy about this at all if it involves him being contained separately. Mostly, the boys are together, but, if they are very active, and I can't be with them, I am being cautious and have Remy one side of the stairgate and

Wolfie the other. Remy shows his displeasure at being separated by barking and whining when this happens. It's not the case that he's anxious that I have left the room, because when he can wander where he likes, he doesn't behave in this way if I leave. He's also been fine if left on his own when Wolfie is out for a walk with Matt.

I've just had my first one-to-one, private teaching session since Remy arrived. Wolfie is used to this, and sits quietly. Remy was asleep until about three minutes before the session ended, and then he awoke and barked. Remy is developing his self-confidence, and, although relying on Wolfie generally, he doesn't follow him around all the time now, and is quite happy to play or wander about on his own, However, he does not want to be without Wolfie in some circumstances, and Remy does not like it when he is shut in or out of a room or the house on his own. This is perfectly normal at this stage; as there will be times when it will be necessary to leave him on his own, we will teach him to be comfortable with this.

Remy's diary
July 30
Day 8 with us: Nine weeks and six days old

Notes
Remy woke at 5.20am, so Matt got up to make breakfast. Remy was quite content, not playful; Wolfie was fast asleep on the settee. Matt left Remy on one settee and Wolfie on the other when he came to wake me. When he got back he found Remy on the settee with Wolfie, lying on Wolfie's bum! Wolfie went out for a walk with Matt; Remy did bark a little when Matt and Wolfie left, but soon settled down to play with me. Remy does ask Wolfie to interact with him a lot, but Wolfie doesn't want to be bothered when he is really tired and trying to get comfy, so it's our job to distract Remy, using in phrases such as 'Leave Wolfie, he's asleep' so that Remy can begin

to understand when it's okay to interact. Once Wolfie has settled he's happy for Remy to sit or sleep with him.

We have also seen Wolfie become protective towards Remy. It's there in how he interacts with Remy, playing carefully, adjusting his actions so that Remy is safe. Wolfie has begun responding to new noises and people by barking at them. He would usually bark a couple of times when there is something new, but the tone of bark is more of an alert with a hint of uncertainty that there is something different. Now that Remy's around there's no mistaking what Wolfie's bark is saying: don't come near. He's fine with visitors to the home – new and

A blossoming friendship.

familiar – and usual callers he sees, such as the postman, but anything that Wolfie is not sure of when we are in the garden or field is very definitely told to stay away. Our response is to reassure Wolfie, and refocus his attention elsewhere.

WOLFIE AND REMY PLAY DIARY

July 30
The boys had a really nice play today, which worked well as Wolfie had already had a good run, so was tired and not excitable,and Remy was calm and not in manic play mode. I manage play by telling Wolfie to be steady and careful, and to wait when I think it's getting a bit much so that they can pause. I never let it get out of hand, and say 'Finish for now' or 'Settle down boys' to call a halt for a while. Wolfie can respond to all these phrases as he knows them. Remy is beginning to understand, but if he becomes manic and his mind goes into over-arousal, he can't think, so I get his attention and we play away from Wolfie to vent the energy that's causing this.

July 31
They've both realised that playing together is great fun, and have been taking every opportunity to do so. Wolfie has begun to interrupt play and stand still so that Remy runs away and Wolfie can chase him, rather than play being up-close with front paws and mouthing activities all the time. They've both overdone it, though, and have struggled to settle down.

August 3
Lots of good play this morning. I've separated them for breakfast as we are still in the early stages, and then for about five minutes when things got a little too excitable. Remy was wearing his harness so that I had something to hold on to if I needed to intervene, but this wasn't needed as things are now stable between the boys.

Wolfie responds fantastically to voice cues when playing with Remy, and I make suggestions to ensure they are both still aware and able to think; also to ensure play runs smoothly and doesn't go wrong. I say 'Carefully,' 'Run away and he'll chase you,' 'This way,' 'Wolfie, just nose,' (for making sure he's gentle with his teeth), 'Rest for a minute,' 'Settle down we'll play later,' and I use 'Wait' for both of them to pause what they are doing. Remy is learning language quickly and responds to this, too, although is also taking direction from what Wolfie does.

5 August
I no longer supervise their play, but keep an eye on them when it gets a little excitable. They're still finding it difficult to calm down together, so I have to separate them by asking Wolfie to settle down, which he does. Remy can't settle down yet; he remains excited and wants to carry on, as he's not got the control over his emotional mind that Wolfie has. Remy is very persistent, and goes back to Wolfie to try and get him to play again. I have to interrupt Remy and refocus him on playing with me, gradually calming him as we engage in slower, quieter play.

August 6
Today sees another step forward. Wolfie is snoozing, and Remy is wandering. When Remy wants Wolfie to play and he doesn't want to, Remy goes off and amuses himself.

They are now coming to the end of play and settling together, without me intervening to help Remy calm down.

This new calmness won't happen every time they play, as Remy is still a young puppy, but will become the usual routine in time. Remy needs to learn as much language as Wolfie so that he, too, can manage his emotional mind and regulate himself. There are still times when Remy is too excited, and Wolfie can't listen to me and disengage because of Remy's insistent, non-stop play!

It's easy to focus on Wolfie, as he is so much further forward in his learning, but that's unfair to him; Remy needs to learn so that he can respond and manage himself as Wolfie does, rather than expect Wolfie to always do this, and compensate for Remy's lack of ability.

Remy has been here for two weeks now, and things have progressed really well. The boys have settled into a nice routine; Wolfie is reliable, and completely trustworthy when it comes to managing himself, whatever Remy does. Remy is as reliable as a young puppy can be.

Our days usually begin with a walk in the field. Both boys are calm, and wander about and relax, watching the world go by for about forty minutes before they get excited and play. Play has moved on again, and they've gone from close together mouthing play, to moving about, and running a little. Now Remy has decided that the best game is chase, wait and ambush, and lets Wolfie know he wants to play this by holding Wolfie's tail in his mouth and gently pulling it side-to-side. Wolfie turns round and play bows, then gets ready to chase. Remy turns and runs around the apple tree, doubles back under Wolfie's legs, and runs the other way, before Wolfie has had a chance to move! They are reciprocating body language, and timing when to pause and when to resume moving together.

I go about my jobs for the day, only pausing to keep an eye on them when they get very excited to check that neither becomes manic. Mostly they don't, and stop at the same time to lie on the grass together. It is wonderful to see them so happy.

An early play session with the boys.

POSITIVE PLAYTIME

It's really important to monitor play properly, along with setting up the environment to facilitate play. An empty garden or field lacks those things that help support good play. Dogs need places they can escape to. They may need a rest, a pause before they continue, or a place that makes them feel safe when the other is doing something. Having objects in the area gives them places to go, be it garden furniture, bushes, a tree, open gates (if, like us, you have some land and have sectioned it into several areas), or even just the side of a shed. All these things can serve as a barrier between dogs, or provide something solid at their back.

Remy did not want to remain in the middle of the garden the first few times that Wolfie stopped play to go and run, and moved to behind an open gate, next to the tree, or by the side of the fence. This made him feel safe, and he's also brave enough to run a little way after Wolfie now he's got used to seeing Wolfie run at top speed.

Remy continues to run after Wolfie, always returning to the safety of an object of some sort when Wolfie is coming towards him, and ambushing Wolfie as he goes past, then again retreating to the side of the gate, or by the fence.

As he grows more confident, and is not knocked over by Wolfie, Remy stays in the open longer, until there is no need to go to a safe place, other than to use it as a good place from which to ambush Wolfie or Chilli the cat!

As Remy grows braver and begins chasing Wolfie more, Wolfie has to look out for where he is. Each time Wolfie runs towards Remy, I remind him by saying, 'Mind Remy.' Wolfie runs past Remy, but never too closely, and on those occasions that Remy moves into his path, Wolfie jumps over him.

The boys also use the objects and furniture in the garden as a way to surprise each other. One

A puppy called Wolfie

will go this way around something, and the other will go that way around it, or they change direction and go around something else, adding an element of 'guess which way I'm going' to their play.

When play is at close quarters, dogs will often mouth each other, jaws open, with movement usually focused on moving their heads as they do this.

Wolfie likes to course or chase, as part of play, and this can involve catching Remy with his mouth. When their play becomes excitable, Wolfie tends to do this, so, I say 'Carefully,' to start with, and every time Wolfie's nose makes contact with Remy, I tell him 'Just nose; don't hold him.' As Wolfie learns this, he spends more time pushing Remy with his nose and mostly does not progress to holding Remy with his mouth, although there have been a couple of occasions where I've told him 'Let go of Remy,' as Wolfie has his leg or an ear in his mouth.

This reminder gives Wolfie an awareness of how to play with Remy, so that when they are running about and his desire to hold when he catches Remy is strong, he can use his nose as an alternative. It takes time, so I keep monitoring and reminding Wolfie each time play becomes excitable, reminding them to disengage if I think they are getting too intense.

I also tell Wolfie to be careful when they are engaged in close play, when Remy is often completely underneath him. There's usually a lot of play bowing and trying to get on the floor, and I don't want Wolfie to sit on Remy! So, as Wolfie stands over Remy him and lowering his body towards the floor, I say, 'Carefully, don't sit on Remy.' Wolfie, bless him, only ever crouches, doesn't go any further to the floor when he feels Remy beneath him.

Remy's play style is to run as fast as he can and body slam, so he gets the instruction to go past Wolfie. 'Go past him,' 'Don't run into him,' 'Mind Wolfie's legs' are the phrases I usually use.

In the field they like to play by pouncing and jumping around each other, which then turns into a long run, when Wolfie keeps his speed in-line with Remy's, and Remy spends his time looking at Wolfie

Close quarters play.

rather than where he is going. Several times we have had to quickly move out of the way as the boys come thundering past.

I teach Remy to look where he is going when he is running, and not just at Wolfie.

A QUICK LEARNER

Amongst the phrases that Remy already knows are: get yourself a drink/this way/come on through/bring it back [after throwing a toy]/mind your feet/mind your nose [for keeping out of the way when I'm opening gates, he's not one to wait]/where's Dad?/where's Wolfie?/follow me/wait [a vague approximation at the moment]/carefully/go round the other way.

Remy wags his tail in his sleep when he turns over, makes lovely little happy noises when he has a cuddle, and runs to me and stands between my legs when we're out playing, and he's happy and wants a cuddle (he also does this if he's a little worried, which is a great response).

It's early days, but things are going wonderfully. Wolfie is really happy to have a little brother, and Remy adores Wolfie, We couldn't have asked for more. It's a joy to see them both so happy and rewarded by their friendship.

Of course, I have done everything possible to ensure that things go well –

- waiting to get a puppy until Wolfie had sufficient control over his emotional mind to regulate himself, and keep it in the background. If his emotions did override his intellectual mind, Wolfie was aware of what was happening and managed himself so that this did not escalate to mania

- choosing the right breed and individual puppy to compliment Wolfie's personality, and the anticipated personality of the new puppy. We went through quite a few breeds before we settled on the French Barbet. Then it was down to finding the right breeder who would be mating dogs with the right temperament to provide us with a puppy

- determining the right temperament based on the lifestyle you intend the puppy to have, as well as the personalities of his sire and dam

- considering what the breed chosen was intended to do, and whether the puppy's parents and grandparents show strong breed traits

- managing Wolfie's and Remy's initial experience of each other, and continuing to do so all the way through their developing relationship to ensure the best opportunity for a wonderful friendship

Wolves, our domestic dog's ancestors, live in family units, in which the previous year's young are still part of the family when new cubs are born.

Along with an adult or two, the yearlings are often left with the cubs whilst the parents hunt. Primarily, the yearlings play with the cubs, and display a degree of protective behaviour towards them, adjusting play to the cubs' capabilities, and assuming the role of protector in the event of danger.

All of this happens because the care system in the brain has been activated, a genetic characteristic that can be seen in modern-day dogs, which is predisposed to activate more strongly in yearlings when a puppy is introduced, making the older puppy more receptive to bonding with the young pup.

All this playing makes a little chap thirsty!

REMY'S DIARY
August 11
Day 20 with us: 11 weeks and four days old

AM
5.15:   Awake, play, a little breakfast
6.15:   Settle down
8.00:   Ready to play, walk up hill, around pond

A puppy called Wolfie

The boys love hanging out together in the field.

8.45: Breakfast. Play, running, play with toys, taking them from the other, no problems, but a little stillness and pausing as the other took the toy, so assessing their responses in case either became worried. Distracted them after a while and helped them play by running around instead of with the toys

10.30: Sleep

PM

12.15: Awake, mooching

1.30: Walk over field, really nice, dog had a good time. Relax. Lunch

2.50: Snooze, then a little light play and out for a walk, mooch

4.30: Dinner, then play, then settle for a sleep

6.15: Awake. Out for a walk, more dinner, play,

8.30: A chew to settle down

9.00: Mooch about

9.30: Asleep

LOVELY THINGS ABOUT MY BOYS
Wolfie –
- smiles in his sleep
- loves it when I bring home some tasty treat for him to eat when I've been shopping
- loves running
- has a really, really long tail
- loves the beach ...
- ... and Remy

Remy –
- wags his tail in his sleep
- sits and barks at me when he is hungry
- loves everyone he meets
- *really* loves his big brother, Wolfie
- loves Camembert!
- is a great kisser! He has so much love to give, and I get huge kisses very often!

Remy has just had his last vaccination, and now weighs 11.5kg (25.4lb). He's a sturdy little sausage, and growing well.

We've all had a lovely walk in South Molton. Remy is less worried about traffic than Wolfie was; he seems to take everything in his stride. Remy has tried to retrieve the plastic ducks in the pond, although he didn't quite know how to hold on to them. He was so pleased with himself that he rushed out of the pond, gave me a huge, soggy cuddle and ran around doing happy dances! When he's all played-out and tired, Remy runs as fast as he can all the way back to the house and jumps on the settee for a snooze.

Hazard avoidance has begun for Remy. Seven weeks of age is the average time at which this happens, with many dogs already experiencing the phase when they go to their new homes. Wolfie was no exception, and we saw the first signs of hazard avoidance when he had been with us for a week. Remy is late starting at 11-and-a half-weeks old, and it is easy to tell that this is what it is as he's been with us for two-and-a-half weeks already, and has only seemed mildly insecure about moving home. A later onset is to be expected with Remy as his breed is one of the least reactive, with hazard avoidance starting earlier for more reactive breeds.

How each dog deals with this is very different:, Wolfie backs away when scared, and barks only a couple of times, whereas Remy leans forward and barks non-stop. As with Wolfie, we must be careful about exposing Remy to new experiences and stimuli, and listen when he says he is not comfortable.

Remy got under the fence and into the field with our Hebridean sheep this afternoon. There is herding instinct in Barbet ancestry, and Remy's is really good considering it was his first time with sheep. He was chasing, but remained at a distance, and chased in a manner that did round up the sheep, rather than dispersing them through random chasing. The sheep are used to dogs, and to being herded a little, albeit at a much slower pace, so I climbed over the fence to fetch Remy. Surprisingly, he came back to my recall. He disengaged with the sheep easily, had a little detour to sniff something, then came and stood with me. I picked him up and lifted him over the fence, then climbed over myself.

Remy did want to go back in with the sheep, so I held onto him, talked to him to help change his focus, and got out some of his favourite food. I released him, feeding him a piece of food every few seconds as we walked away from the sheep. Once we were a distance away, and his focus was back on scenting, Remy lost interest in the sheep. Knowing that the sheep are a strong motivation for Remy, and that herding is rewarding, I made sure I had his attention on the food as we went past that part of the fence for the next couple of walks.

PARTY TIME!
It's September and time for the Barbet Summer Party, which we've really been looking forward to, as it's a chance to meet fellow Barbet owners, and, of course other wonderful Barbets. Remy's sire and dam will be there, along with three of his sisters. Wolfie has been invited, too, so it's a day out for all of us.

The journey takes just over an hour, and we

A puppy called Wolfie

Remy watching our Hebridean sheep with great interest.

almost get there before Remy is sick. Poor boy, he doesn't become anxious, or refuse to get in the car (although he is still too small to do this on his own), and it doesn't seem to matter what length the journey is, he is usually sick just before we arrive. Strangely, he's never sick on the return journey, even if he's eaten. We've been driving slowly and carefully, particularly around corners, and also timing journeys to when Remy has not just eaten. None of this makes a difference: he's still sick, and if his tummy is empty, it's just bile he sicks up.

The one thing I have noticed is that he is worse if excited. On those occasions when he can lay down and relax he may not be sick, but if he is excited and barking, looking around and moving, he *always* is.

We continue driving carefully, and timing meals to journeys, and add in measures to help Remy remain calm. It's no good timing going out to when he is already calm, as the prospect of a car journey makes him excited, so we say the calming words he already knows – settle down/we won't be long/ – using our voices to convey the feeling of calmness, and in the car one of us gives Remy a slow, calming massage.

We have a fantastic day at the party,

with around 20 Barbets in attendance. There is a fun agility course, a mini fun show, talks and demonstrations on showing and grooming, a very large field for the dogs to run about in off-lead, a barbecue, and a professional photographer to capture the day.

Remy does really well – he and his siblings are exactly sixteen weeks old today, and this is the first time he has been around so many people and dogs in one place. His sire, Duplo, is huge! We were already aware that Remy will be a big boy, and now we can see exactly how big he might get! Chatting with Duplo's owners, we find that a couple of features and characteristics (Remy has the same white markings as his dad, and he likes standing in-between legs for a cuddle) have passed from father to son. Remy also meets up with his dam, Anouk, and sisters, Maddie, Olive, and Zelda.

Entering the fun show, I have to say we are not great, although I'm good at getting in the way so that the judge sees me and not Remy, and, with so much going on, Remy is not walking quietly by my side ... never mind, it was good fun.

Wolfic and Matt show us how to do agility, which is hilarious, a combination of man and dog competing to jump over the same hurdles! Wolfie is much better at agility these days, though he still doesn't really see the point of it. But if his Dad's doing it, then so will Wolfie.

By the time the day has ended, both boys are completely exhausted, and we've made some lovely new friends.

Meet the family (l-r): Anouk, Maddie, Remy, Zelda, Olive and Duplo.
(Courtesy ruralshots.com)

Chapter 12
Best brothers

The friendship between Wolfie and Remy is blossoming: they're open and easy with one another, and neither has felt the need to be worried. As time goes by they become closer, and want to do more things together. Mealtimes now happen in the same area, although I supervise them, and will always do so, as it takes only one misunderstanding for the relationship to go wrong. Both boys must feel perfectly comfortable about eating together, and if either shows signs that this is not the case – doesn't eat/eats too quickly/watches the other for too long/body language changes/vocalises – then it cannot continue. As it is, they are fine, and both are comfortable with this progression.

Going from having one dog to two brings the possibility of issues. We've brought up Wolfie, and know what he likes, dislikes, how much space he wants, when he wants a cuddle, and when he wants to be left alone. Adding another dog changes the dynamic, so everything is monitored for the tiniest hint of Wolfie not coping.

The same goes for Remy. We don't know as much about him as we do Wolfie, but we are able to tell if there's cause for concern.

For example, If Matt is cuddling on the settee with Wolfie, how does Wolfie respond when Remy approaches? What if Remy tries to put his head right next to Wolfie? What happens if Wolfie is on the settee and Remy wants to get on, too? How are they when a door is closed, and both become excited waiting for us to open it? What happens if they find a scent that they each want to sniff at the same time? The possibilities are endless, and I am bracing myself in case something should happen: each new experience they share triggers an expectation that they may disagree. My role is to not let my feelings influence how I behave, however, because, if I did, I'd avoid doing things because of my fear. There is nothing about their friendship that suggests I should act on my fears, so I remain calm and in control, even if I am tense on occasion.

We have two settees now that Remy is with us, so that there is one for each dog. Wolfie lays on his usual one, and Remy has the new one. However, sometimes, Remy likes to get on Wolfie's settee when Wolfie isn't on it, and sometimes, Wolfie wants to get on it when Remy is already there. Wolfie hasn't yet sat on the new one, and I do not want to tell Wolfie that he can't sit on his comfy settee when he wants to, so initially I ask Remy to get off when Wolfie wants to get on. This doesn't require any effort from me, as Remy gets off himself once he feels Wolfie leaning against him, and happily settles down somewhere else. There's a fine line between teaching them that they can share, and move over for each other, or inadvertently teaching them that they cannot be on or near something when the other is there. I make sure that the situation is fine, and talk them through it, to give them awareness of what their actions mean.

I say to Wolfie, 'Mind Remy, don't sit on him,' and I ask Remy to get off and sit on the other settee until Wolfie is aware and considers where his bum is going. Then I monitor in case I need to intervene,

Where one is, there, too, is the other ...

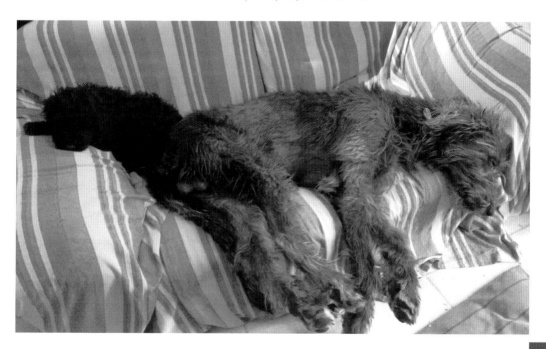

but otherwise leave it to them to sort out how to sit. Wolfie does try to sit next to Remy, so sometimes they are on the settee together, but it doesn't give Wolfie enough room to lay down properly, so often Remy gets off as Wolfie is a little too close.

The fact that they are both comfortable being on the settee together is a huge advantage when Chilli the cat decides that, instead of coming in through the open window, she will try and go past the dogs, which entails dodging Remy, who is comfy on the floor, and jumping over Wolfie's head resting on the arm of the settee, so she can get to the counter where her biscuits are.

Unfortunately, Remy cannot resist chasing her, so Chilli runs to avoid Remy, lands on Wolfie's head, and jumps from there to the counter, with Remy in close pursuit (who also jumps on Wolfie's head). Wolfie looks up as if to ask, 'Why are you disturbing me?' then lays down again.

Having two dogs means that we have to revisit self-confidence, in order to bring up Remy as we did Wolfie, but also to ensure that neither dog becomes dependent on the other, or lack self-confidence when on their own. Wolfie is used to going out without another dog, of course, but this does not automatically mean he wants to go out without Remy, but if we never take them out separately, they may not cope as well if that situation becomes unavoidable. We take them out together, and Matt and Wolfie go in a different direction to Remy and I. Matt will take out Wolfie whilst me and Remy stay home, and Wolfie will stay in the house whilst we are out with Remy, and vice versa. We take it at the pace they are comfortable with, and both get used to doing things together *and* on their own.

RESOURCE GUARDING

We've bought them some new toys, and Remy has very definitely told Wolfie to stay away from these. Remy happily shows Wolfie existing toys and sticks that he has found in an attempt to get Wolfie to play with him, and once play has begun they each try to take the object from the other's mouth if it's a toy they can both hold, or one of them will quickly run

and pick up the toy when the other is not looking, or at a distance from it. This is great fun and not once have they had any kind of disagreement.

However, a new toy is a problem, and our solution is to let Wolfie have a look at the toy first, so that he is not as interested in it, making it less likely he will try to see what it is when Remy has it. Then we play with the new toy with Remy for a while, after which we do something else. When Remy subsequently remembers the new toy and picks it up and runs away with it, Wolfie is not very interested. It's not long, then, before Remy decides that it's not much fun playing with the toy on his own, so shows it to Wolfie, and play resumes its normal pattern.

It's possible that if we had expected and encouraged Remy to share the new toy with Wolfie from the start, he may have developed more of a resource-guarding response. As we have adjusted how a new toy is introduced to the two of them, it is simply the novelty aspect of the toy that prompts Remy to want to investigate it on his own first, before sharing it with Wolfie.

Dogs resource guard for a variety of reasons. Sometimes, as in Remy's case, it is easily dealt with, and never becomes an issue, but it can be with some dogs. Resolving issues entails understanding why they are occurring in the first place, and then instigating a plan specifically tailored to the dog involved. It's not possible to have a strategy that resolves *all* resource guarding issues, although things can be done to minimise or, in some cases, avoid these.

Properly monitor dogs when there are resources around. At the very first sign of one dog becoming uneasy, adjust the situation to alleviate this, which usually means working with the other dog, getting his attention to distract him from looking at the uneasy dog, or increasing the distance between the two of them. Once an issue or potential issue has been identified, adjust how the resource in question is accessed, to minimise the dog who has it needing to use guarding behaviour. Ignoring the fact that a dog is uneasy in a given situation in the hope that he will get used to it, will most likely result in an increase in resource guarding. Some dogs can overcome this response, given time and the right support that enables them to feel safe, but some may require ongoing strategies to manage resource guarding in multi-dog situations.

HORMONES AGAIN!

Remy now weighs 17.55kg (38.69lb), at nearly five months of age, and his first hormonal phase has begun ... very obviously as he has begun humping Wolfie. Wolfie is the recipient of Remy's amorous feelings as Remy usually places his paws on Wolfie's neck when they are sitting together: an ideal position for expression of his sexual feelings. Remy is going through the motions, as his motor pattern for this has activated, but there is no intent and no real understanding until sexual maturity at the second hormonal phase.

How we deal with this is relevant. If a puppy was humping a toy or cushion, there may be less inclination to interrupt the behaviour than if he was doing it to another dog or a person. It

Remy in his first hormonal phase.

A puppy called Wolfie

needs interrupting, nonetheless, because the more a behaviour is practised, the more reinforced it becomes, and performed more often, to the point of obsession. This may have serious implications when the puppy reaches sexual maturity, as he will be much bigger and stronger by then, and, rather than just going through the motions as in this first phase, will have a higher drive to see the behaviour through to resolution. Trying to stop a dog intent on humping someone or something can lead to him experiencing strong feelings of frustration and irritation, and result in a reactive response. Many dogs will be inclined hump when they reach sexual maturity, but this is much easier to deal with when the behaviour has not been reinforced at the first hormone phase.

There is also a chance that Wolfie will object to Remy doing this, and a disagreement might ensue, and this will also be so much worse if I don't deal with the situation now, and it happens when Remy is older. The tolerance that Wolfie affords Remy now may not extend to when he is older, and so there is a risk my boys will fight. So my distract, diffuse and refocus strategy is used to redirect Remy to do something else when he feels a sexual urge, and one of the games we play is chase and fetch with toys, putting them in and taking them out of a bucket (see image, right). This is a great game for refocusing puppies who are grabbing at clothes, or who are overly-focused on a person or dog.

Remy is naturally enthusiastic, and, aside from the humping, the only other effect of his hormonal phase is that he is even more enthusiastic than usual, and it takes a little effort to distract him. During his first hormonal phase. Wolfie really struggled to regulate his emotional mind, and went into over-arousal very easily, whilst Remy remains pretty well balanced throughout this phase.

It's interesting to note that the male hormone cycle for Remy in this phase is just over half the time it was for Wolfie. With Wolfie each part of the cycle was 3-4 days long, with the whole cycle lasting 10-12 days. Remy's cycle is 2-3 days for each stage, and 6-9 days for the entire cycle. It is also much less distinct with Remy than it was with Wolfie. Another

(Courtesy Mighty Dog Graphics)

difference is that, when Wolfie was in the withdrawal phase as testosterone levels dipped, he would be jumpier and more scared. Remy is also feeling this, but he expresses it by barking and being more reactive.

MANAGING OVER-EXCITEMENT

More enthusiastic now that his hormones are influencing his mind, Remy has become much more exuberant when he plays with Wolfie, and has taken to standing on the low wall and jumping on Wolfie when he goes past. Every gateway is a suitable ambush point, and he pulls Wolfie's tail until what to do when he becomes over-aroused. As he does not find the same joy in running on his own that Wolfie does, I have a different approach.

When Remy stands on the wall and jumps on Wolfie, I use my hand to focus his attention so that he jumps at my hand instead of Wolfie. I add in the phrase 'Don't jump on Wolfie.' It takes a few tries, but Remy is now jumping at me rather than Wolfie. Once this is established, I begin to concentrate on my voice cue rather than the hand signal, gradually reducing the latter so that Remy does not continue to jump at me, but simply jumps off the wall onto the ground, and we progress to Remy jumping off the wall just ahead of Wolfie instead of on top of him.

However, this manoeuvre has just delayed Remy's desire to interact, because, once he's on the ground, he begins jumping at Wolfie, and is too excited not to do this. Another redirection is required.

Remy loves walking through my legs, and when he wants a cuddle he stops between them. I already ask him to go through my legs rather than jump at me when I come home after being out, so, as he knows this cue and can do it as an alternative to jumping at me, I use it to stop him jumping at Wolfie. Using my hand as a visual cue when I interrupt Remy, I say to him 'Leave Wolfie; go through.' We have to do this several times as we walk the short distance from the yard to the gate into the field, by which time Remy has calmed down enough to stop jumping.

The next thing is to distract Remy from trying to ambush Wolfie every time he comes through a gate. Remy goes through a gate and lies down in ambush position, so Wolfie refuses to come through, knowing that Remy will once again run and jump at him. I use toys to get Remy's attention, make myself exciting so that he wants to come to me, and engage his scenting instinct by telling him to find a rabbit or pheasant. He knows these phrases, and finds scenting extremely enjoyable, so if I can encourage Remy to find something, this takes his mind off Wolfie and gives him something pleasurable to do instead, whilst Wolfie comes through the gate. Sometimes, I stand by the gate and feed Remy

Wolfie plays with him. As you can imagine, Wolfie is now not keen to go past the wall or through gates, and stands to one side, not moving, until Remy's attention is focused elsewhere. He's usually so tolerant with Remy, but I can see it's not so evident now when Remy refuses to let go of his tail until he plays. This is something that Remy has always done, but now his hormones are influencing his mind, he's more insistent about it: previously, if Wolfie didn't respond, Remy would give up, but now he won't stop, and tries harder. It's clear that Wolfie needs some help!

I am now managing Remy so that he knows

A puppy called Wolfie

Remy insists on playing ...

... but it's Wolfie's turn to pounce!

Wolfie is all played out.

tasty tidbits, whilst Wolfie walks through. Once in the field, things return to normal and Remy is not overly-focused on Wolfie. We go through the same process on the way back.

Wolfie, balanced and not influenced by his hormones, likes his usual relaxation time. Remy, in the grip of hormone influence, has forgotten what relaxation is, so to give Wolfie some quiet time I'm playing more with Remy, and taking him to the field without Wolfie to exhaust some of his energy.

When we've finished our play, I make sure that Remy also settles down, and does not become overtired by being on the go all the time. Remy likes having his chest massaged, and this is a good way of concluding an activity and helping to re-balance his mind. It doesn't always work straight away, however, as Remy is sometimes too aroused, and either asks me to play, or tries to get Wolfie to do so.

Now, focus: trick training
I add in some trick training to help focus and quiet his mind, which Remy loves.

I began by teaching him to touch and target my hand, and from here I guide him through each new trick. This removes the need to use food as an incentive to follow to learn a movement, and also means he's not dependent on food, and we have created a really strong bond. Food *is* used as a reward each time he carries out a trick or part of it. Once he's learnt one trick, we add this to other tricks he knows, with a food reward at the end of a sequence, rather than after each trick. Remy likes to be on the move, so the tricks he is learning are those where movement is involved. Amongst the tricks he knows are –

- go fast/slow
- circle me
- weave through my legs
- turn around
- walk at various speeds next to me
- stand between my legs and then walk forwards or backwards with me, or on his own

It's a common misconception that any dog will sit, particularly if food is on offer, but not all dogs do, and Remy usually remains on his feet in a ready-to-move stance. Any attempts to teach a sit using food result in him stepping backwards, or lifting his head higher to reach the food. Never mind: as Remy does not want to keep still, tricks involving a sit can wait until he is ready.

Not all activities for puppies need to be high-energy, so it's sensible to have a range of different levels of physical and cognitive activities to do with your puppy. There's definitely something in the saying 'if you bring up a busy dog, you will have a busy dog.' Some puppies find it difficult to be calm and to relax, and are always wanting to be on the go. Relaxation is a very important part of overall physical and psychological health and well being, but some dogs need help in accessing this. If you are always doing things with your puppy he will have an expectation that this will always be the case, along with a diminishing ability to be content to sit and watch the world go by on occasion. This can lead to frustration as he struggles to cope when you are not doing anything with him, and there is inherent frustration in not being able to relax, anyway.

Finding something that helps your puppy to come out of a manic state and relax can be difficult, but persevere. With Wolfie it was running that naturally led to relaxation. Remy's activities do not always naturally lead to relaxation, so finishing off with a massage does this for him.

Barking mad
Remy has become quite the barker recently; another result of hormonal influence. Where Wolfie sits in the garden and watches the world go by when I am teaching, Remy stands at the gate and barks for the entire hour. There's not a lot I can do about this, unfortunately. I do go and check him, telling him I'll be back soon, but as I am with clients I can't interrupt the session for any length of time.

Remy also barks when I leave the room to fetch chews from another room. If I leave him and Wolfie in one field whilst checking another before

A puppy called Wolfie

opening the gate, Remy barks at that. He barks at the horses and the sheep. His impulse control and self-restraint are not quite there yet: he is enthusiastic, anticipatory, and struggling to wait for anything. This is the complete opposite to Wolfie, who has a calm nature. If I am close to him, I talk to Remy as I am doing things, telling him he's fine, and 'I'll be back in a minute.' When I get back I say something like 'Silly boy, there's no need to bark,' 'You can be quiet now, I've come back.' It's not making much difference at the moment, but we will get there!

Remy has also started a rather amusing game, which, although potentially annoying, I can't help but laugh at! It goes like this –

Remy: *Let me out, Mum ...*
I open the door, let him out and close it.
Remy: *Mum, let me back in ...*
I let him in, close the door ... and it starts over again.

It really is hilarious. I say 'What are you like? I can't keep opening and closing the door!' Remy looks, smiles, and wags his tail, and I indulge him once again! I do tell him we've finished when he decides to do it at bedtime, but mostly it is during the day. The door would normally be open, but now we are into October it's cold so the door is closed. Now, if this activity was in any way the result of distress or displacement, I would be addressing the underlying problem that causes it. But this is simply Remy finding fun in a new game, and as long as he doesn't become obsessed with it (which won't happen as there are times I tell him we've finished playing), it is fine.

REMY'S DIARY
October 22
With us for 3 months: now five months old

I decided I just had time to take the boys for a run in the fields before Clive arrived to trim the horses' feet.

How wrong I was ...

We wandered across the first field and arrived at the gate to the next. Two male pheasants were in the field, face-to-face, clearly disagreeing about something. As I opened the gate for the boys, the pheasants flew off, and Wolfie stood and watched – sensible boy: no point running after something that's flown away. Remy is more interested in scenting, and ran straight over to where they had been. Picking up something he ran back to Wolfie.

I was quite surprised to see that he had a pheasant in his mouth! This one had clearly being trying to pretend he didn't exist, whilst the two who flew off had been having a go at him. Wanting to check the pheasant and manage a situation where I had two off-lead dogs, and no idea how they would react, I went to have a look. Remy still had the pheasant, and had turned away from Wolfie when he tried to sniff it to let him know he wasn't letting go. Wolfie did not try to engage with Remy or the pheasant, but stood waiting.

I asked Remy to let me see, and, little pudding, he dropped the bird at my feet. The pheasant was alive, with no obvious injuries from either the other pheasants or Remy.

Once Remy had released the pheasant, the bird gave up the pretence of being dead, thus quickly reigniting Remy's interest. With both boys in tow, I relocated the pheasant to the next field and the safety of the other side of the fence. I turned to go back across the field, only to find that Remy had no intention of leaving whilst he could still see the pheasant.

By now, Clive's arrival was imminent, and we were two fields away from home ... Had there been time, I would have waited, and distracted and refocused Remy, but there wasn't, so, there I was, with nearly 20kg (44lb) of puppy in my arms, staggering across the field to the gate as quickly as I could. It was just as well that Wolfie was happy to walk back rather than also being distracted by the pheasant as there was no chance I could carry him, too!

BREED INSTINCTS

The Barbet is a versatile breed, bred with various instincts, and Remy has already shown aptitudes to herd, retrieve, scent, and guard. He has a natural affinity for water, and a very soft mouth, which is essential for game retrieval. When Remy is working he is focused and calm; his work drive is obvious to see, although this is less evident when he becomes aroused, or other emotions take over, when he becomes playful and excited. Of all his abilities, we are focusing on retrieving, scenting and water.

I find herding to have a frustration aspect to it that I don't want to see reinforced in Remy. We have only a small flock of sheep, and rarely need to do anything with them, so the opportunities for Remy to develop his herding abilities are limited in any case. We also do not need a guard dog, and would rather bring out the Barbet trait of being good with people and dogs, rather than develop a guarding instinct. Remy really loves retrieving, scenting, and water, and these activities are more rewarding for him than herding or guarding.

Remy is still a young puppy, and we have no desire to try and force his instincts, so we let him explore and develop naturally. We can guide him by attaching phrases to what he is doing to create a word association, which also serves to give him a better understanding of doing things in different contexts. As it is, Remy is very capable, with a very natural ability, but at the moment he lacks the

Thankfully, the bird that Remy retrieved was unharmed.

competence and precision that comes with practice and/or maturity.

Puppy problems

Whilst Remy is generally sailing through his hormonal phase, there are a couple of issues that we did not experience with Wolfie, one of which is that Remy seems to become 'stuck.' This happens when he has had a busy time, and, whereas Wolfie would go into over-arousal and struggle to calm his mind, Remy simply stands still away from us somewhere in the garden or on the yard when this happens, and no matter what we do, he cannot seem to go from this state to coming back to the house for meals, comfort, or play (although does sometimes still want to play if he's not been too active). He stays where he is, not moving, statue-like, for as long as we leave him. Strangely, this behaviour also seems to coincidence with when it is raining. If we go to him he walks away, and then stands aqain.

This behaviour is problematic in two ways –

• his mind is unable to transition out of this mode, which is not a good thing

• he is becoming too wet which makes him cold

Remy becomes 'stuck.'

When Wolfie didn't want to come in, he was happy for us to go to him and guide him in, but Remy is not, and I can't even get near him as he runs away and then stands again. The first time this happened it took me nearly an hour to get to him, by which time he was thoroughly soaked and very cold. Holding him around his chest and walking him inside, his mind clicked out of being stuck and he was fine, and drying him off and cuddling him warmed him.

The second issue we have with Remy is that lead walking is a total nightmare, because he is very sure that once his harness and lead are on, he is competing in World's Strongest Man doing the truck pull. I have never seen a dog – let alone a puppy – pull with such strength and single-mindedness. I have clients with dogs who are also like this on-lead, and we do get through to them, even if it's only for a

few seconds to begin with, but this does not happen with Remy. He has always pulled on the lead, and is so intense about it that I haven't been able to get through to him at all.

We do all of the things that promote a bond when we are out walking. We've taught language, disengage techniques, and distract, diffuse and refocus. We play games and continue to develop our bond, and Remy is encouraged to scent and explore. We practise tricks that incorporate walking and doing things together. We practise lead walking at home and in the field. But none of this is any use when we are out, because I cannot get through to him to actually do any of them: he is oblivious to any and all stimuli. His mind is not present, and he doesn't scent, wee, or even look around: all he does is pull as hard as he can to get from A to B as quickly as possible. When we get home he is either exhausted or a little excitable in a normal puppy way. Emotionally, he is always exhausted and does not show any positivity, which is not a good state to be in. He appears totally unaware during his walks, so is certainly not able to enjoy them.

The only thing that has ever registered when he's like this is when he sees another dog, and then he focuses on the dog, but is almost just as unaware otherwise. He's met, said Hi, and had a play with the dogs he meets when we are out, and, once he gets close enough to them, he's in the present, and he is happy and engaging. Once the dog has gone, however, he reverts to pulling, and there is no let-up. Tiring him out first doesn't help, either, whether it's a run off-lead in the field, or a run on-lead for the first part of our walk.

Remy is getting bigger and stronger, and I am struggling to hold onto him when he's like this. His pull is so strong that I have to lean back in order to stay in control of where he goes. Catch me off guard and not braced and I am pulled along for quite a few steps before I am again in control. If I run with him, I cannot go fast enough to reduce any pull on the lead, let alone have any hope of being alongside him, but at least I am less likely to be pulled over.

Wolfie's lead walking was perfect by the time he was four months old, and he was already competent at changing speed and matching ours so that he didn't pull. Aside from the usual puppy exuberance that meant he pulled when there was something exciting, Wolfie was, and still is, always by our side.

As we do more walks, there is some awareness with Remy, and I am able to talk to him, but this is only when we are in the park and other dogs are about. We've had a couple of good walks around town after we've been in the park, and there are the odd few times he does walk nicely by my side, but this is not exactly progressing much.

FUN WITH LEARNING

We've had lots of fun focusing on Remy's natural instincts. As a water retriever he is trying to retrieve

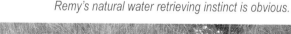

Remy's natural water retrieving instinct is obvious.

A puppy called Wolfie

the plastic ducks that live in the pond, so has been in and out of this many times. He's not bad considering his age: he knows what to do, even if his efforts are a little haphazard at times. He goes into the water and retrieves the ducks almost every time, now, mostly dropping them on the bank next to me. Trips to the pond are regular events as he really loves water retrieving.

He's great at retrieving on land, too, and will happily play this game for ages. Scenting is really enjoyable for him, also, and he is exceedingly good at finding and flushing game. Whilst Remy is busy using his nose to find things, Wolfie does sometimes join in, or else simply stands and looks. There have been a few occasions when Remy is following a scent, and Wolfie has seen movement and flushed the game before Remy has reached it! Remy is good at listening to me and roughly following directions when he is scenting, unless he is on to a fresh scent, when he can't respond until he's finished.

We've introduced Remy to the beach, and he is as excited about being here as Wolfie is. When it's quiet, this is a great place to practise off-lead and recall with Remy. The opposite to Wolfie, who can go quite a distance from me when off-lead, Remy stays close, and where I go, he goes ... not necessarily straight away, but he won't be without me. He also enjoys going in the sea whilst Wolfie is not at all sure about the waves.

Remy becoming 'stuck' has been going on for a good two months now, and I have some strategies in place to manage it. I always close all of the gates at home, so he is only in the immediate garden – which is a relatively small area. – after we have been busy doing different activities, and it is time to relax.

When we return from playing or walking I have food at the ready, and give Remy a little every few steps to encourage him back to the house – sometimes this works. I have also been putting his harness on him so that I can hold on to him easily if I get close enough.

It was fine, physically guiding him back to the house a couple of months ago, but he is bigger and

Wolfie introduces Remy to his favourite place.

stronger now, and resists until we get to the door.

I cannot possibly leave him out in the rain for hours, shaking with cold, though do so if it's dry, and change strategy to going out every so often and talking to him to interrupt his mindset. He is beginning to do this himself and come to the house, but not always, and when it is raining he appears not to be able to do it at all.

TAKING STOCK

Wolfie is now a year and eight months old, and Remy is seven months old. Things are going well, and the boys love running around in the snow. Due to reduced daylight hours we are taking them out at dawn and dusk, which is proving great fun.

One word describes Remy perfectly – joyful – and he is the happiest, most waggy-tailed puppy we have ever known: his tail rarely stops wagging. He's brought a happiness to Wolfie that we never could. Remy's joy is infectious, and Wolfie can't rest for long before Remy is asking him to play. Remy jumps, barks, pounces, and pulls Wolfie's tail. He

The boys love being out in the snow.

licks Wolfie's nose, and doesn't give up. He runs in and out the door, saying 'Come on, Wolfie, get up and chase me.' Wolfie does take his time to respond, although it's clear from his body language and actions that he is receptive to this, and not irritated by it. I'm happy to let Remy continue to entice Wolfie to play as he is not much influenced by his hormones now, and will give up if Wolfie is unresponsive (Remy is too insistent sometimes, so we redirect him to play with us or on his own).

Finally, Wolfie gets up, wags his tail, play bows, and does a little pounce, and they are off, running around the garden chasing and ambushing each other, stopping every so often to wag tails, play bow and begin again. The close friendship and having a brother to do things with are what have been missing for Wolfie. Remy completes Wolfie's life, and Wolfie does the same for Remy.

A regular stream of clients and dogs visit for courses, etc, and I had imagined that, with two dogs looking over the gate, now, rather than one, dogs with anxiety and fear issues around other dogs might not be as comfortable about seeing both boys. Happily, this is not the case, as Remy is giving off

A puppy called Wolfie

Misty dawn walks are hugely exciting!

the same safe vibes as Wolfie, and clients' dogs appear as interested in both of them as they were Wolfie on his own. Even Remy's tendency to bark has not caused any worry.

Things are not so great when we are out, however, as Remy's lead walking is getting worse, not better! I see plenty of clients with dogs who have this issue, which generally improves once we put strategies in place. I am obviously missing something as I still haven't figured out how to interrupt Remy's single-minded attitude to even begin to use the strategies we have in place.

To make matters worse, currently, I am suffering from a condition which is set off by movement and impact, so lead walking with Remy has been put on hold. When I feel up to it we are occasionally still going to the park and into town, so that Remy can get out and meet people and dogs, but not as often as I would like in order to practise and progress Remy's pulling issue. Whilst his mind goes into manic state every time we go out there is a chance that this will become harder to interrupt the longer it goes on.

The relationship between Wolfie and Remy goes from strength to strength. Remy's second hormonal phase goes as smoothly as the first, albeit he is a little more enthusiastic this time. It's easier to interrupt a particular mindset this time, and humping has been replaced by kissing, which is what Wolfie does when he feels amorous. Best of all, the problem with Remy becoming 'stuck' has resolved itself. If he gets stuck now it lasts for just a minute or so, and then he runs back to the house with his tail wagging.

Play is very interesting: my boys have been learning by observation and practise. Remy is very quick to turn and change direction; Wolfie is very slow to do this. Wolfie has a very long stride when he runs, and Remy has a short one, though pumps his legs more quickly. As time has gone by the boys have learnt from each other. Wolfie has tried more turning and changing direction, following Remy as he does it, and has really improved these skills. Remy, who had no hope of keeping up with Wolfie, has

learnt to lengthen his stride when he is running and increase his stamina. The only time Remy can't keep up is when Wolfie is running as fast as he possibly can.

As previously noted, Wolfie is a real daddy's boy, and is Matt's shadow; always with him. They do lots of things together and have a really close bond. I also have a wonderful bond with Wolfie, though not as close. Remy is turning out to be a mummy's boy: my shadow, always wanting to do things with me. Matt takes out both boys for an early morning walk most days, and they help him with jobs around the farm. If I am about, Remy is usually by my side, and if he's been with Matt he comes rushing back to tell me what he's been doing, delivering kisses as if we've been apart for weeks! Wolfie loves helping on the farm and being involved; he loves long walks, running and exploring new places – all of the things that Matt likes doing, too, and which fit in around his work. Remy has a yearning to learn and do things, using his mind. He also loves running and walking, but activities such as trick training and scenting really capture his interest, which is great as I also love to learn new activities to increase my knowledge and expand my perception. It is also so rewarding to teach Remy, and I am lucky in that I have the time to practise and attend courses/events with him.

NEW STUFF TO DO

Wolfie is two years and four months old, now, and Remy a year and three months.

Remy and I have begun learning competition obedience. As I do so much teaching for a living, it's nice to get out and learn something new myself, plus it provides an opportunity for dedicated me and Remy time. We are adding another aspect to our relationship with this new activity, and Remy is learning to listen to me when we are in an unfamiliar environment ... part of my ongoing strategies to address our lead-walking issue. What is very interesting is that the language, understanding, and tricks that are ongoing and part of Remy's life have given us a good foundation to build on as we learn competition obedience.

A puppy called Wolfie

Wolfie – Dad's boy.

A PROBLEM SOLVED

I've been looking at how we actually walk on the lead. Different things can be done and various positions used with a lead to ease pulling, but, having tried, there's no possibility of employing these techniques with Remy pulling so much. I have a brainwave, and have engaged the help of a friend when we go out walking.

First, we need to experiment. My friend, Anne, has a long line attached to the back ring on Remy's harness, with the idea that she can take the strain of Remy pulling with the long line, giving me the ability to try different lead techniques with the short lead, which won't be pulled taught. I will also be closer to Remy and able to walk by his side, so can get his attention and interrupt his manic state.

We begin with me attaching the regular short lead to the back ring, so that I can walk next to Remy with Anne taking the strain of his pulling with the long line. Unfortunately, nothing I say or do has any effect with Remy, and it doesn't matter what I do with the lead either. We move to trying a double-ended lead with both sides clipped to the back ring forming a loop so that I can have my hands in different positions to help dissipate from behind some of the pressure from Remy pulling. This doesn't have any effect, either!

Next, we unclip one end of the lead from the back ring and clip it to the front ring, which doesn't make any difference to Remy's pulling, except to make him significantly off-balance.

These techniques work well for many dogs, giving the owners a way to break through their dog's pulling and get his attention, so that they can teach him how to walk without doing this. But they are just not having any effect whatsoever on Remy.

Remy does slow very slightly occasionally, but this is more due to the fact that he is tired. We finish our walk and come home, where Remy flops on the floor, worn out. We are also both exhausted – Anne more than me as she has been doing all the holding whilst I have been experimenting. Thankfully, Anne agrees to return for another walk.

In the meantime, I mention our unsuccessful walk to another friend, Jen, who also owns a Barbet. She suggests we clip both ends of the lead to the front ring, and hold the lead as I would reins on a horse.

On our next walk, Anne is again on the long line taking most of the strain, both ends of the short lead are clipped to the front ring, and I move the lead over Remy's head so that it forms a loop around his body, holding it with my hands shoulder-width apart.

Finally, we make a breakthrough! This approach seems to reduce the pull from the back of the harness, and results in Remy slowing his pace a little ... which also means he is pulling a little less. As we walk a little further, Remy seems to click out of his manic state and is able to look around, take the odd sniff, and have a wee: he even looked back at me and wagged his tail. He is still pulling significantly, but, now that we have found a way to make his mind aware, we can progress. Thank goodness!

The next couple of walks sees Remy becoming more aware, more involved with the environment, and better able to listen and respond to me. His pulling has reduced again, to the point where there is no resistance on the long line that Anne is holding for part of the walk. Remy is so much happier, he looks at me, wags his tail, and is interested in what's going on around him. When we get home, he rushes up the garden to Matt and Wolfie, excited and wagging his tail. He does this when he been out doing something he enjoys with one of us; he comes home and tells us how happy he is.

This is such a wonderful thing to see, and a huge step forward in our lead walking. To go from being exhausted and flat to happy and bouncy is a big improvement in Remy's emotional well being. Having help has been really beneficial, as Anne has provided the means for me to work with Remy rather than be dragged behind him; she's also given me much-needed back-up and confidence. When you are on your own, difficult situations can be worrying and cause anxiety, and it can be hard to be optimistic. Matt is unable to walk with me and Remy

A puppy called Wolfie

as often as we need to practise because he is at work, so having Anne's help has been a huge bonus.

So far, we've been along the lanes where it is quiet so that Remy can get used to his new awareness, and also improve his lead-walking skills. We've done three walks with our new lead-walking approach, and Remy is due his vaccination boosters, so we must take him into town.

He has a good pull when we first get out of the car, but by the time we've walked down the road he is much better. Remy is able to stand and watch dogs without pulling to get to them, and listens to me and disengages when I say 'Let's carry on.' He says Hi to several dogs and, again, is much more restrained as we approach them.

Anne has the long line attached for only the first part of our walk, when we unclip it as Remy is not pulling much at all. I am able to hold him on my own and walk at a normal pace without any undue pulling. He has not become manic or unresponsive at all, despite the extra excitement and stimulation of being in town. It looks like that particular mood state is now behind us.

For the first time, of his own volition Remy has done something typical of younger puppies learning to lead walk, Twice, now, he has sat down and not wanted to move. This is wonderful, because, up until now, Remy has never even let up his pace, let alone stopped. Not wanting to move is something usually worked through when puppies are younger than Remy; Wolfie did it for the first couple of months he was with us. This has been delayed in Remy, but as he is older and has so much more learning and understanding, it is quite easy to get him up and moving again.

This is our fourth walk, and the change in Remy's mindset is profound. The specific way of attaching and holding the lead as suggested by Jen, complimented by Anne on the long line giving me the ability to practise, has resulted in success, and already I feel confident that Remy will not revert to how he was, and I can take him out on my own, along with continuing to meet up with Anne for a walk. The long line is unlikely to be needed for much longer, if at all. Remy has progressed on every walk, and is engaging in and really enjoying his outings.

THE FUTURE

It feels like our boys have been with us forever. We've had the usual puppy issues to deal with, ranging from easy to more difficult, but they've all been resolved.

The individual personalities that Wolfie and Remy have really compliment each other. Wolfie is pure sunshine, and he's easy-going, calm, and gentle. He is happy to be busy, and equally happy to simply sit. Wolfie has a mischievous side which comes out when he plays. He is brave and sure of himself, confident around other dogs, people and new experiences, approaching all things with a happy, laidback attitude. Remy's personality is pure joy, and he is outgoing and gregarious. He has a drive to be on the go more than does Wolfie, and likes to engage his mind. He is quick to tell you what he wants, and to express himself. His self-restraint is not at Wolfie's level, yet, but he'll get there as he matures. Remy is enthusiastic and happy in everything he does, and although he has the occasional moment of uncertainty due to his age and still-maturing mind, he, too, is confident around other dogs, people, and new situations.

Both boys had the benefit of the best start in life with good breeders,which has contributed to their personalities and success of their relationship with each other. From the first moment they met, Wolfie and Remy liked each other, and it has been wonderful and a real privilege to see their relationship progress and mature. The happiness they find in being with each other and the joy they have for life is very evident: together and when they are apart, they are independently confident and emotionally resilient.

Matt and I give Wolfie and Remy a lifestyle framework that nurtures, teaches, and supports them. They are surrounded by love, and live in an environment that provides safety, and the complete understanding that they are individuals with their own free will. We encourage them to express themselves, develop their personalities, and achieve their potential, having done all we can to ensure they have everything they need to enjoy life to the fullest.

Wolfie and Remy are part of us and our family; we look forward to many years of happiness with them.

The best of friends.

★ ★ ★ ★ ★ Amazon reviews

"Fantastic book recommended for every pet owner!"

"It is a lovely book which is easy to read. Suitable for both dog owners and professionals"

"Great reading - makes you think about your relationship with your dog and how to improve it"

HH4576 • Paperback • 20.5x20.5cm • £12.99* • 96 pages • 153 colour pictures
• ISBN: 978-1-845845-76-6 • UPC: 6-36847-04567-0

For more info on Hubble and Hattie books please visit www.hubbleandhattie.com;
email info@hubbleandhattie.com; tel 44 (0) 1305 260068
*prices subject to change/p&p extra

Also by Kathie Gregory –

A tale of two horses

Hubble & Hattie

A passion for free will teaching

Kathie Gregory

"... a celebration of the harmony that can be achieved when we take time to observe, listen to, and learn from animals" – Sarah Fisher, author and animal behaviour counsellor

"... Kathie's commitment to actively engaging the horse's intelligence and enthusiasm for learning, and cultivating his ability to make wise decisions" – Horsemanship Magazine

HH4794 • Paperback • 22x170cm • £14.99* • 144 pages • 80 colour pictures • ISBN: 978-1-845847-94-4 • UPC: 6-36847-04794-8

Index